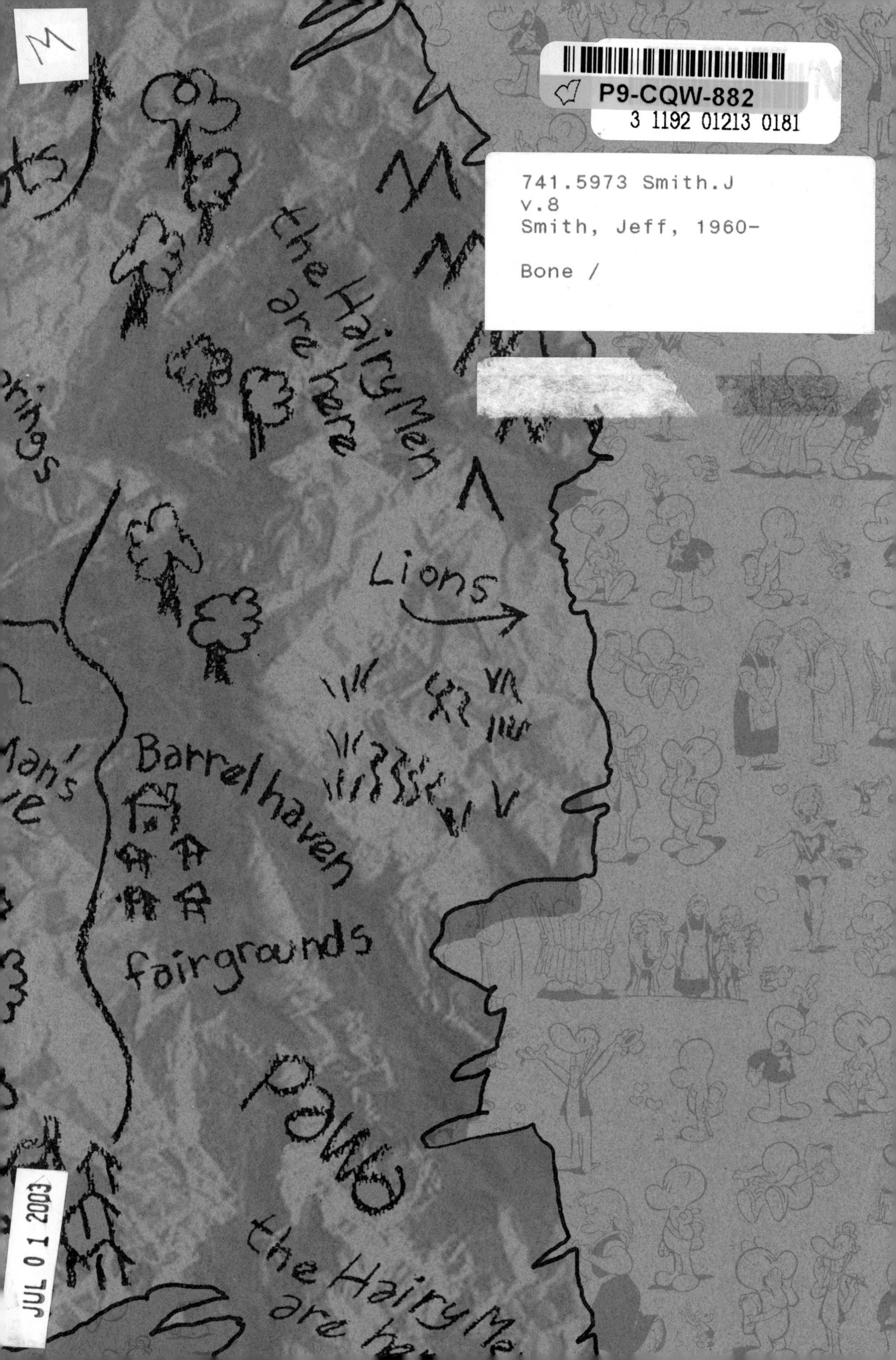
the Hairy Men are here
Lions
Barrelhaven
fairgrounds
Pawo

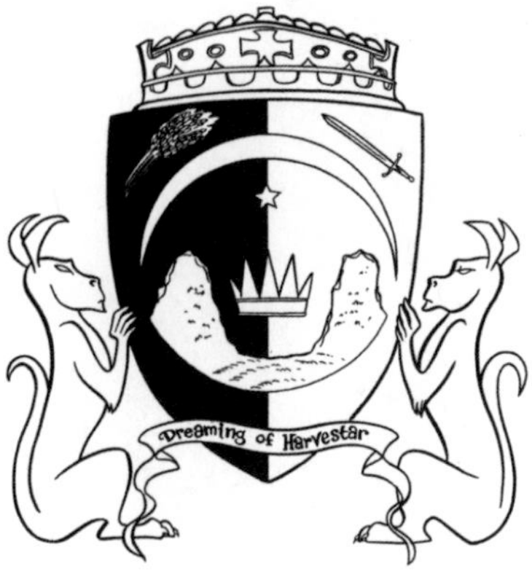
Dreaming of Harvestar

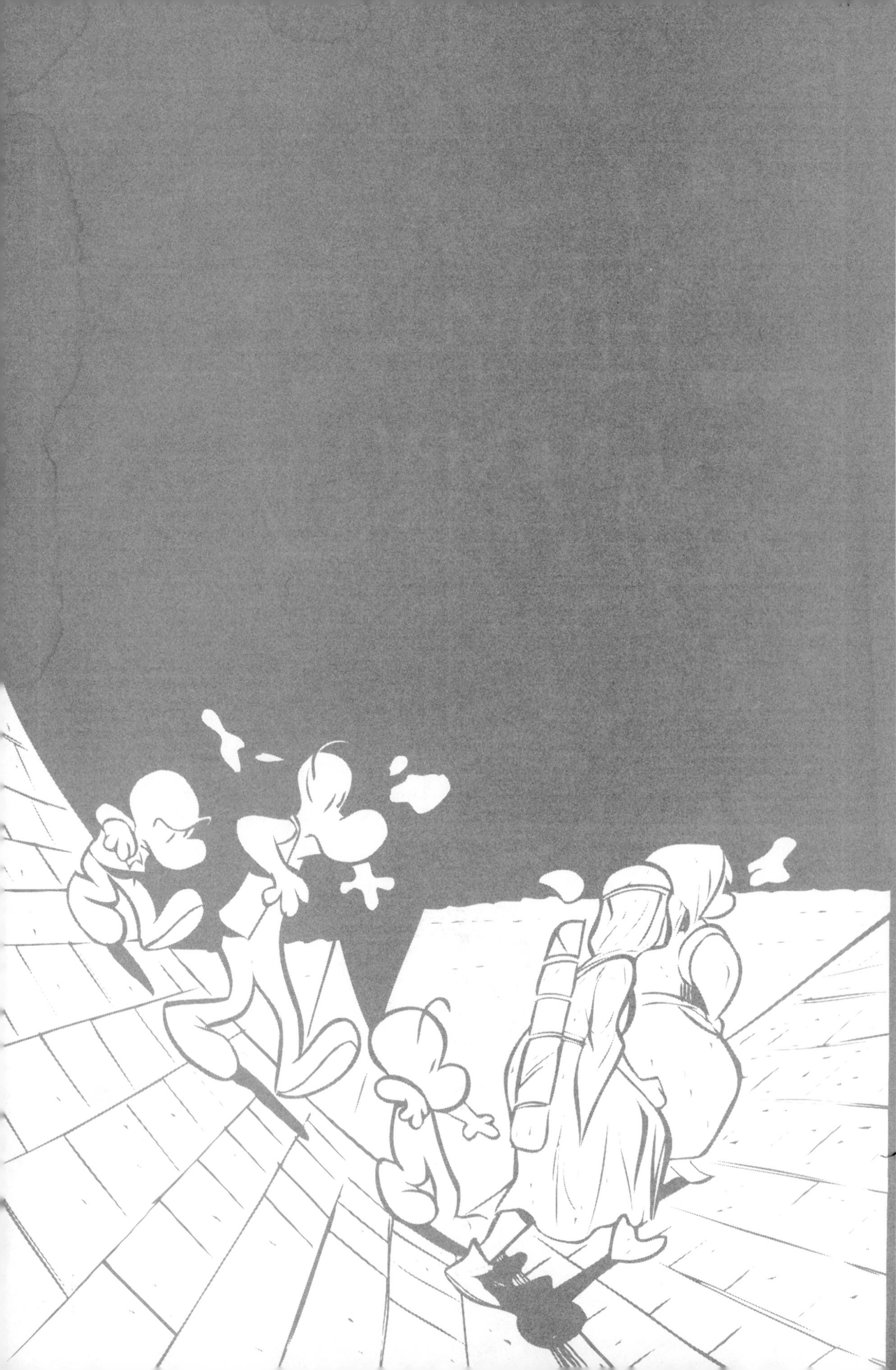

VOLUME EIGHT:
TREASURE HUNTERS

JEFF SMITH

CARTOON BOOKS
COLUMBUS, OHIO

THIS BOOK IS
FOR
KATHLEEN
GLOSAN

Acknowledgements: The Harvestar Family Crest designed by Charles Vess.
Color by Steve Hamaker.

For information write:
Cartoon Books
P.O. Box 16973
Columbus, OH 43216

Hardcover ISBN: 1-888963-12-3
Softcover ISBN: 1-888963-13-1
Library of Congress Catalog Card Number: 95-68403

10 9 8 7 6 5 4 3 2 1

Printed in the United States

FTER A GRUELING JOURNEY THROUGH LANDSCAPES DESTROYED BY THE PHENOMENON KNOWN AS GHOST CIRCLES, THE BONE COUSINS AND THEIR COMPANIONS, THORN AND GRAN'MA BEN, REACH THE ANCIENT LAND OF ATHEIA

BUT THE FRIENDS AND VILLAGERS THEY LEFT BEHIND STILL STRUGGLE IN THE GHOSTLY WASTELANDS . . .

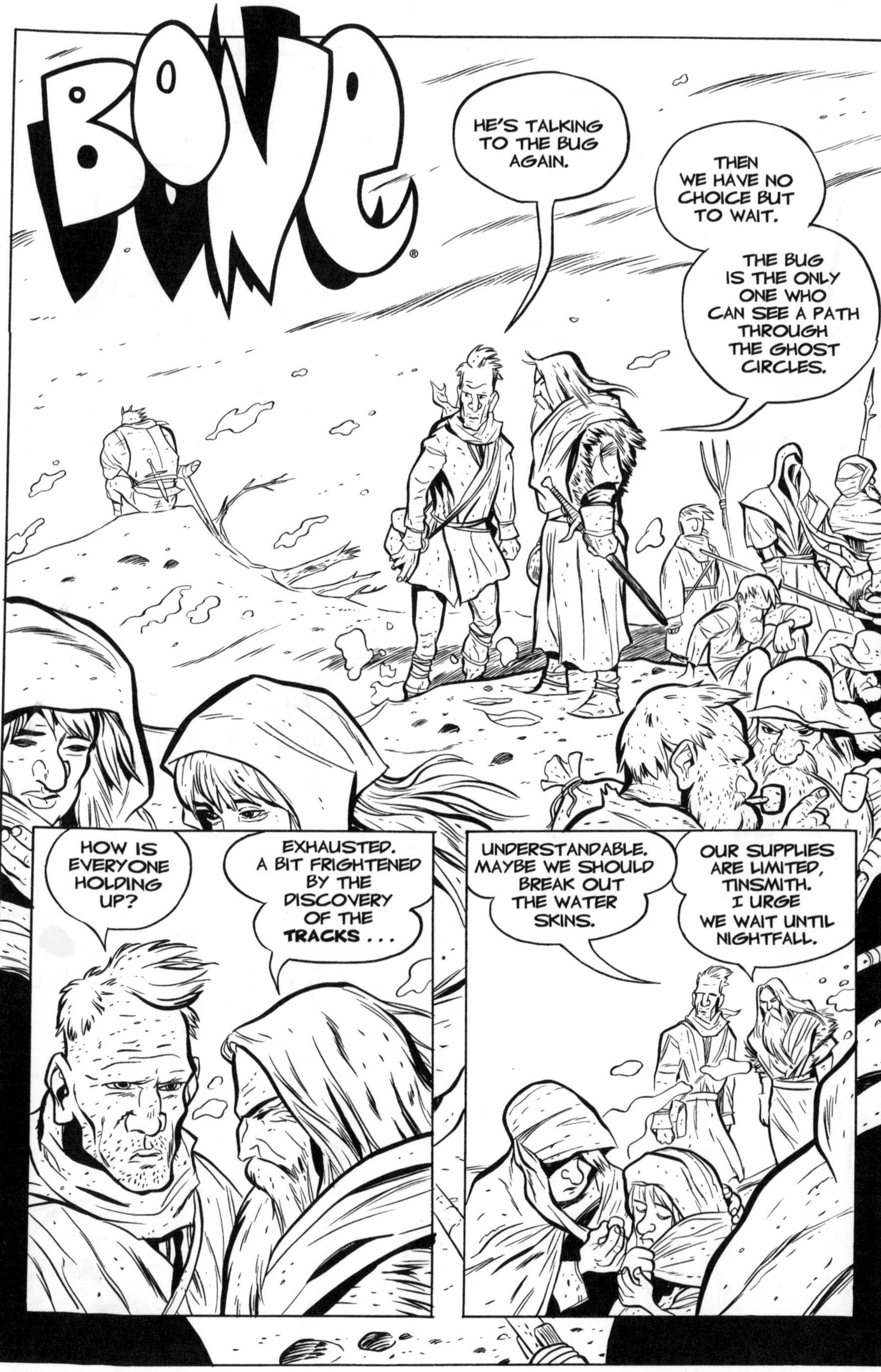
BONE®
HE'S TALKING TO THE BUG AGAIN.
THEN WE HAVE NO CHOICE BUT TO WAIT.
THE BUG IS THE ONLY ONE WHO CAN SEE A PATH THROUGH THE GHOST CIRCLES.
HOW IS EVERYONE HOLDING UP?
EXHAUSTED. A BIT FRIGHTENED BY THE DISCOVERY OF THE **TRACKS** . . .
UNDERSTANDABLE. MAYBE WE SHOULD BREAK OUT THE WATER SKINS.
OUR SUPPLIES ARE LIMITED, TINSMITH. I URGE WE WAIT UNTIL NIGHTFALL.

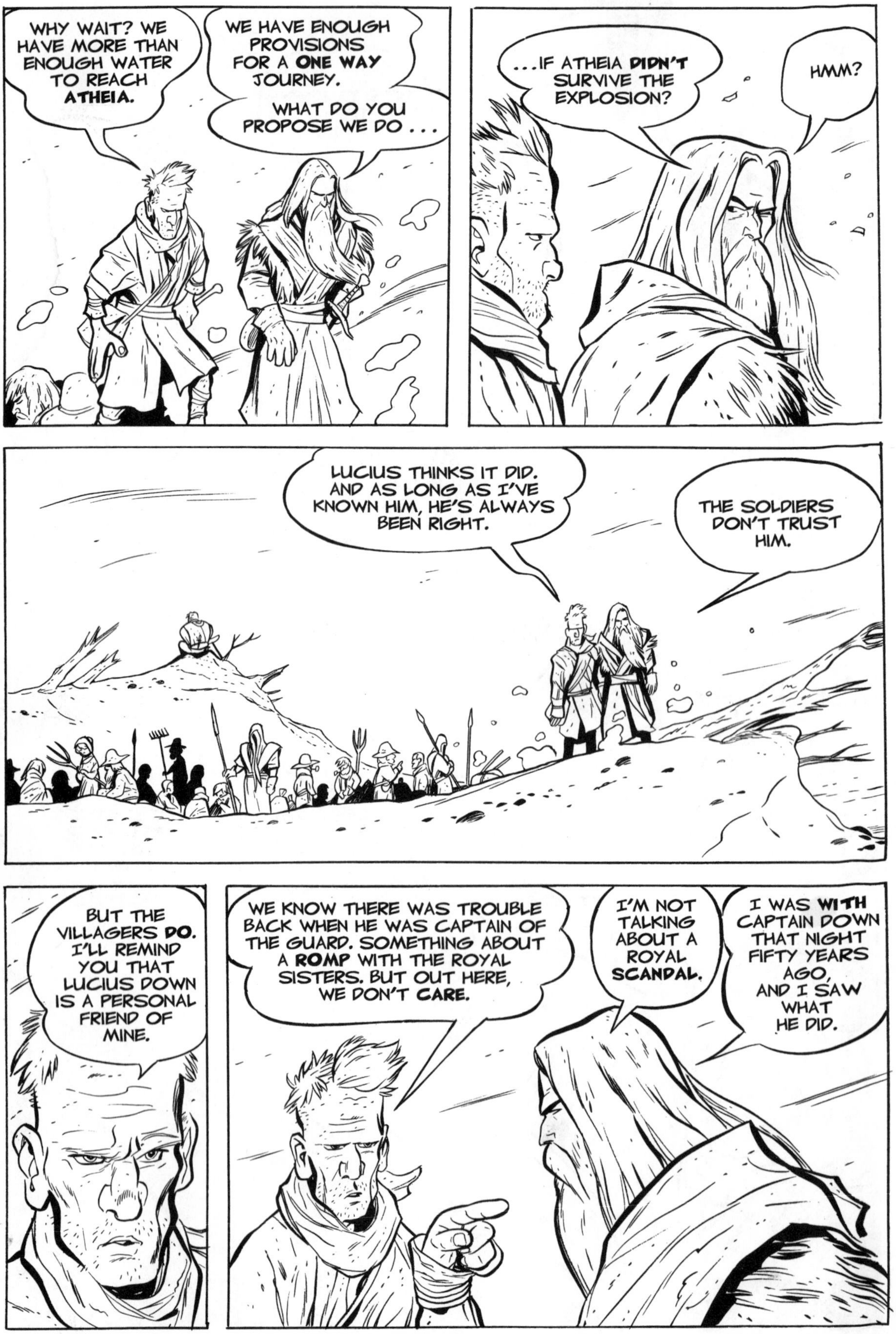
WHY WAIT? WE HAVE MORE THAN ENOUGH WATER TO REACH **ATHEIA.**
WE HAVE ENOUGH PROVISIONS FOR A **ONE WAY** JOURNEY.
WHAT DO YOU PROPOSE WE DO . . .
. . .IF ATHEIA **DIDN'T** SURVIVE THE EXPLOSION?
HMM?
LUCIUS THINKS IT DID. AND AS LONG AS I'VE KNOWN HIM, HE'S ALWAYS BEEN RIGHT.
THE SOLDIERS DON'T TRUST HIM.
BUT THE VILLAGERS **DO.** I'LL REMIND YOU THAT LUCIUS DOWN IS A PERSONAL FRIEND OF MINE.
WE KNOW THERE WAS TROUBLE BACK WHEN HE WAS CAPTAIN OF THE GUARD. SOMETHING ABOUT A **ROMP** WITH THE ROYAL SISTERS. BUT OUT HERE, WE DON'T **CARE.**
I'M NOT TALKING ABOUT A ROYAL **SCANDAL.**
I WAS **WITH** CAPTAIN DOWN THAT NIGHT FIFTY YEARS AGO, AND I SAW WHAT HE DID.

HE MARCHED OUR ARMY STRAIGHT INTO A **RAT CREATURE TRAP**. THE BLOODBATH THAT FOLLOWED WAS THE BEGINING OF THE **GREAT WAR** ITSELF.

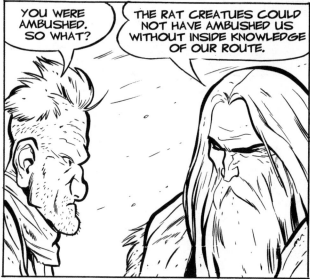

YOU WERE AMBUSHED. SO WHAT?

THE RAT CREATUES COULD NOT HAVE AMBUSHED US WITHOUT INSIDE KNOWLEDGE OF OUR ROUTE.

WHY WOULD HE DO IT? LUCIUS DOESN'T LIKE RAT CREATURES. HE **FIGHTS** THEM!

HE WAS THE ONLY ONE WHO KNEW OUR ROUTE THAT NIGHT.

ONLY HE COULD HAVE ALERTED THE ENEMY.

FIFTY YEARS LATER, WHERE'S YOUR **PROOF?!**

A YOUNG FARMER NAMED **JONATHAN OAKS** HAS GIVEN US OUR PROOF.

JON -- ?

OH, BLOODY STARS.

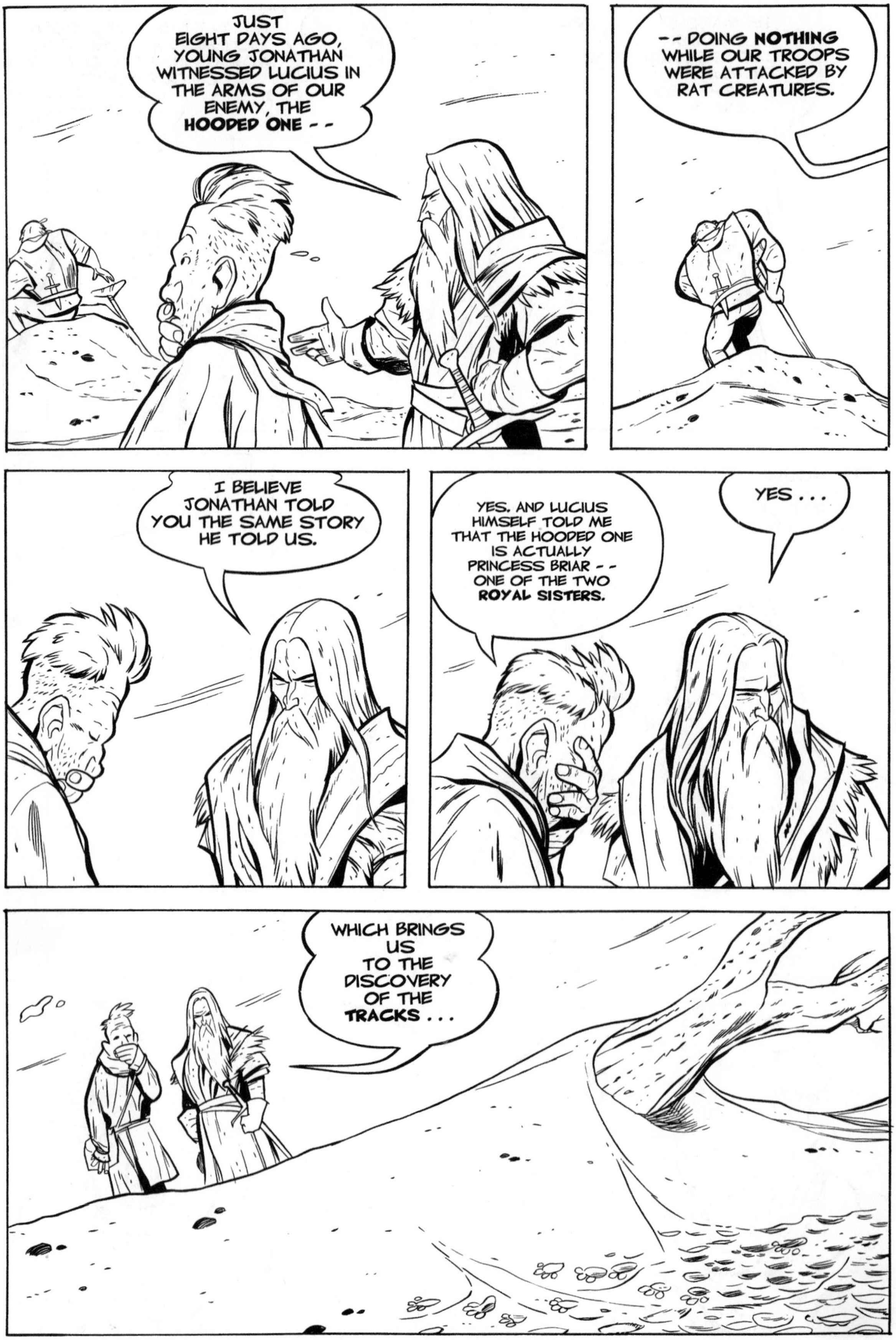
JUST EIGHT DAYS AGO, YOUNG JONATHAN WITNESSED LUCIUS IN THE ARMS OF OUR ENEMY, THE **HOODED ONE** - -
- - DOING **NOTHING** WHILE OUR TROOPS WERE ATTACKED BY RAT CREATURES.
I BELIEVE JONATHAN TOLD YOU THE SAME STORY HE TOLD US.
YES. AND LUCIUS HIMSELF TOLD ME THAT THE HOODED ONE IS ACTUALLY PRINCESS BRIAR - - ONE OF THE TWO **ROYAL SISTERS.**
YES . . .
WHICH BRINGS US TO THE DISCOVERY OF THE **TRACKS** . . .

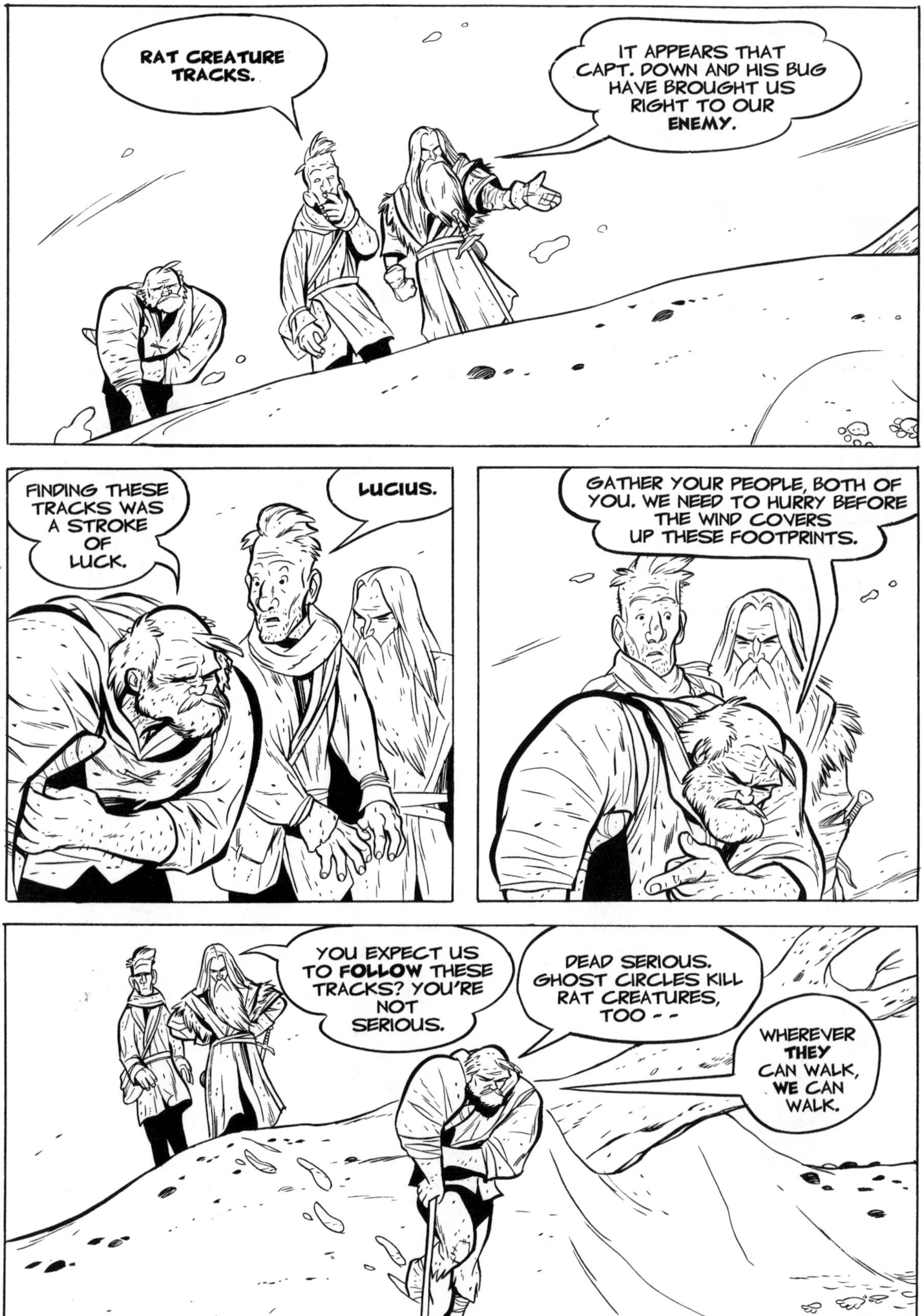
RAT CREATURE TRACKS.
IT APPEARS THAT CAPT. DOWN AND HIS BUG HAVE BROUGHT US RIGHT TO OUR ENEMY.
FINDING THESE TRACKS WAS A STROKE OF LUCK.
LUCIUS.
GATHER YOUR PEOPLE, BOTH OF YOU. WE NEED TO HURRY BEFORE THE WIND COVERS UP THESE FOOTPRINTS.
YOU EXPECT US TO FOLLOW THESE TRACKS? YOU'RE NOT SERIOUS.
DEAD SERIOUS. GHOST CIRCLES KILL RAT CREATURES, TOO - -
WHEREVER THEY CAN WALK, WE CAN WALK.

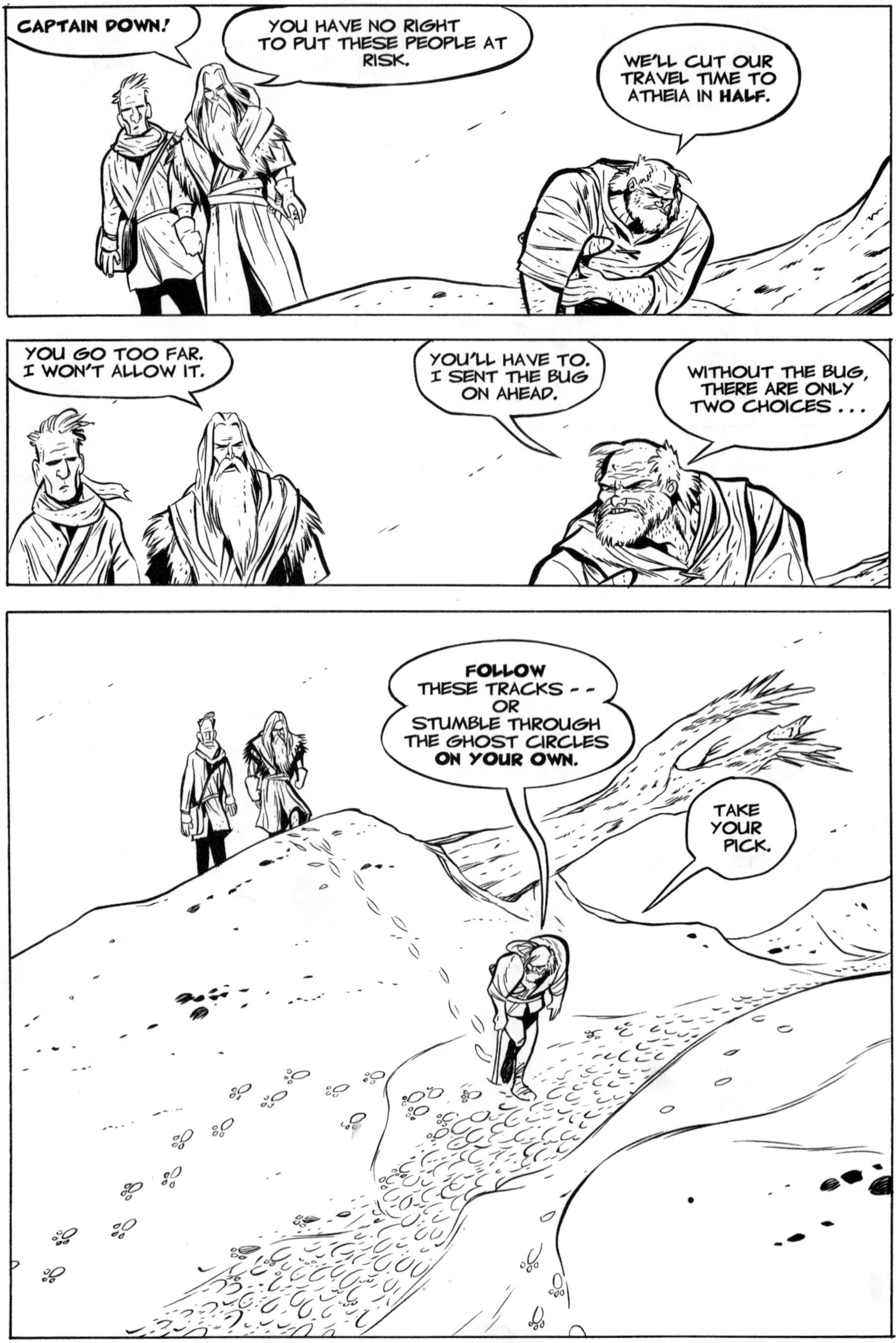
CAPTAIN DOWN!
YOU HAVE NO RIGHT TO PUT THESE PEOPLE AT RISK.
WE'LL CUT OUR TRAVEL TIME TO ATHEIA IN HALF.
YOU GO TOO FAR. I WON'T ALLOW IT.
YOU'LL HAVE TO. I SENT THE BUG ON AHEAD.
WITHOUT THE BUG, THERE ARE ONLY TWO CHOICES . . .
FOLLOW THESE TRACKS - - OR STUMBLE THROUGH THE GHOST CIRCLES ON YOUR OWN.
TAKE YOUR PICK.

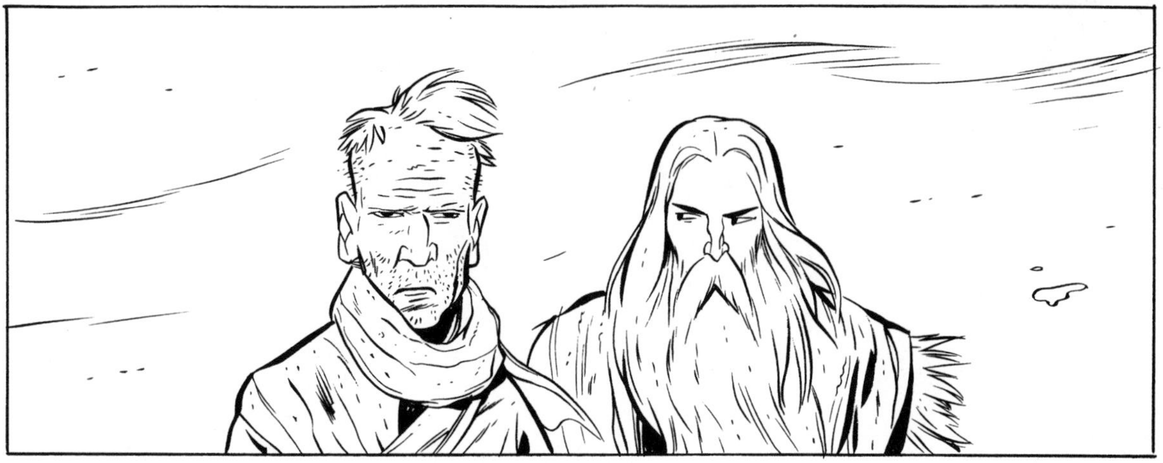

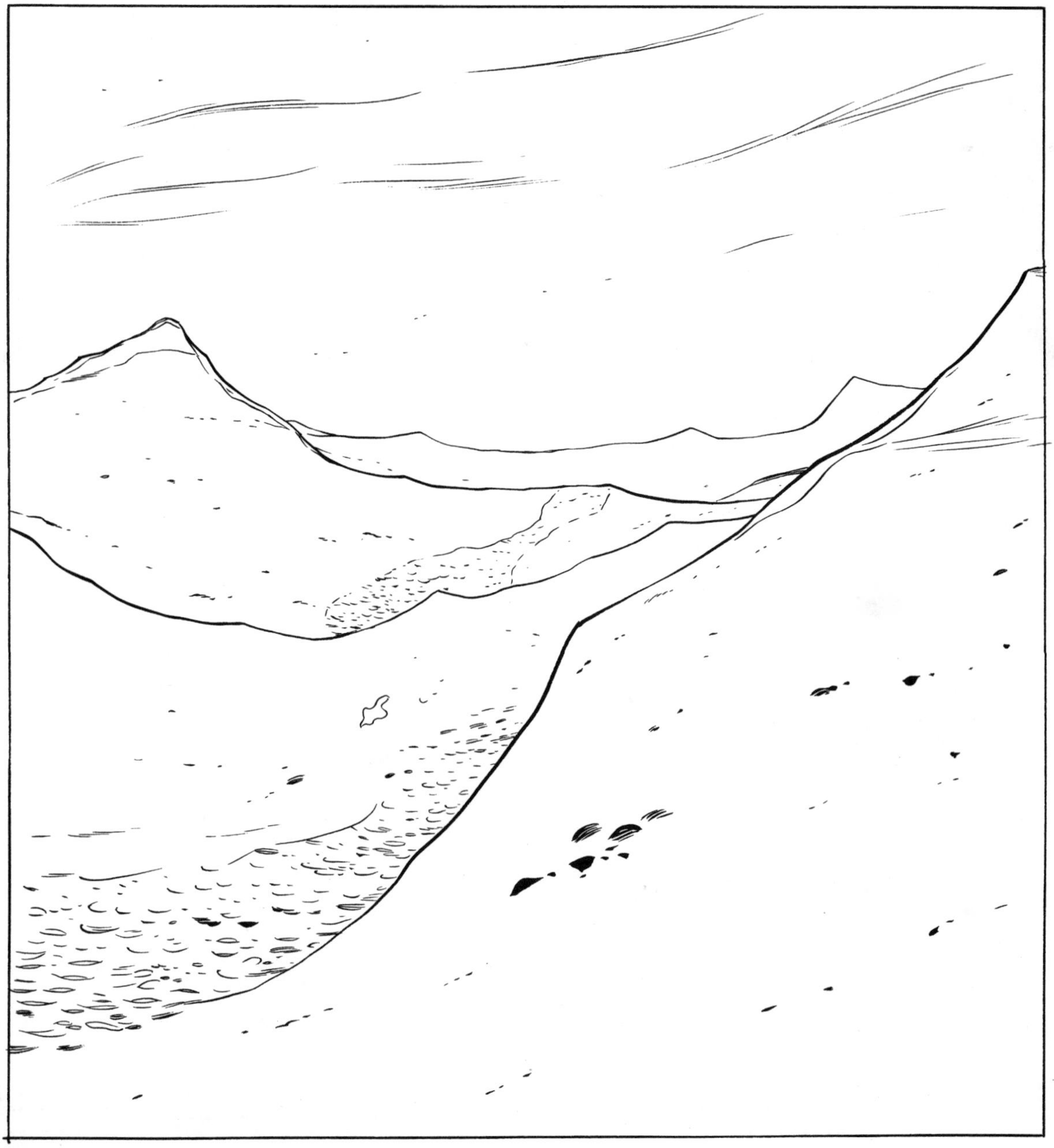

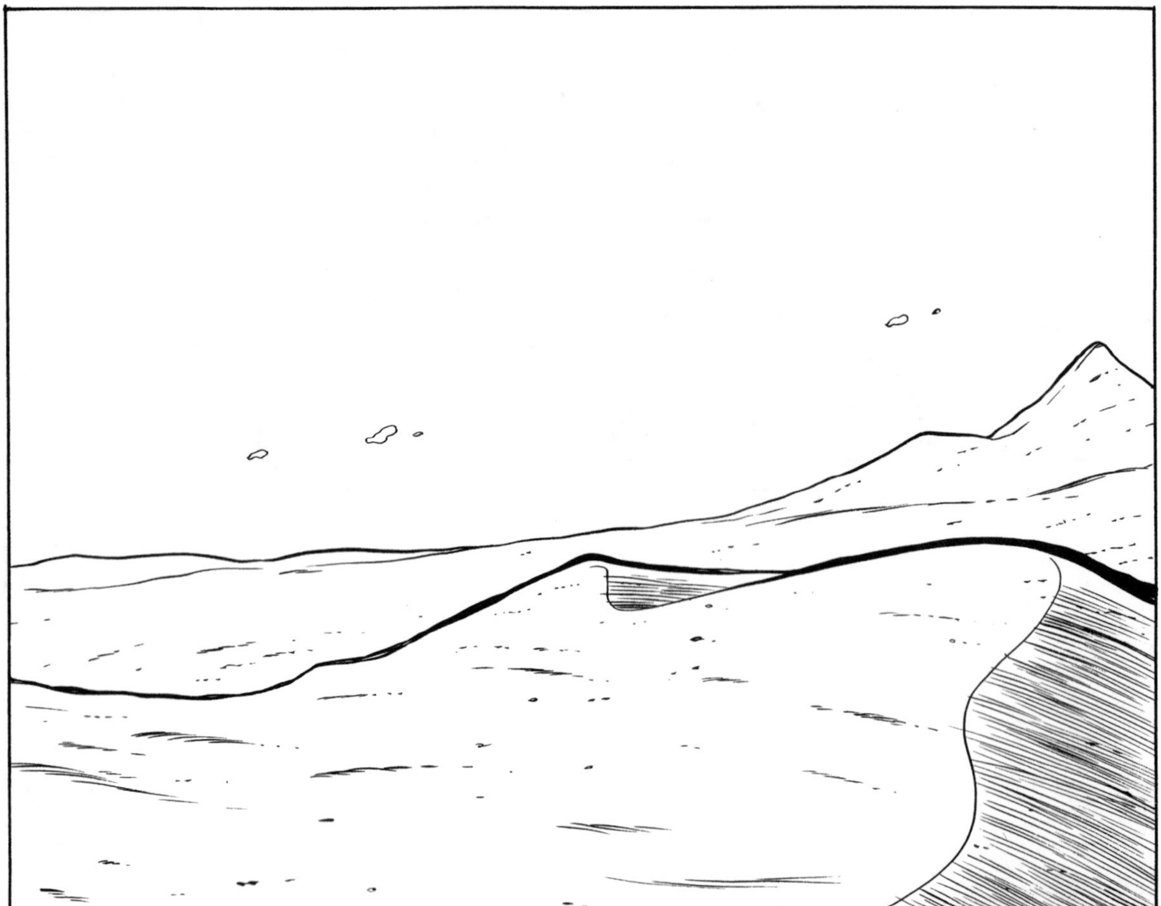

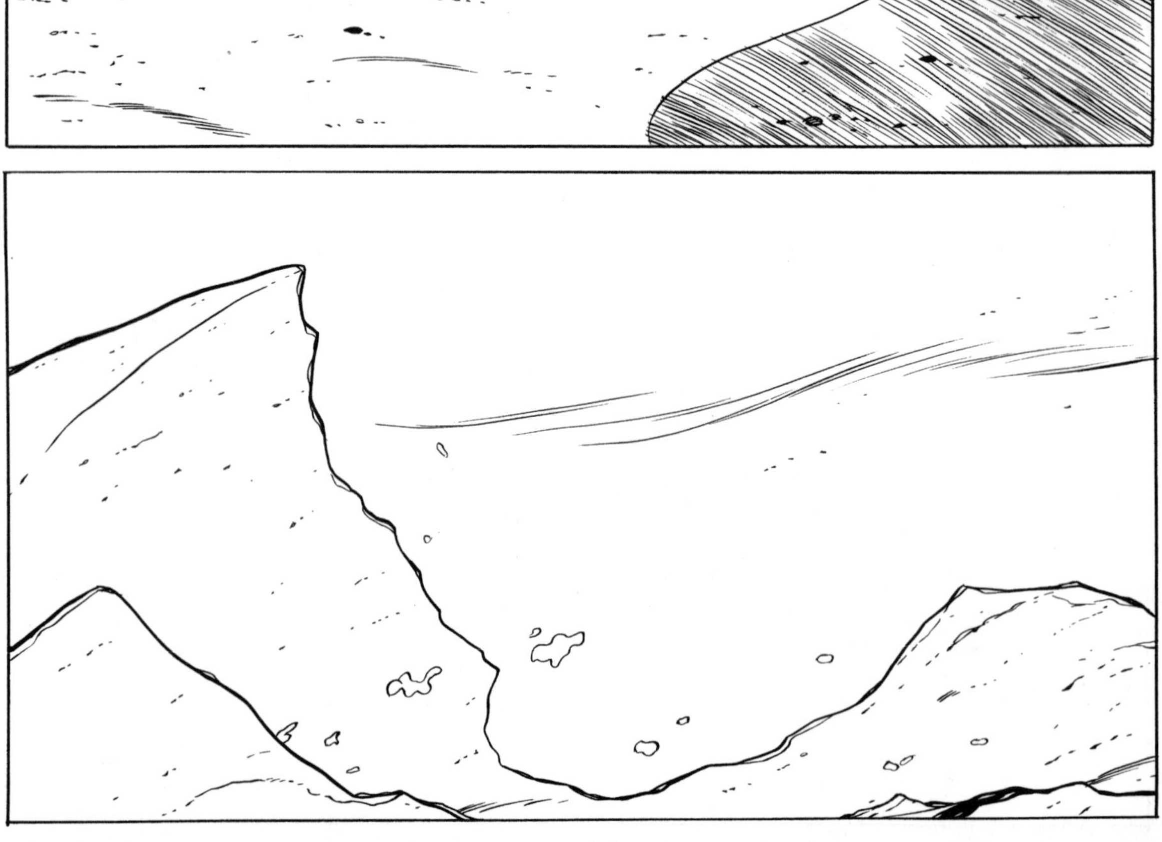

TREASURE HUNTERS

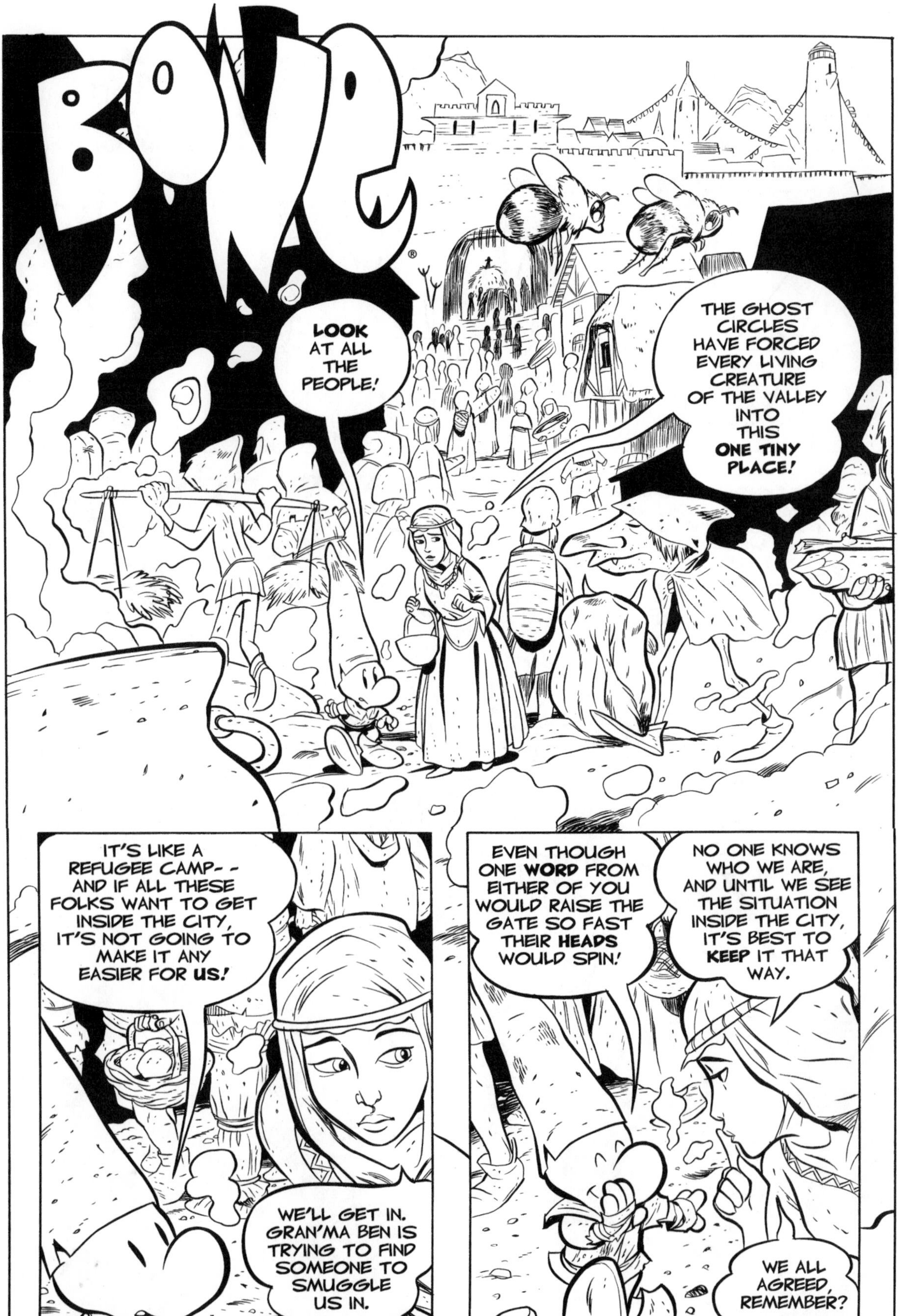
BONE®
LOOK AT ALL THE PEOPLE!
THE GHOST CIRCLES HAVE FORCED EVERY LIVING CREATURE OF THE VALLEY INTO THIS ONE TINY PLACE!
IT'S LIKE A REFUGEE CAMP-- AND IF ALL THESE FOLKS WANT TO GET INSIDE THE CITY, IT'S NOT GOING TO MAKE IT ANY EASIER FOR US!
WE'LL GET IN. GRAN'MA BEN IS TRYING TO FIND SOMEONE TO SMUGGLE US IN.
EVEN THOUGH ONE WORD FROM EITHER OF YOU WOULD RAISE THE GATE SO FAST THEIR HEADS WOULD SPIN!
NO ONE KNOWS WHO WE ARE, AND UNTIL WE SEE THE SITUATION INSIDE THE CITY, IT'S BEST TO KEEP IT THAT WAY.
WE ALL AGREED, REMEMBER?

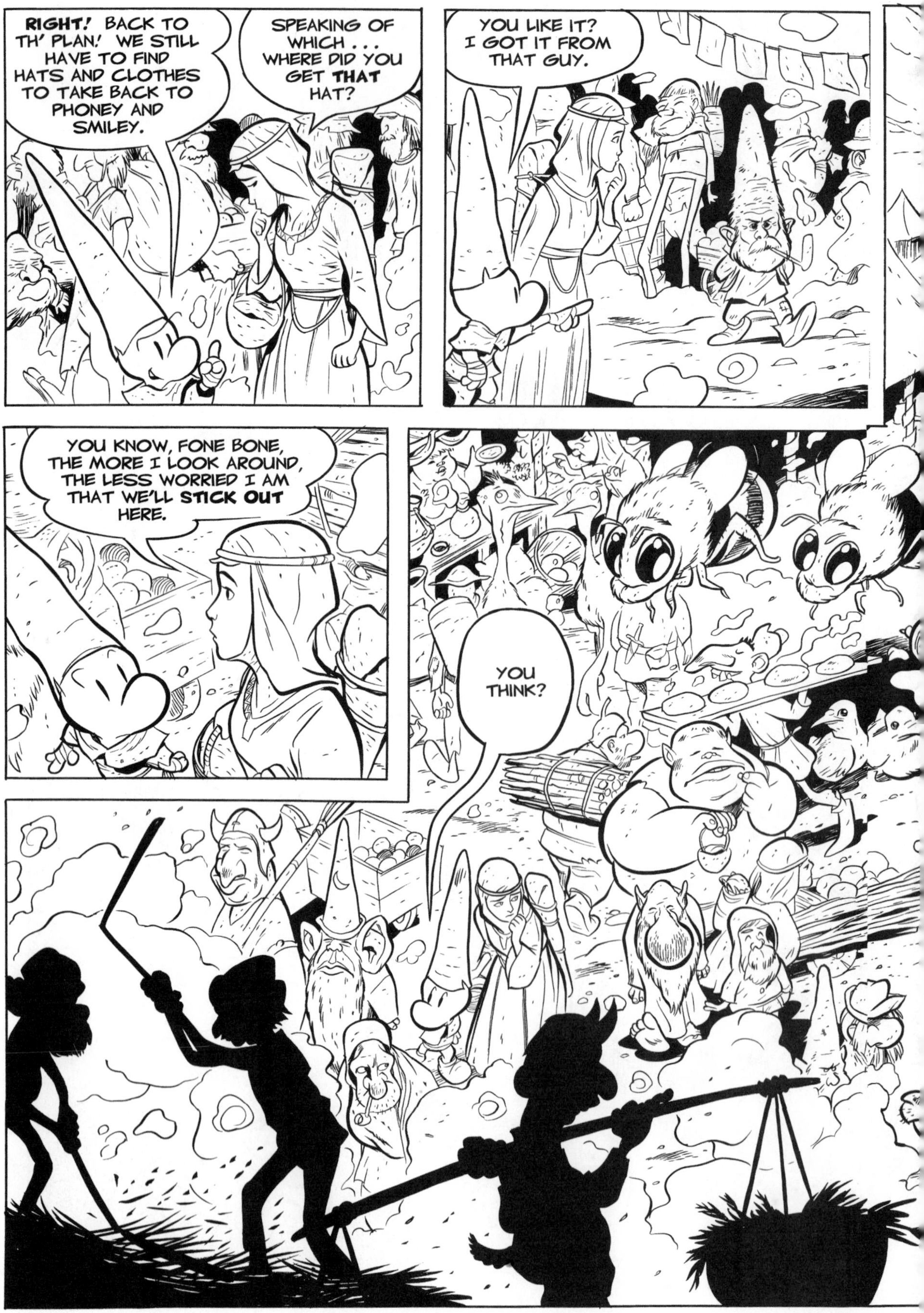
RIGHT! BACK TO TH' PLAN! WE STILL HAVE TO FIND HATS AND CLOTHES TO TAKE BACK TO PHONEY AND SMILEY.
SPEAKING OF WHICH . . . WHERE DID YOU GET **THAT** HAT?
YOU LIKE IT? I GOT IT FROM THAT GUY.
YOU KNOW, FONE BONE, THE MORE I LOOK AROUND, THE LESS WORRIED I AM THAT WE'LL **STICK OUT** HERE.
YOU THINK?

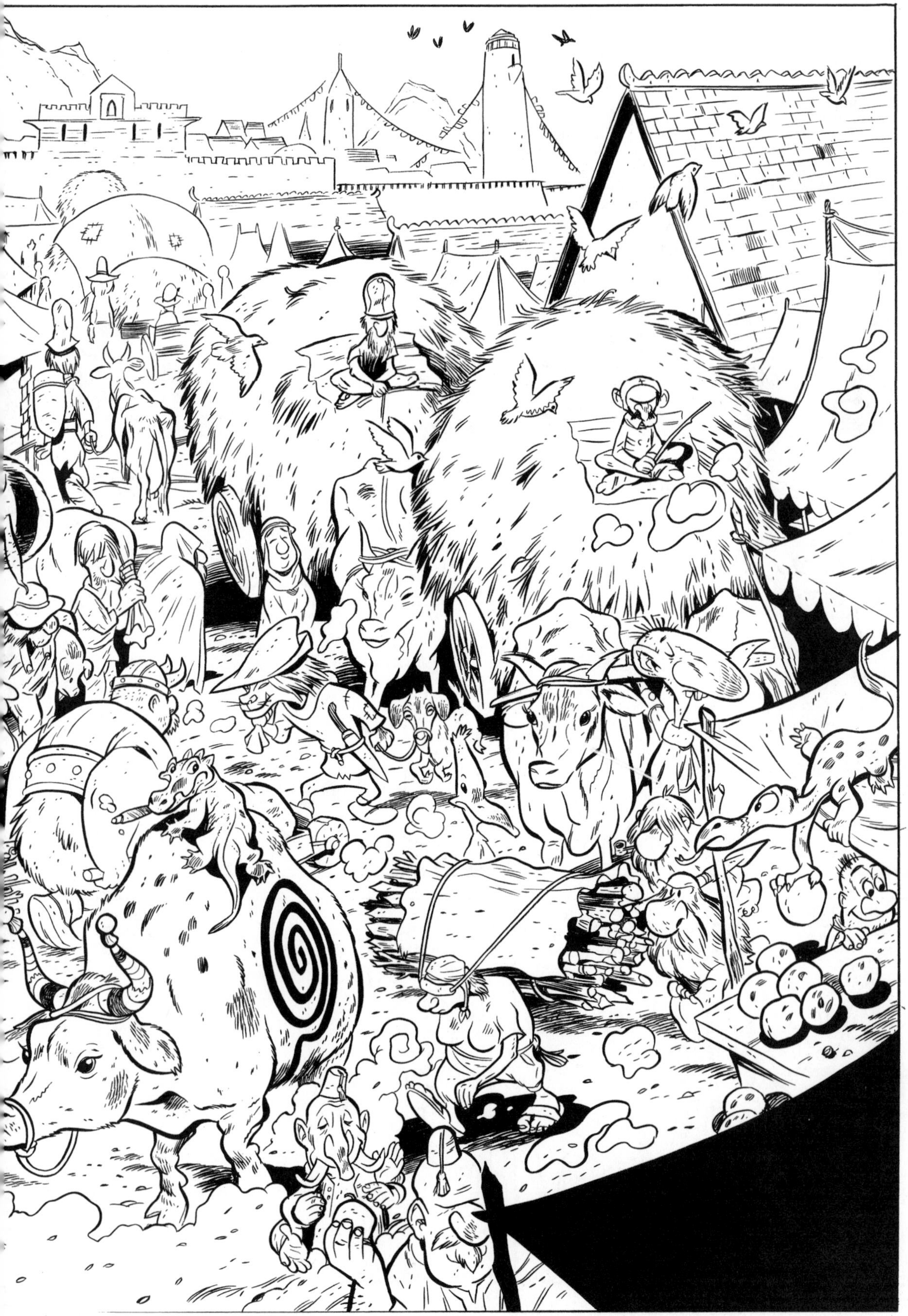

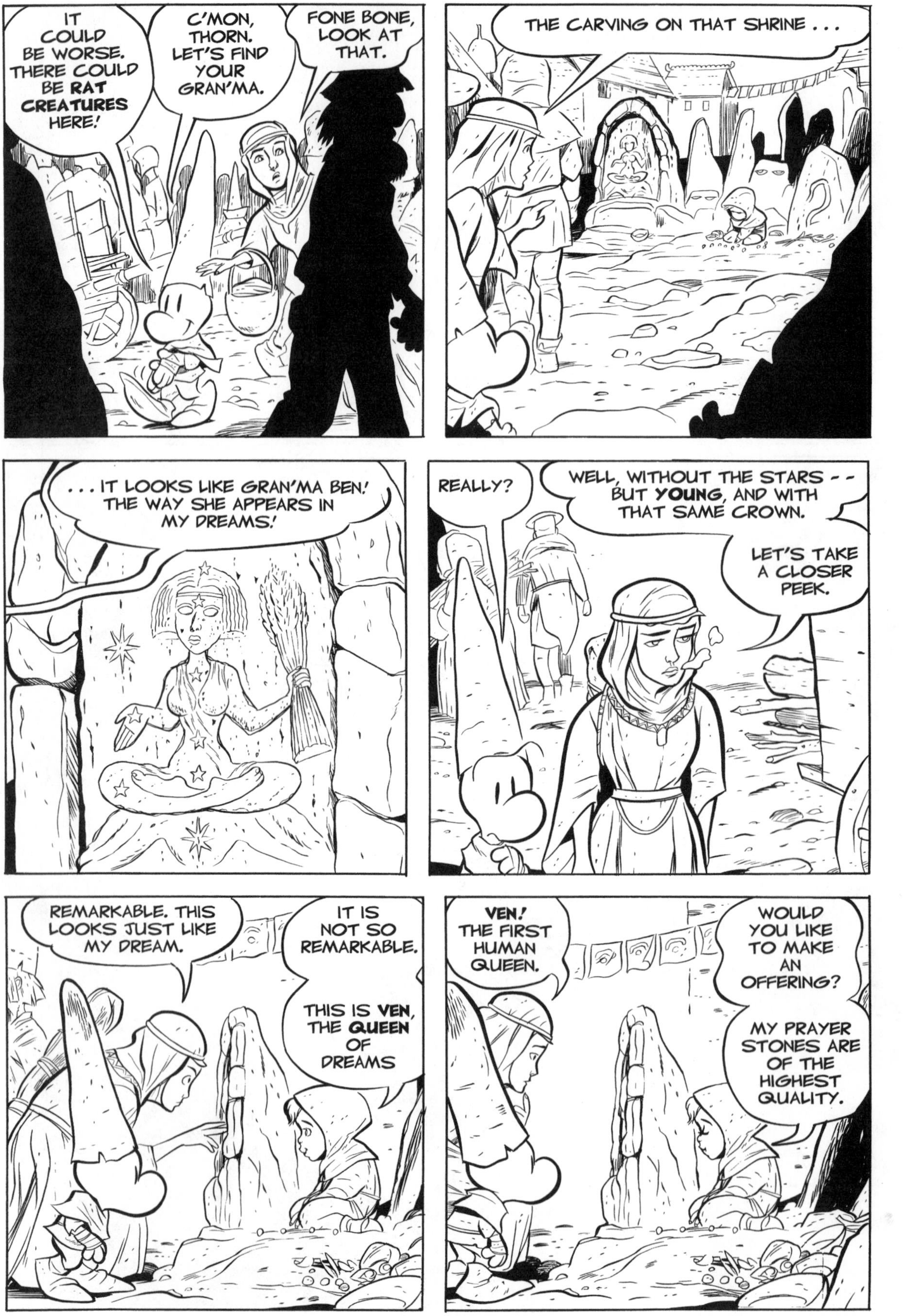
IT COULD BE WORSE. THERE COULD BE RAT CREATURES HERE!
C'MON, THORN. LET'S FIND YOUR GRAN'MA.
FONE BONE, LOOK AT THAT.
THE CARVING ON THAT SHRINE . . .
. . . IT LOOKS LIKE GRAN'MA BEN! THE WAY SHE APPEARS IN MY DREAMS!
REALLY?
WELL, WITHOUT THE STARS -- BUT YOUNG, AND WITH THAT SAME CROWN.
LET'S TAKE A CLOSER PEEK.
REMARKABLE. THIS LOOKS JUST LIKE MY DREAM.
IT IS NOT SO REMARKABLE.
THIS IS VEN, THE QUEEN OF DREAMS
VEN! THE FIRST HUMAN QUEEN.
WOULD YOU LIKE TO MAKE AN OFFERING?
MY PRAYER STONES ARE OF THE HIGHEST QUALITY.

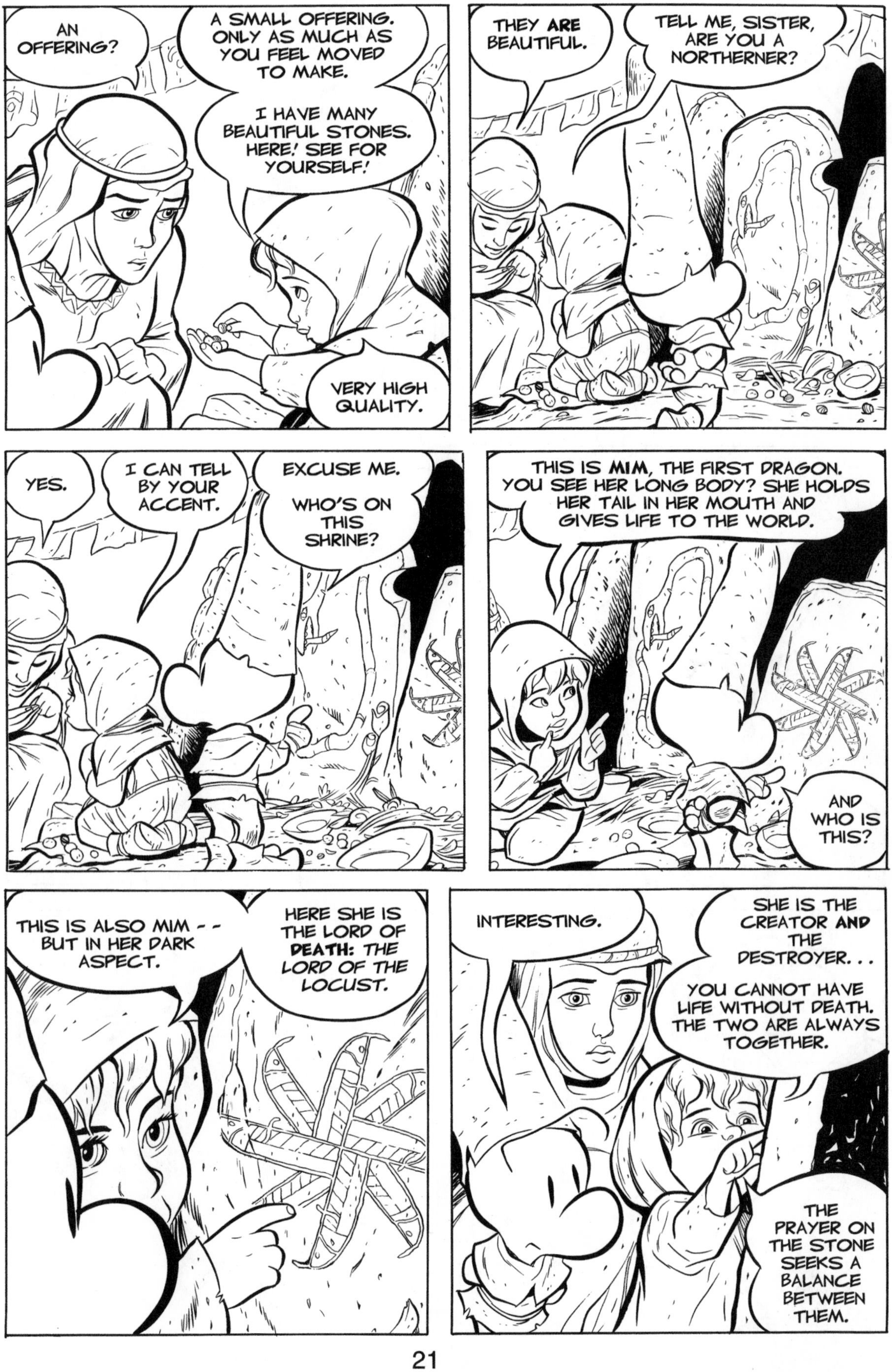
AN OFFERING?
A SMALL OFFERING. ONLY AS MUCH AS YOU FEEL MOVED TO MAKE.
I HAVE MANY BEAUTIFUL STONES. HERE! SEE FOR YOURSELF!
VERY HIGH QUALITY.
THEY **ARE** BEAUTIFUL.
TELL ME, SISTER, ARE YOU A NORTHERNER?
YES.
I CAN TELL BY YOUR ACCENT.
EXCUSE ME.
WHO'S ON THIS SHRINE?
THIS IS **MIM**, THE FIRST DRAGON. YOU SEE HER LONG BODY? SHE HOLDS HER TAIL IN HER MOUTH AND GIVES LIFE TO THE WORLD.
AND WHO IS THIS?
THIS IS ALSO MIM - - BUT IN HER DARK ASPECT.
HERE SHE IS THE LORD OF **DEATH:** *THE LORD OF THE LOCUST.*
INTERESTING.
SHE IS THE CREATOR **AND** THE DESTROYER. . .
YOU CANNOT HAVE LIFE WITHOUT DEATH. THE TWO ARE ALWAYS TOGETHER.
THE PRAYER ON THE STONE SEEKS A BALANCE BETWEEN THEM.

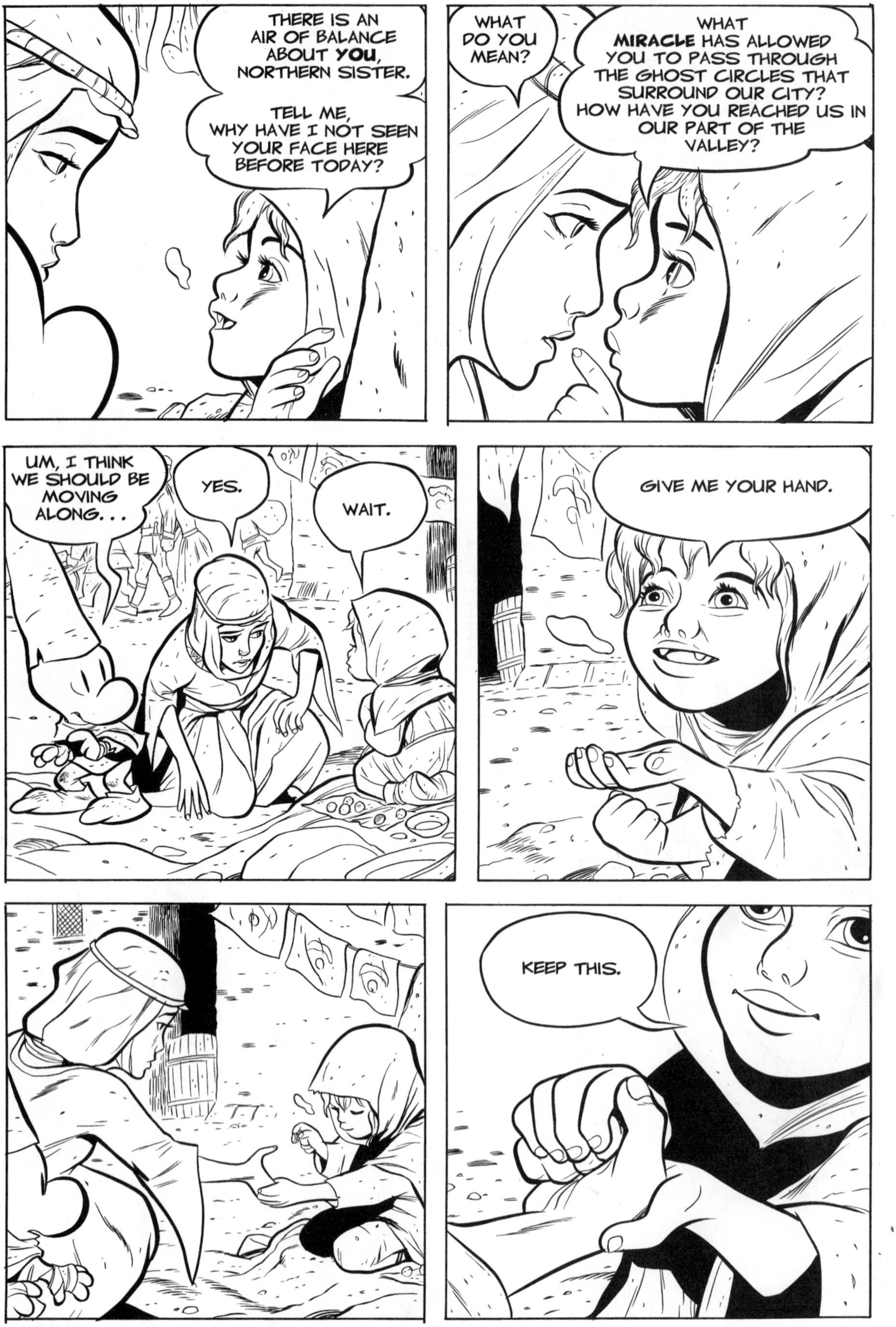
THERE IS AN AIR OF BALANCE ABOUT **YOU**, NORTHERN SISTER.
TELL ME, WHY HAVE I NOT SEEN YOUR FACE HERE BEFORE TODAY?
WHAT DO YOU MEAN?
WHAT **MIRACLE** HAS ALLOWED YOU TO PASS THROUGH THE GHOST CIRCLES THAT SURROUND OUR CITY? HOW HAVE YOU REACHED US IN OUR PART OF THE VALLEY?
UM, I THINK WE SHOULD BE MOVING ALONG...
YES.
WAIT.
GIVE ME YOUR HAND.
KEEP THIS.

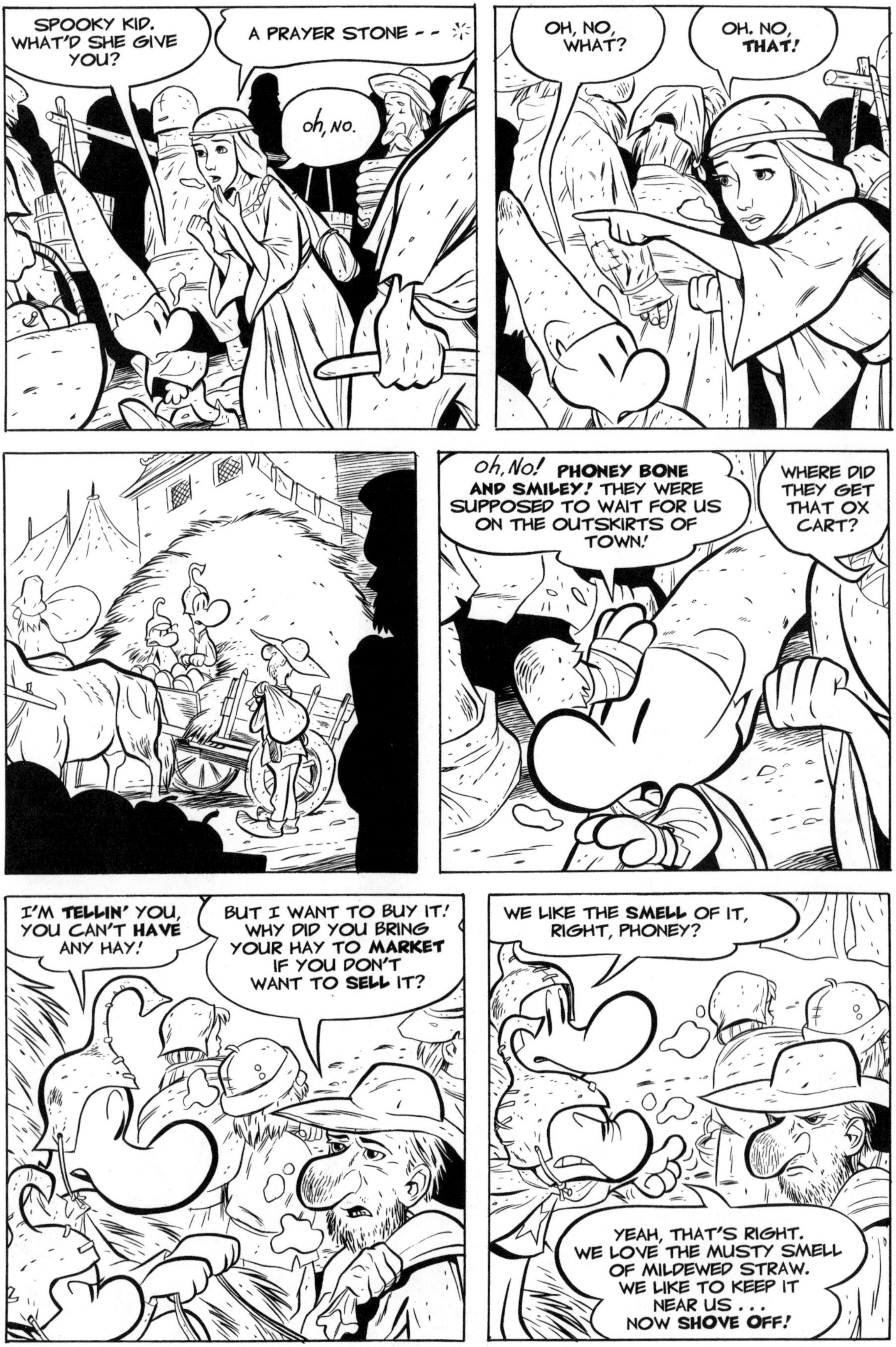
SPOOKY KID. WHAT'D SHE GIVE YOU?
A PRAYER STONE - -
oh, NO.
OH, NO, WHAT?
OH. NO, **THAT!**
oh, No! **PHONEY BONE AND SMILEY!** THEY WERE SUPPOSED TO WAIT FOR US ON THE OUTSKIRTS OF TOWN!
WHERE DID THEY GET THAT OX CART?
I'M **TELLIN'** YOU, YOU CAN'T **HAVE** ANY HAY!
BUT I WANT TO BUY IT! WHY DID YOU BRING YOUR HAY TO **MARKET** IF YOU DON'T WANT TO **SELL** IT?
WE LIKE THE **SMELL** OF IT, RIGHT, PHONEY?
YEAH, THAT'S RIGHT. WE LOVE THE MUSTY SMELL OF MILDEWED STRAW. WE LIKE TO KEEP IT NEAR US . . . NOW **SHOVE OFF!**

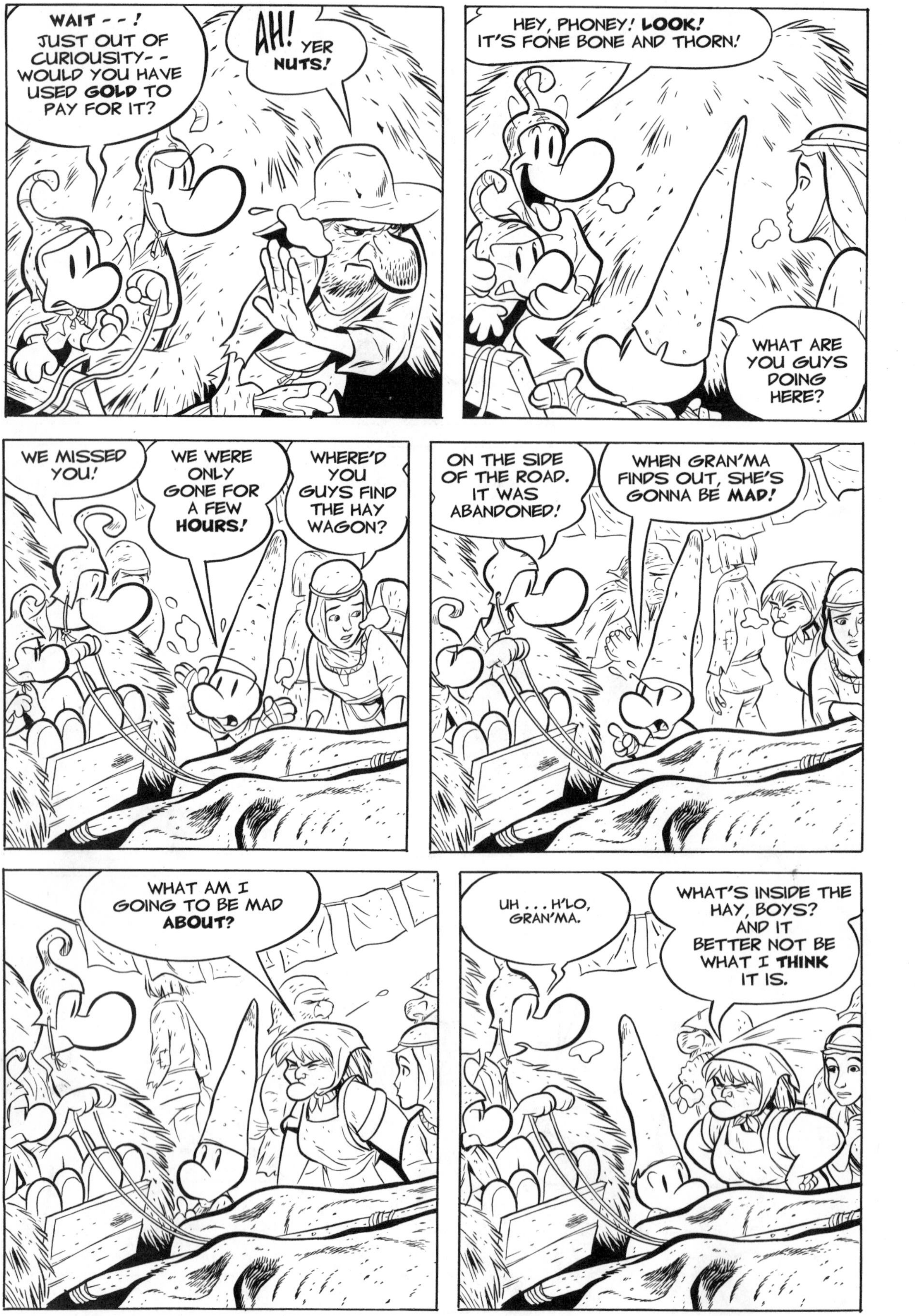
WAIT - - ! JUST OUT OF CURIOUSITY- - WOULD YOU HAVE USED **GOLD** TO PAY FOR IT?
AH! YER **NUTS!**
HEY, PHONEY! **LOOK!** IT'S FONE BONE AND THORN!
WHAT ARE YOU GUYS DOING HERE?
WE MISSED YOU!
WE WERE ONLY GONE FOR A FEW **HOURS!**
WHERE'D YOU GUYS FIND THE HAY WAGON?
ON THE SIDE OF THE ROAD. IT WAS ABANDONED!
WHEN GRAN'MA FINDS OUT, SHE'S GONNA BE **MAD!**
WHAT AM I GOING TO BE MAD **ABOUT?**
UH . . . H'LO, GRAN'MA.
WHAT'S INSIDE THE HAY, BOYS? AND IT BETTER NOT BE WHAT I **THINK** IT IS.

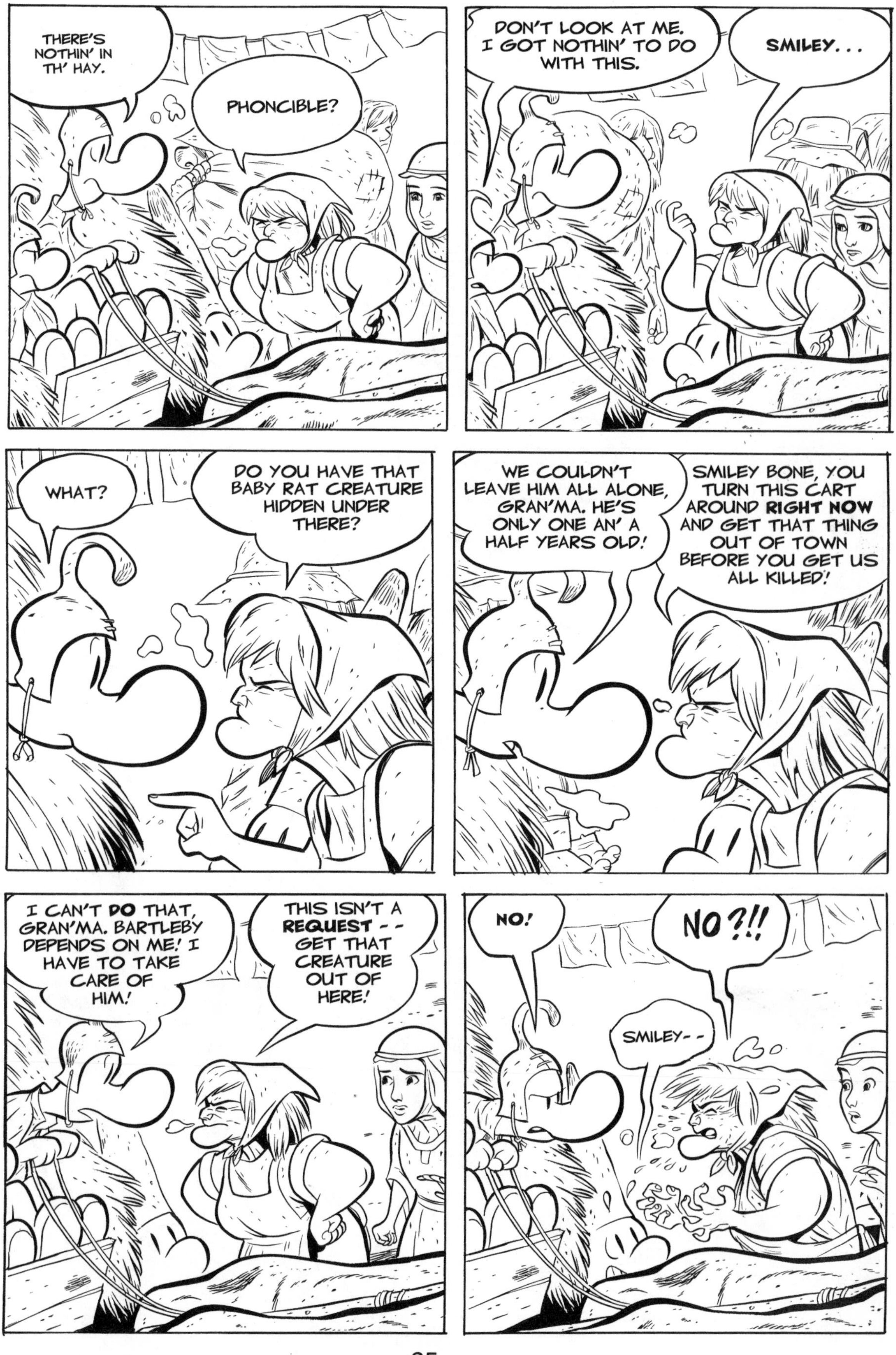
THERE'S NOTHIN' IN TH' HAY.
PHONCIBLE?
DON'T LOOK AT ME. I GOT NOTHIN' TO DO WITH THIS.
SMILEY. . .
WHAT?
DO YOU HAVE THAT BABY RAT CREATURE HIDDEN UNDER THERE?
WE COULDN'T LEAVE HIM ALL ALONE, GRAN'MA. HE'S ONLY ONE AN' A HALF YEARS OLD!
SMILEY BONE, YOU TURN THIS CART AROUND RIGHT NOW AND GET THAT THING OUT OF TOWN BEFORE YOU GET US ALL KILLED!
I CAN'T DO THAT, GRAN'MA. BARTLEBY DEPENDS ON ME! I HAVE TO TAKE CARE OF HIM!
THIS ISN'T A REQUEST - - GET THAT CREATURE OUT OF HERE!
NO!
NO?!!
SMILEY- -

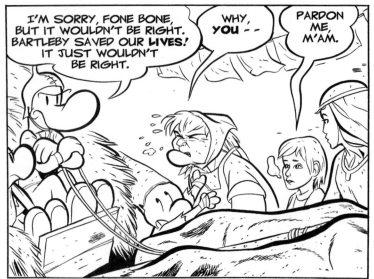

I'M SORRY, FONE BONE, BUT IT WOULDN'T BE RIGHT. BARTLEBY SAVED OUR LIVES! IT JUST WOULDN'T BE RIGHT.

WHY, YOU --

PARDON ME, M'AM.

YES?

I HEAR YOU WANT TO BUY A COYOTE?

WHO SENT YOU?

WILLIAM THE BAKER.

THE GHOST CIRLCLES AND THE CROWDS ARE MAKING THE CITY LEADERS NERVOUS. VERY FEW OUTSIDERS ARE ALLOWED THROUGH THE GATES.

CAN YOU GET US INSIDE THE CITY-- PAST THE GUARDS, WITHOUT ANY QUESTIONS?

HOW MANY IN YOUR PARTY?

FIVE.

FIVE PLUS A HAYCART.

A HAYCART WILL NOT BE SO EASY.

DO YOU KNOW ANYONE ON THE INSIDE? PERHAPS THAT WILL HELP...

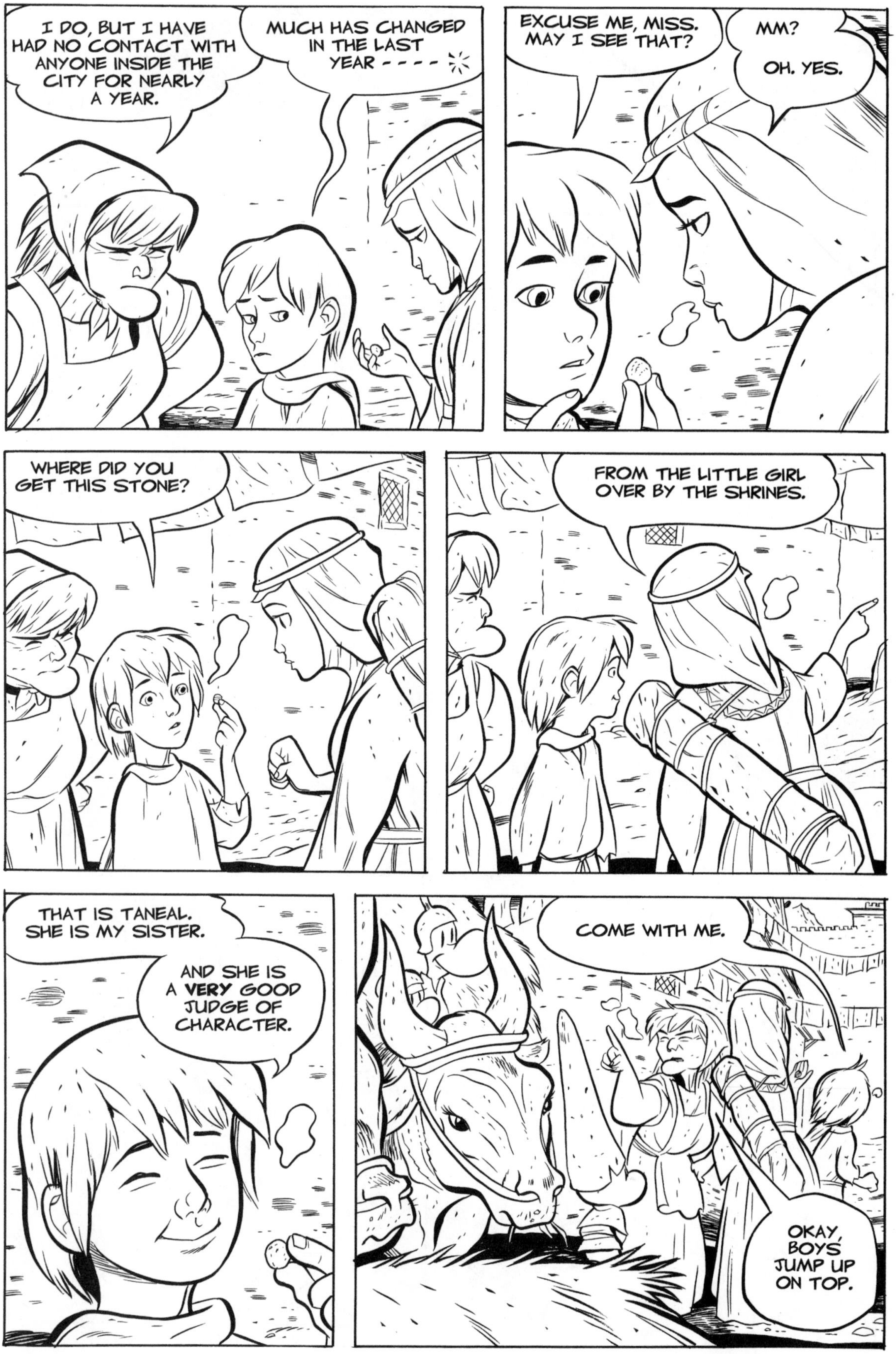
I DO, BUT I HAVE HAD NO CONTACT WITH ANYONE INSIDE THE CITY FOR NEARLY A YEAR.
MUCH HAS CHANGED IN THE LAST YEAR - - - -
EXCUSE ME, MISS. MAY I SEE THAT?
MM?
OH. YES.
WHERE DID YOU GET THIS STONE?
FROM THE LITTLE GIRL OVER BY THE SHRINES.
THAT IS TANEAL. SHE IS MY SISTER.
AND SHE IS A **VERY** GOOD JUDGE OF CHARACTER.
COME WITH ME.
OKAY, BOYS JUMP UP ON TOP.

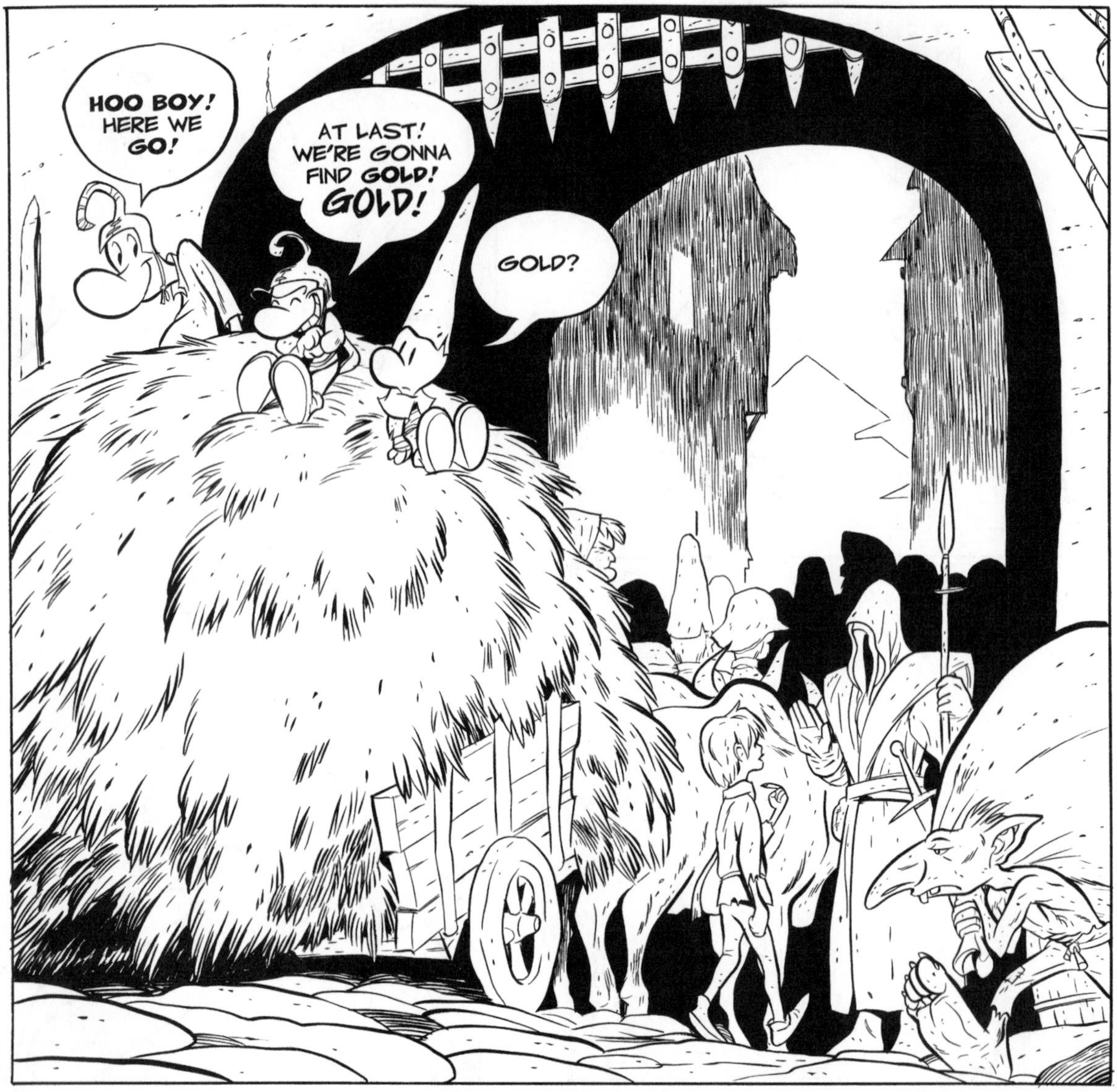
HOO BOY! HERE WE GO!
AT LAST! WE'RE GONNA FIND GOLD! GOLD!
GOLD?

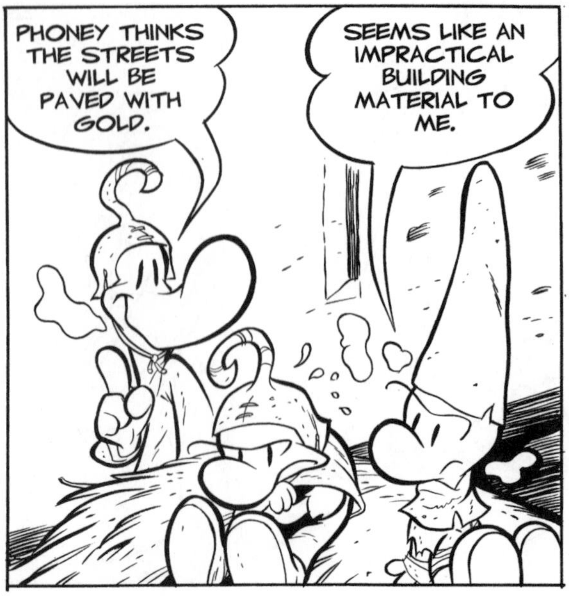
PHONEY THINKS THE STREETS WILL BE PAVED WITH GOLD.
SEEMS LIKE AN IMPRACTICAL BUILDING MATERIAL TO ME.

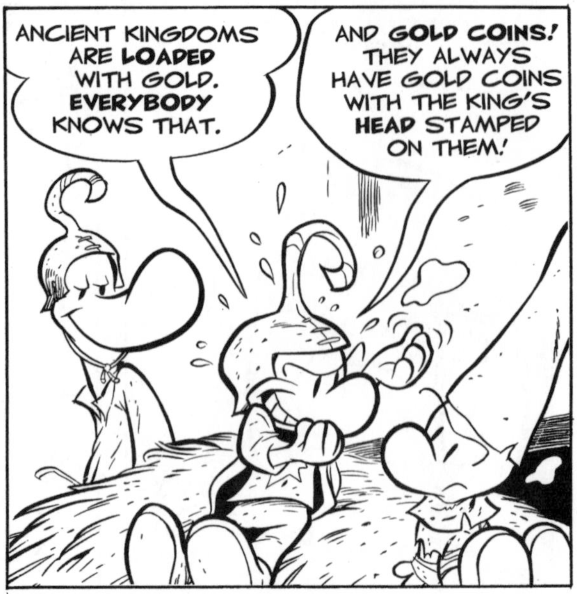
ANCIENT KINGDOMS ARE LOADED WITH GOLD. EVERYBODY KNOWS THAT.
AND GOLD COINS! THEY ALWAYS HAVE GOLD COINS WITH THE KING'S HEAD STAMPED ON THEM!

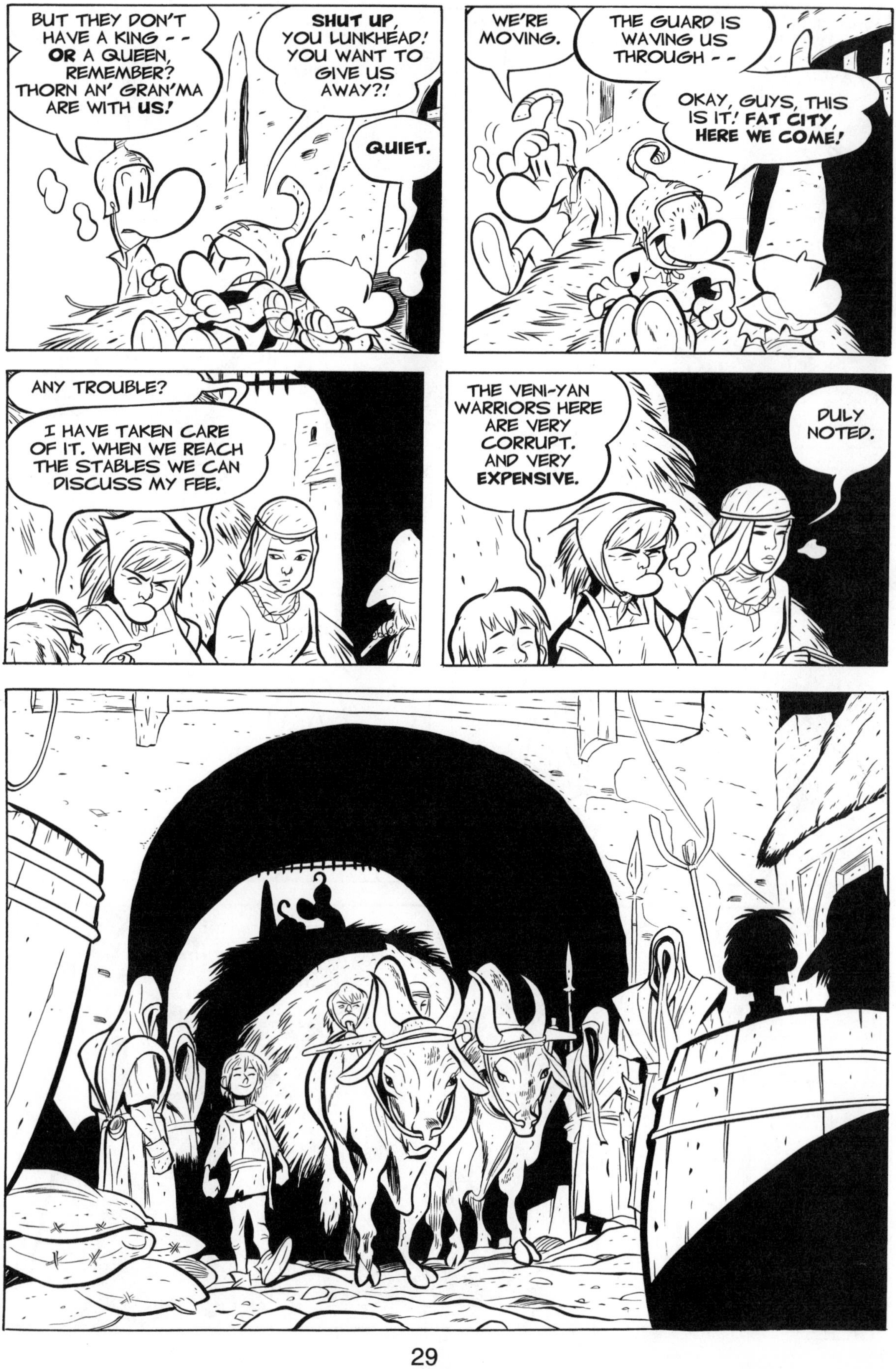
BUT THEY DON'T HAVE A KING - - OR A QUEEN, REMEMBER? THORN AN' GRAN'MA ARE WITH US!
SHUT UP, YOU LUNKHEAD! YOU WANT TO GIVE US AWAY?!
QUIET.
WE'RE MOVING.
THE GUARD IS WAVING US THROUGH - -
OKAY, GUYS, THIS IS IT! FAT CITY, HERE WE COME!
ANY TROUBLE?
I HAVE TAKEN CARE OF IT. WHEN WE REACH THE STABLES WE CAN DISCUSS MY FEE.
THE VENI-YAN WARRIORS HERE ARE VERY CORRUPT. AND VERY EXPENSIVE.
DULY NOTED.

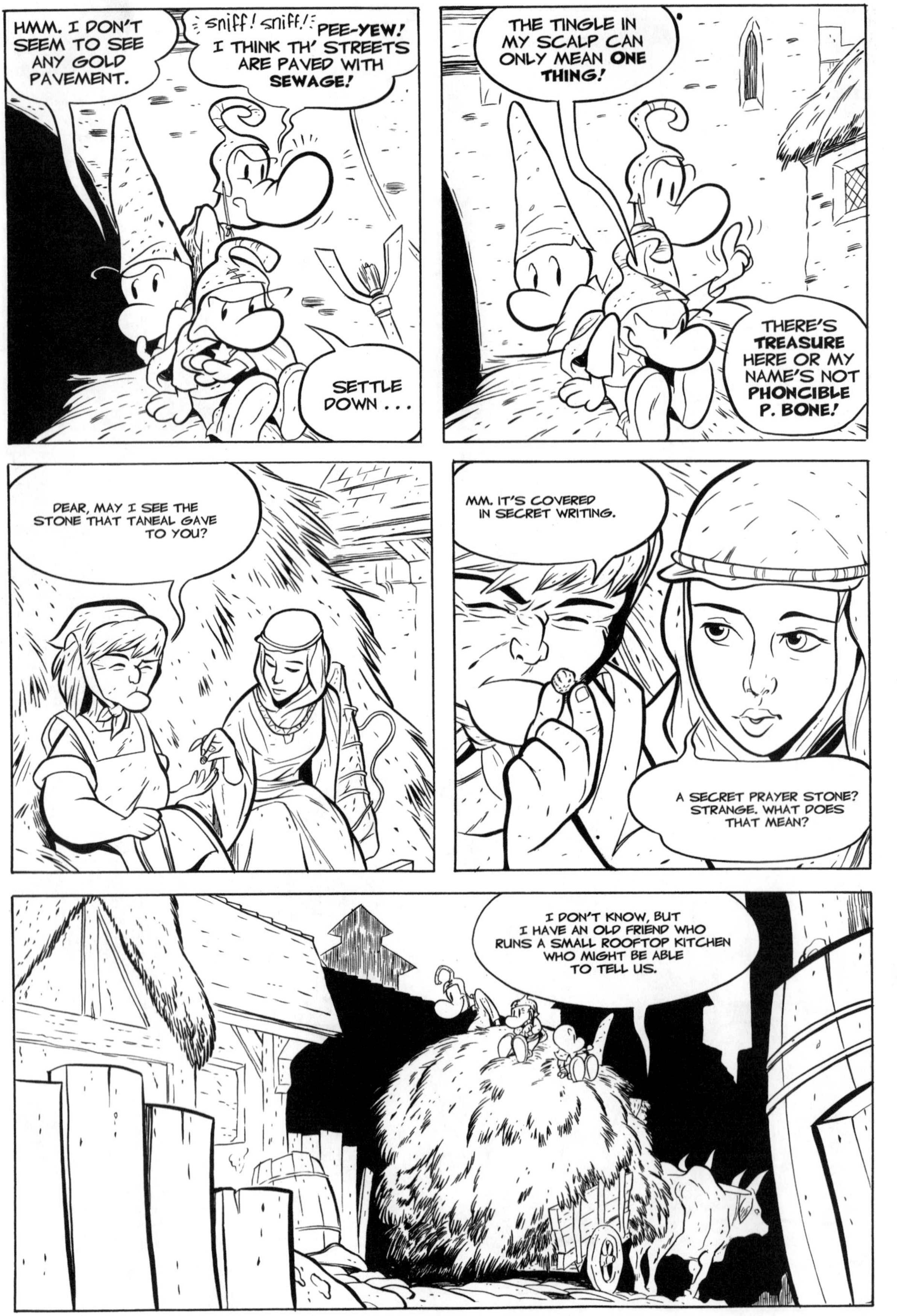

HMM. I DON'T SEEM TO SEE ANY GOLD PAVEMENT.
sniff! sniff!
PEE-YEW! I THINK TH' STREETS ARE PAVED WITH SEWAGE!
SETTLE DOWN . . .
THE TINGLE IN MY SCALP CAN ONLY MEAN ONE THING!
THERE'S TREASURE HERE OR MY NAME'S NOT PHONCIBLE P. BONE!
DEAR, MAY I SEE THE STONE THAT TANEAL GAVE TO YOU?
MM. IT'S COVERED IN SECRET WRITING.
A SECRET PRAYER STONE? STRANGE. WHAT DOES THAT MEAN?
I DON'T KNOW, BUT I HAVE AN OLD FRIEND WHO RUNS A SMALL ROOFTOP KITCHEN WHO MIGHT BE ABLE TO TELL US.

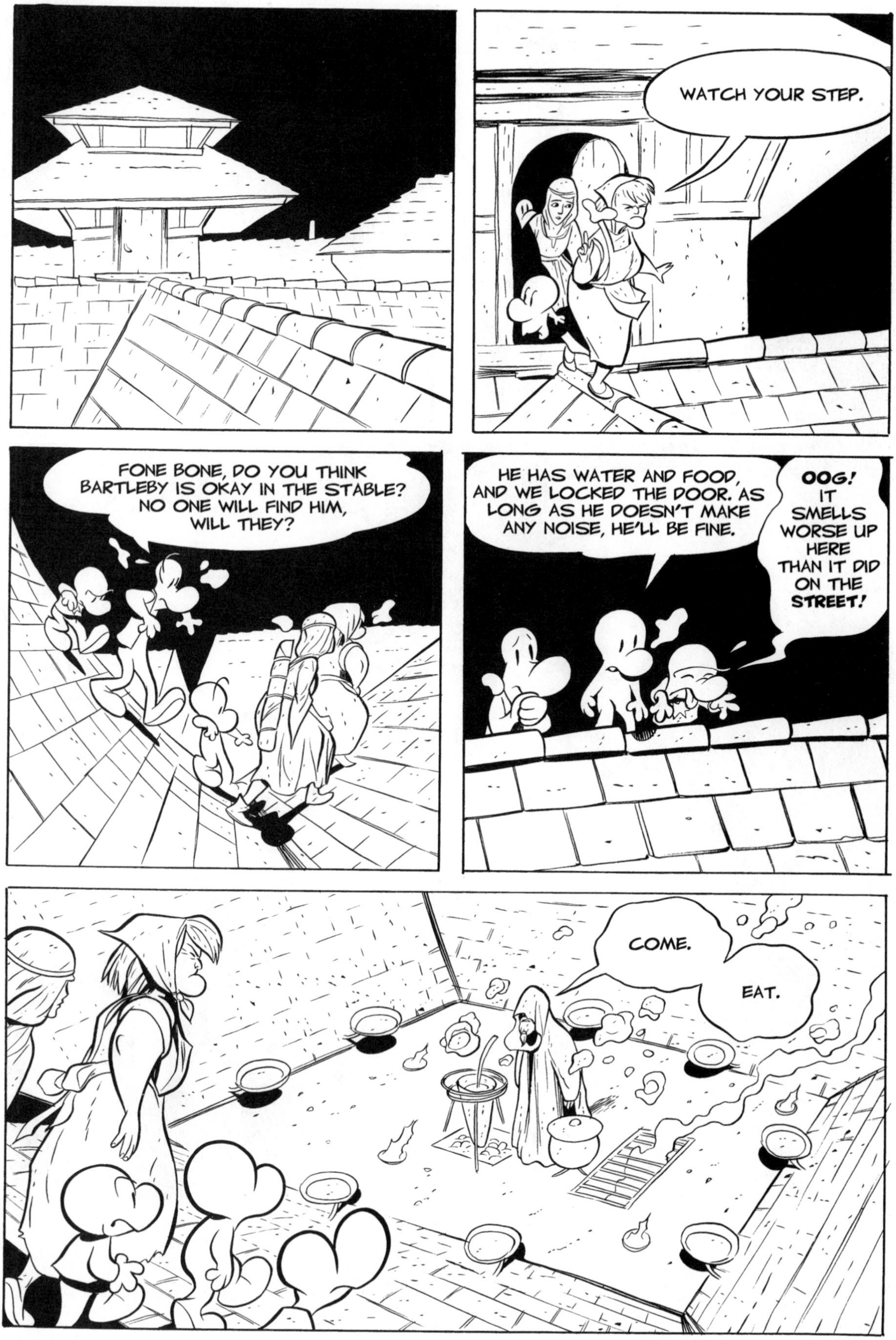
WATCH YOUR STEP.
FONE BONE, DO YOU THINK BARTLEBY IS OKAY IN THE STABLE? NO ONE WILL FIND HIM, WILL THEY?
HE HAS WATER AND FOOD, AND WE LOCKED THE DOOR. AS LONG AS HE DOESN'T MAKE ANY NOISE, HE'LL BE FINE.
OOG! IT SMELLS WORSE UP HERE THAN IT DID ON THE STREET!
COME.
EAT.

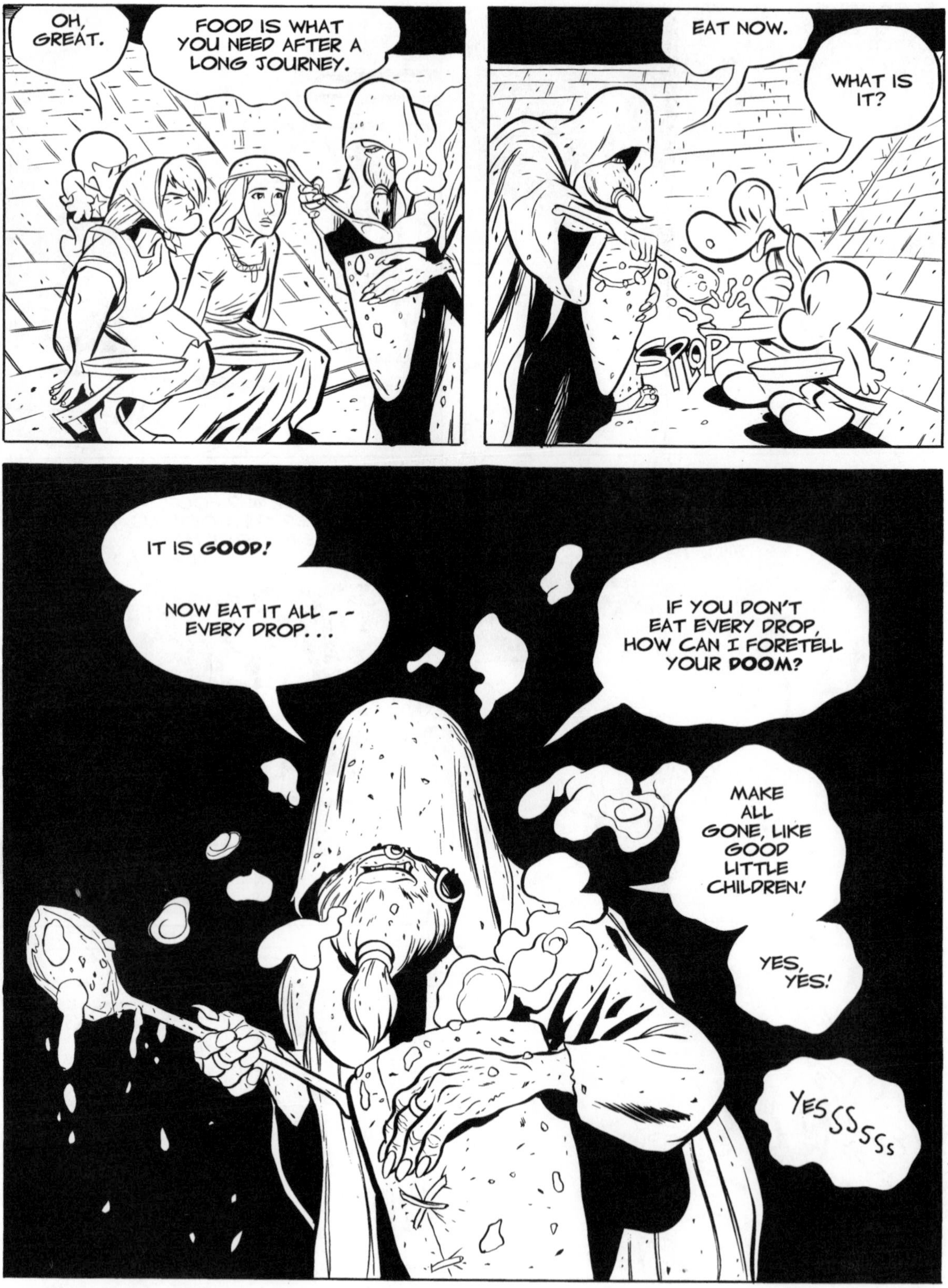
OH, GREAT.
FOOD IS WHAT YOU NEED AFTER A LONG JOURNEY.
EAT NOW.
WHAT IS IT?
SPLOP
IT IS GOOD!
NOW EAT IT ALL -- EVERY DROP...
IF YOU DON'T EAT EVERY DROP, HOW CAN I FORETELL YOUR DOOM?
MAKE ALL GONE, LIKE GOOD LITTLE CHILDREN!
YES, YES!
YESSSSSS

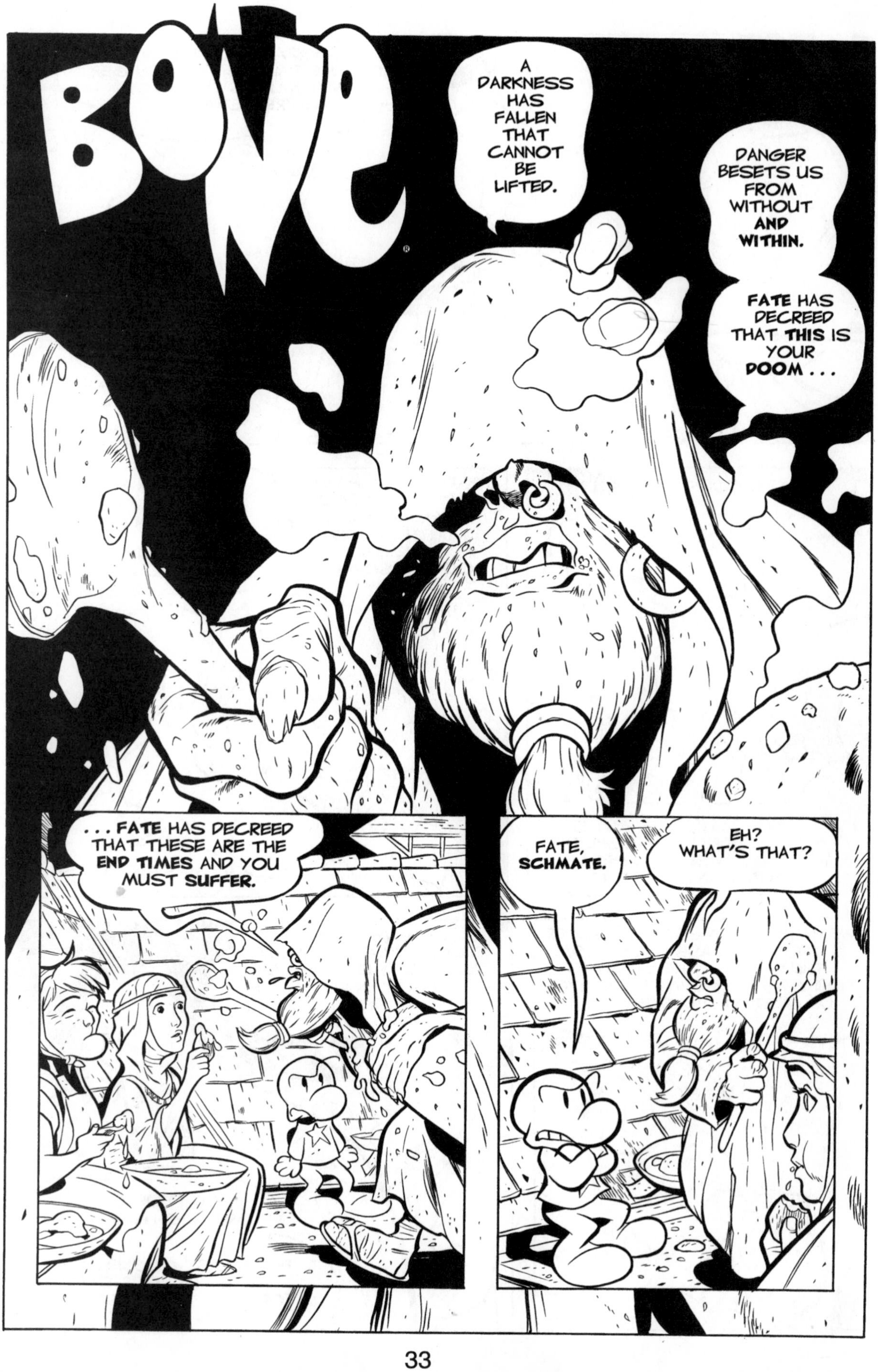
BONE®
A DARKNESS HAS FALLEN THAT CANNOT BE LIFTED.
DANGER BESETS US FROM WITHOUT AND WITHIN.
FATE HAS DECREED THAT THIS IS YOUR DOOM . . .
. . . FATE HAS DECREED THAT THESE ARE THE END TIMES AND YOU MUST SUFFER.
FATE, SCHMATE.
EH? WHAT'S THAT?

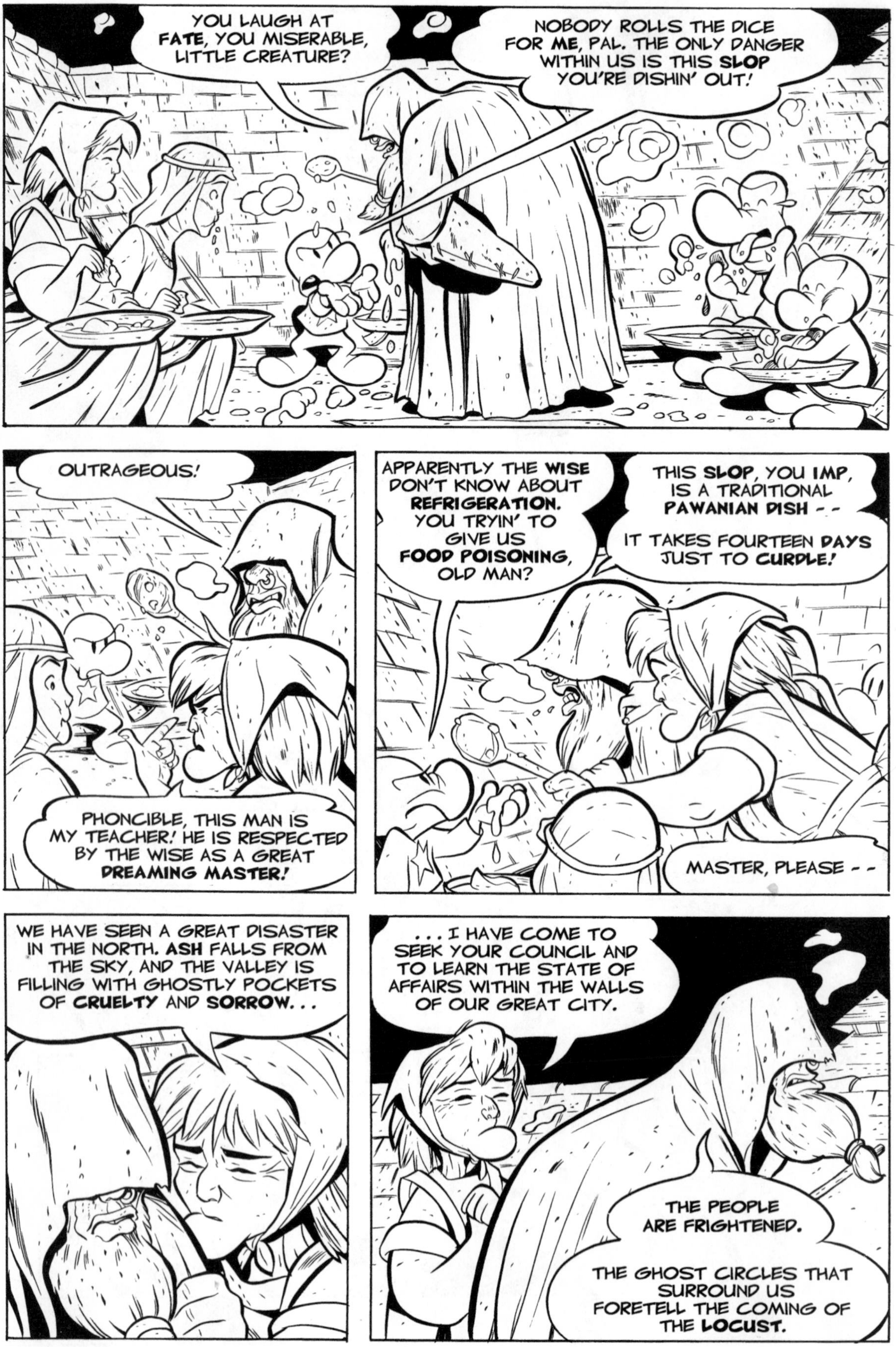
YOU LAUGH AT FATE, YOU MISERABLE, LITTLE CREATURE?
NOBODY ROLLS THE DICE FOR ME, PAL. THE ONLY DANGER WITHIN US IS THIS SLOP YOU'RE DISHIN' OUT!
OUTRAGEOUS!
PHONCIBLE, THIS MAN IS MY TEACHER! HE IS RESPECTED BY THE WISE AS A GREAT DREAMING MASTER!
APPARENTLY THE WISE DON'T KNOW ABOUT REFRIGERATION. YOU TRYIN' TO GIVE US FOOD POISONING, OLD MAN?
THIS SLOP, YOU IMP, IS A TRADITIONAL PAWANIAN DISH - -
IT TAKES FOURTEEN DAYS JUST TO CURDLE!
MASTER, PLEASE - -
WE HAVE SEEN A GREAT DISASTER IN THE NORTH. ASH FALLS FROM THE SKY, AND THE VALLEY IS FILLING WITH GHOSTLY POCKETS OF CRUELTY AND SORROW...
...I HAVE COME TO SEEK YOUR COUNCIL AND TO LEARN THE STATE OF AFFAIRS WITHIN THE WALLS OF OUR GREAT CITY.
THE PEOPLE ARE FRIGHTENED.
THE GHOST CIRCLES THAT SURROUND US FORETELL THE COMING OF THE LOCUST.

ISN'T THERE ANYTHING IN OUR **LORE** THAT MIGHT TELL US HOW TO ESCAPE OUR DOOM?

YOU WERE NEVER THE MOST ATTENTIVE PUPIL, YOUR MAJESTY. YOU PREFERED THE **STABLES** TO YOUR LESSONS. YOU HAD A PARTICULAR FONDNESS FOR **COWS**, AS I RECALL.

I'LL TAKE THAT AS A NO. YOUR KITCHEN LOOKS NEGLECTED, OLD FRIEND. HAS SOMETHING **HAPPENED**?

WHEN MY NATIVE **PAWA** DECLARED ITSELF FOR THE LOCUST, MY CUISINE AND I FELL OUT OF FAVOR.

MUCH HAS CHANGED...

I SHOULD NEVER HAVE LEFT.

THE INNER COUNCIL THAT WATCHED OVER THE CITY HAS BEEN DISSOLVED. THEY HAVE BEEN REPLACED BY DISCIPLES OF VENU WHO CALL THEMSELVES THE **VEDU**.

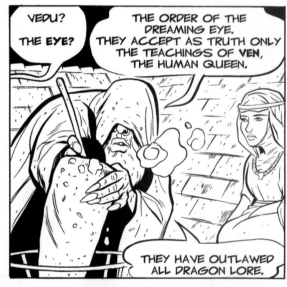

VEDU?

THE **EYE**?

THE ORDER OF THE DREAMING EYE. THEY ACCEPT AS TRUTH ONLY THE TEACHINGS OF **VEN**, THE HUMAN QUEEN.

THEY HAVE OUTLAWED ALL DRAGON LORE.

WHAT? HOW CAN THEY SEPARATE **VEN** FROM THE **DRAGONS**? VEN WAS **TAUGHT** BY THE DRAGONS!

BE **CAREFUL**, YOUR HIGHNESS. SUCH WORDS WILL GET YOU ARRESTED OR **WORSE**! THE VEDU BELIEVE THE DRAGONS ARE **ANIMALS**, AND ARE **IMPURE**.

HOW DID THIS HAPPEN?

I'M VERY SORRY, YOUR MAJESTY.

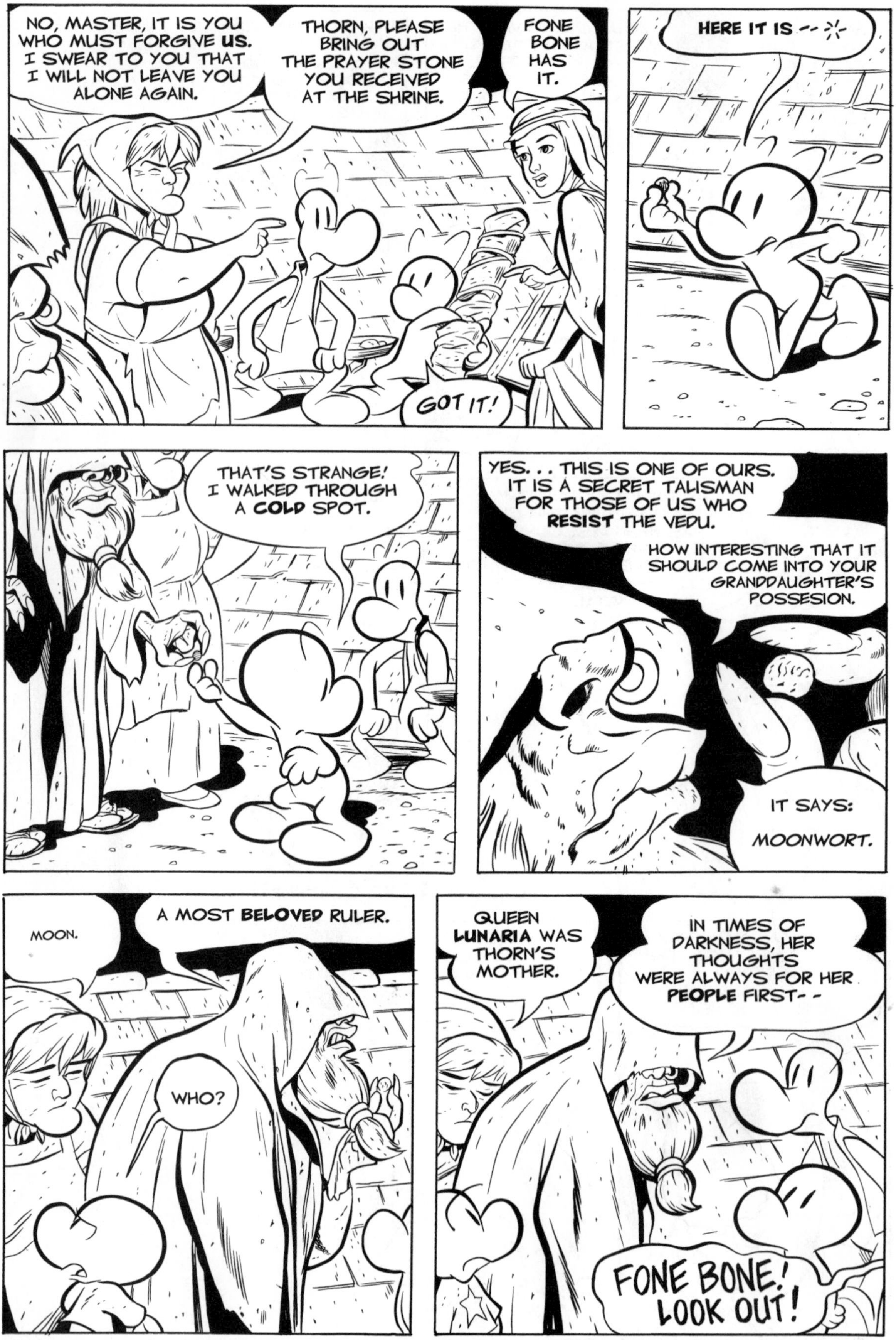
NO, MASTER, IT IS YOU WHO MUST FORGIVE US. I SWEAR TO YOU THAT I WILL NOT LEAVE YOU ALONE AGAIN.
THORN, PLEASE BRING OUT THE PRAYER STONE YOU RECEIVED AT THE SHRINE.
FONE BONE HAS IT.
GOT IT!
HERE IT IS --
THAT'S STRANGE! I WALKED THROUGH A COLD SPOT.
YES. . . THIS IS ONE OF OURS. IT IS A SECRET TALISMAN FOR THOSE OF US WHO RESIST THE VEDU.
HOW INTERESTING THAT IT SHOULD COME INTO YOUR GRANDDAUGHTER'S POSSESION.
IT SAYS:
MOONWORT.
MOON.
A MOST BELOVED RULER.
WHO?
QUEEN LUNARIA WAS THORN'S MOTHER.
IN TIMES OF DARKNESS, HER THOUGHTS WERE ALWAYS FOR HER PEOPLE FIRST--
FONE BONE! LOOK OUT!

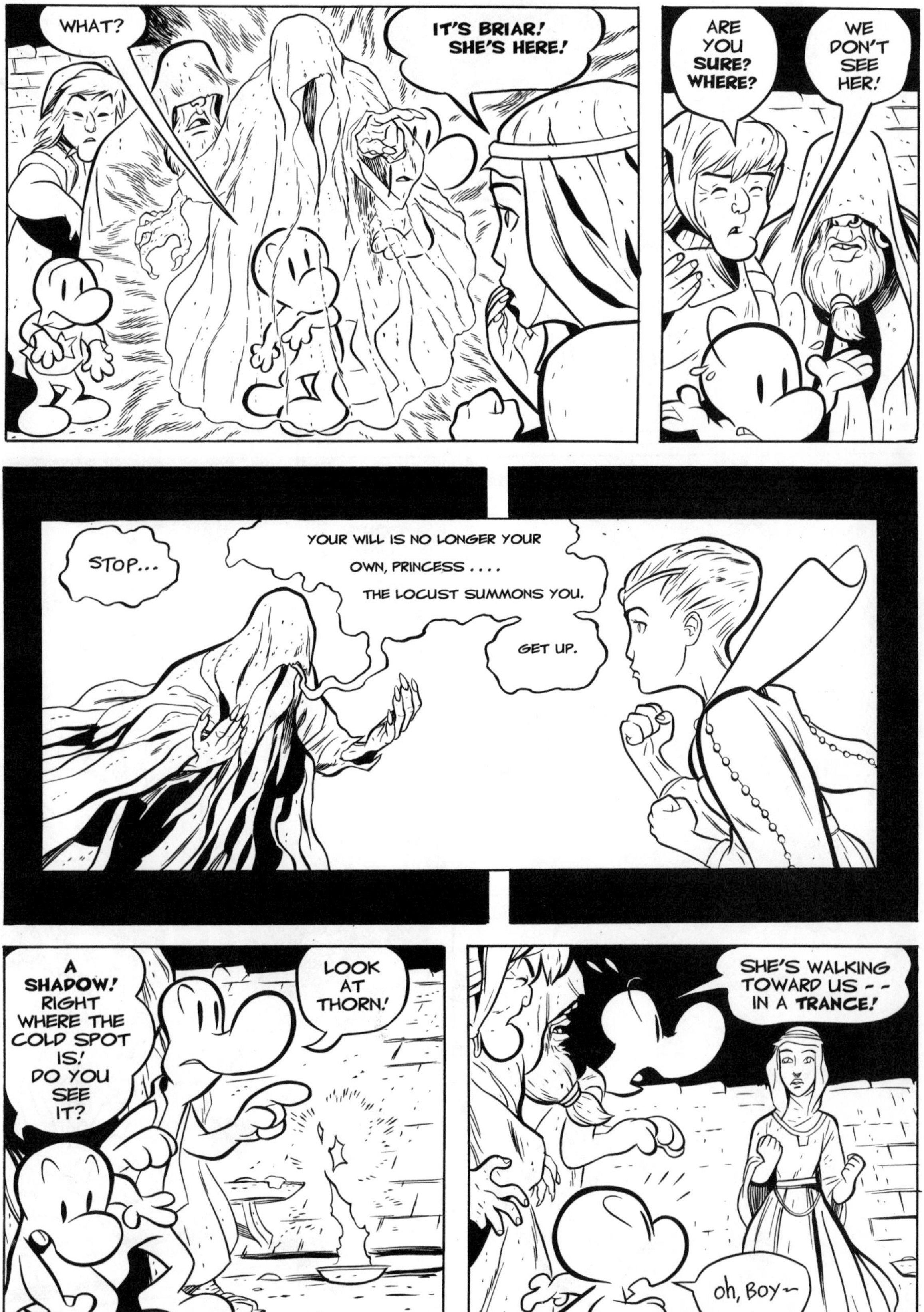
WHAT?
IT'S BRIAR! SHE'S HERE!
ARE YOU SURE? WHERE?
WE DON'T SEE HER!
STOP...
YOUR WILL IS NO LONGER YOUR OWN, PRINCESS ....
THE LOCUST SUMMONS YOU.
GET UP.
A SHADOW! RIGHT WHERE THE COLD SPOT IS! DO YOU SEE IT?
LOOK AT THORN!
SHE'S WALKING TOWARD US -- IN A TRANCE!
oh, Boy~

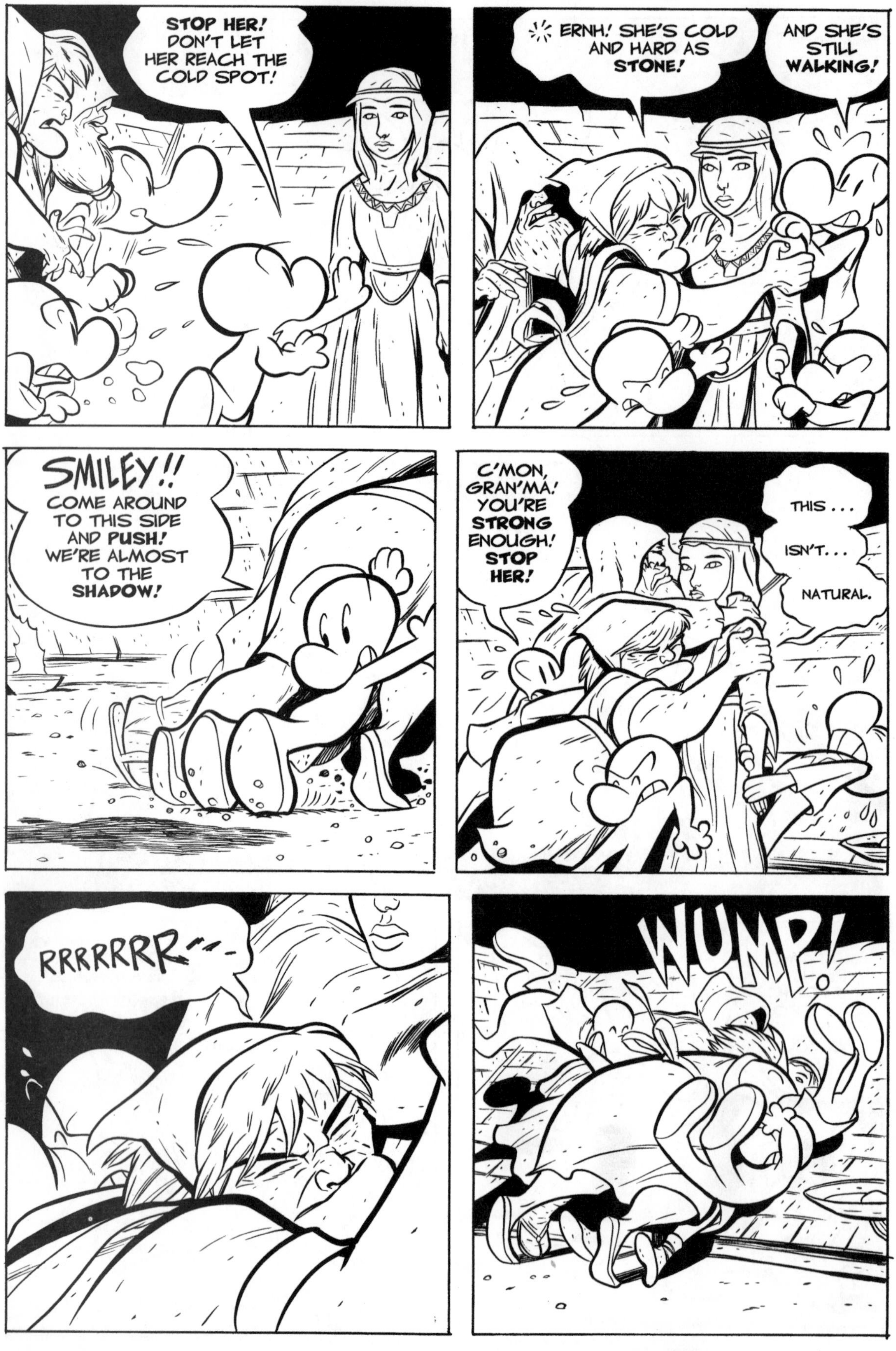
STOP HER! DON'T LET HER REACH THE COLD SPOT!
ERNH! SHE'S COLD AND HARD AS STONE!
AND SHE'S STILL WALKING!
SMILEY!! COME AROUND TO THIS SIDE AND PUSH! WE'RE ALMOST TO THE SHADOW!
C'MON, GRAN'MA! YOU'RE STRONG ENOUGH! STOP HER!
THIS . . .
ISN'T. . .
NATURAL.
RRRRRRR
WUMP!

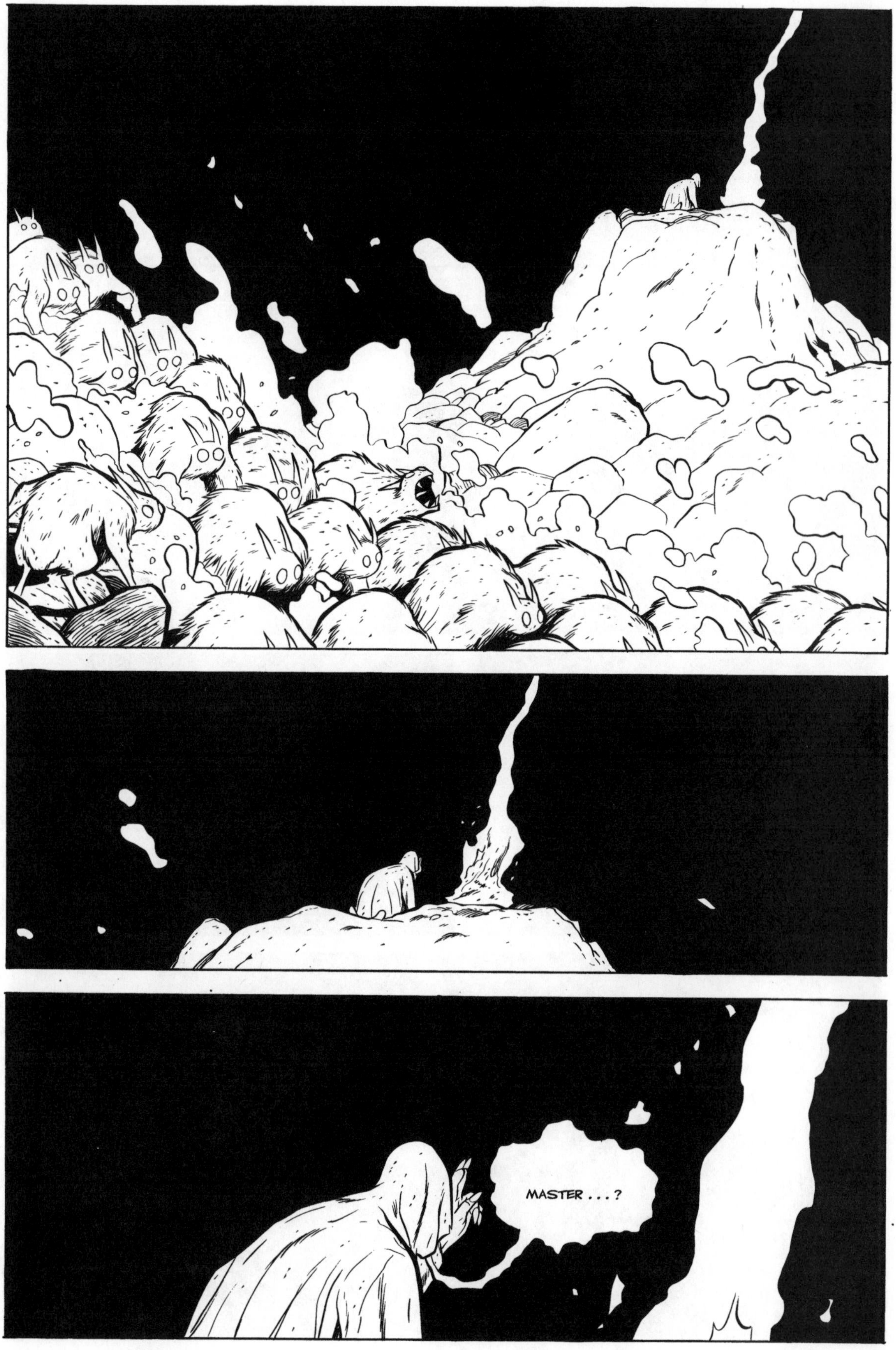
MASTER . . . ?

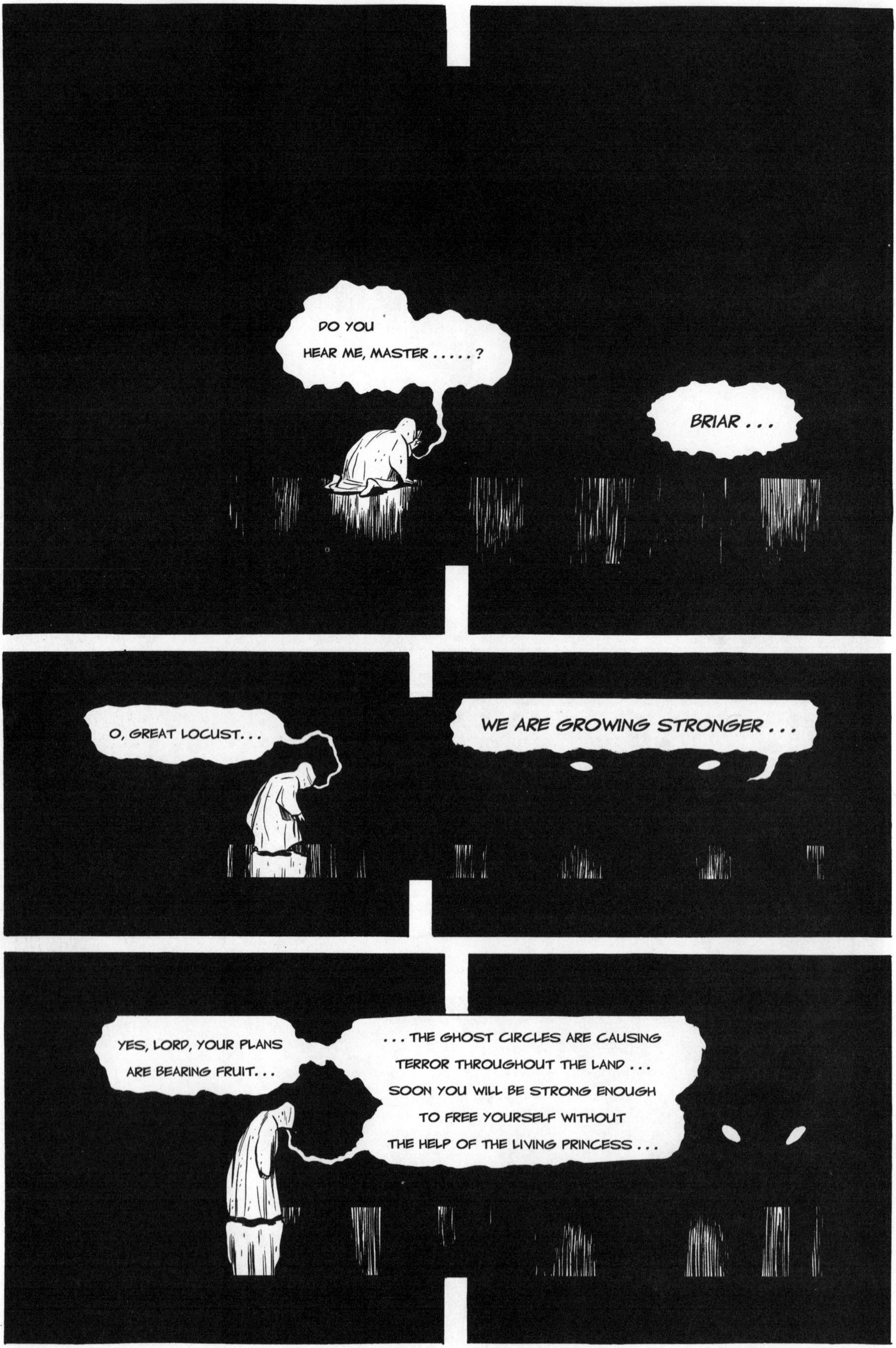
DO YOU HEAR ME, MASTER . . . . . ?
BRIAR . . .
O, GREAT LOCUST . . .
WE ARE GROWING STRONGER . . .
YES, LORD, YOUR PLANS ARE BEARING FRUIT . . .
. . . THE GHOST CIRCLES ARE CAUSING TERROR THROUGHOUT THE LAND . . . SOON YOU WILL BE STRONG ENOUGH TO FREE YOURSELF WITHOUT THE HELP OF THE LIVING PRINCESS . . .

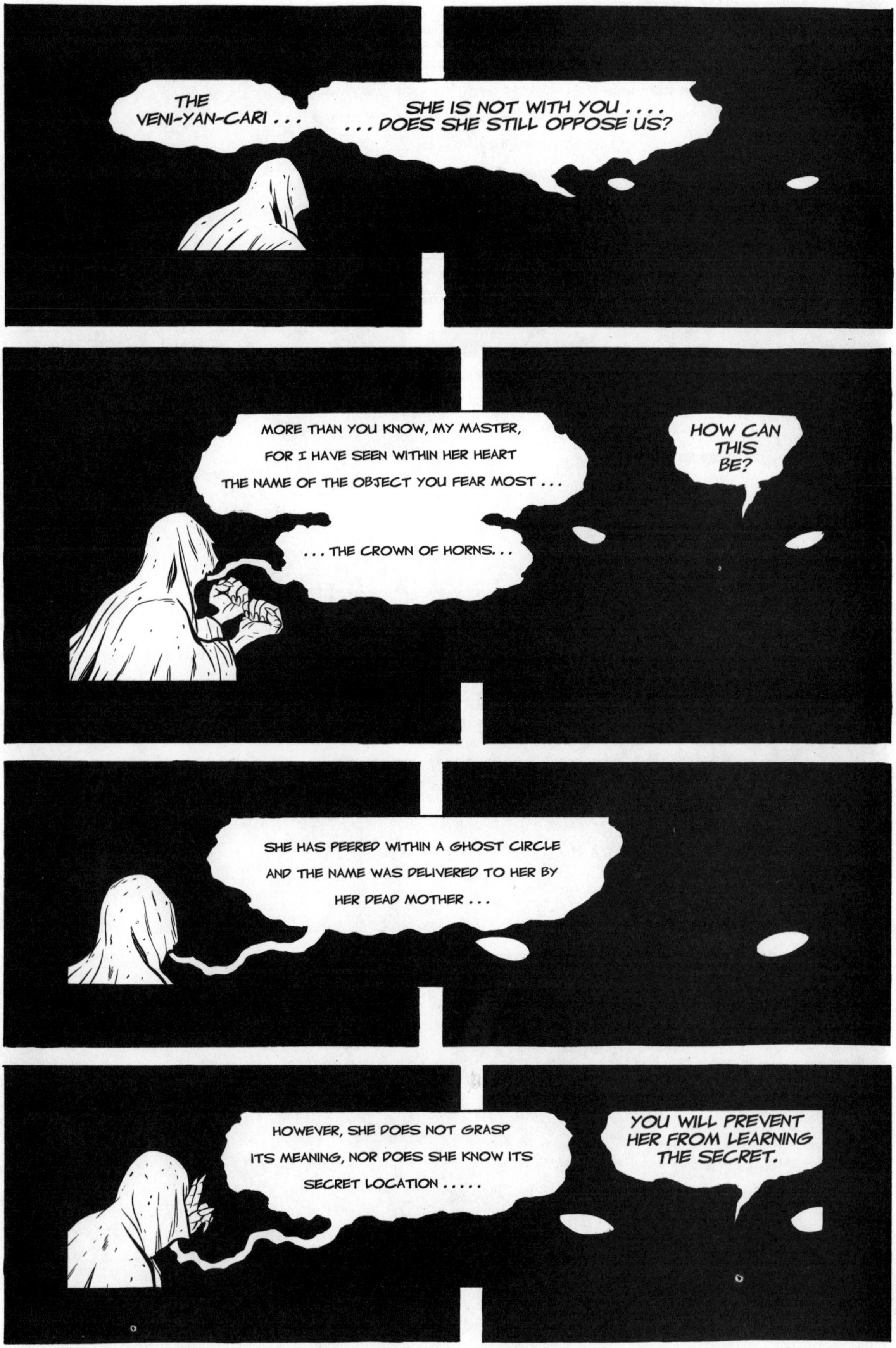
THE VENI-YAN-CARI . . .
SHE IS NOT WITH YOU . . . .
. . . DOES SHE STILL OPPOSE US?
MORE THAN YOU KNOW, MY MASTER, FOR I HAVE SEEN WITHIN HER HEART THE NAME OF THE OBJECT YOU FEAR MOST . . .
. . . THE CROWN OF HORNS. . .
HOW CAN THIS BE?
SHE HAS PEERED WITHIN A GHOST CIRCLE AND THE NAME WAS DELIVERED TO HER BY HER DEAD MOTHER . . .
HOWEVER, SHE DOES NOT GRASP ITS MEANING, NOR DOES SHE KNOW ITS SECRET LOCATION . . . . .
YOU WILL PREVENT HER FROM LEARNING THE SECRET.

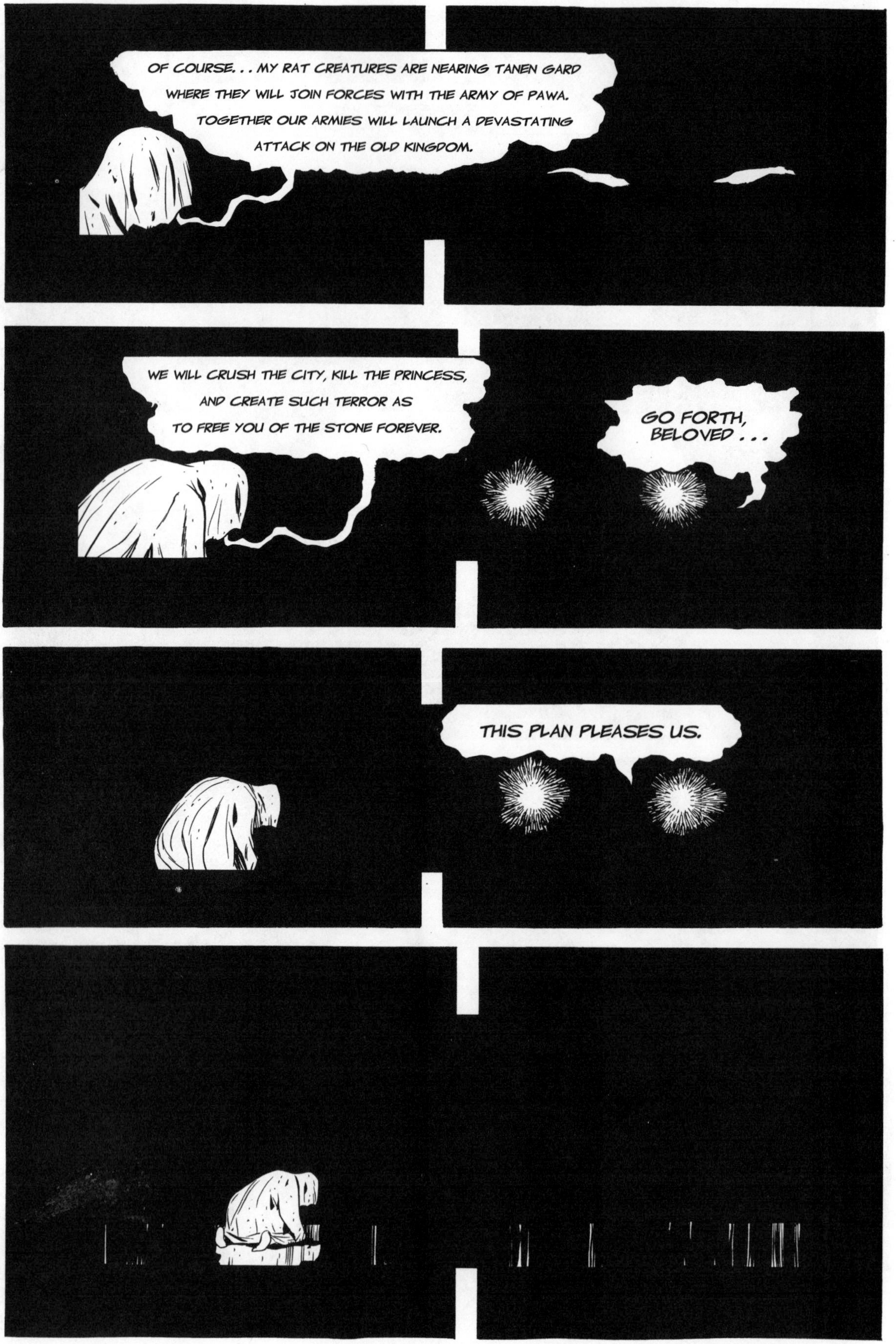
OF COURSE. . . MY RAT CREATURES ARE NEARING TANEN GARD WHERE THEY WILL JOIN FORCES WITH THE ARMY OF PAWA. TOGETHER OUR ARMIES WILL LAUNCH A DEVASTATING ATTACK ON THE OLD KINGDOM.
WE WILL CRUSH THE CITY, KILL THE PRINCESS, AND CREATE SUCH TERROR AS TO FREE YOU OF THE STONE FOREVER.
GO FORTH, BELOVED . . .
THIS PLAN PLEASES US.

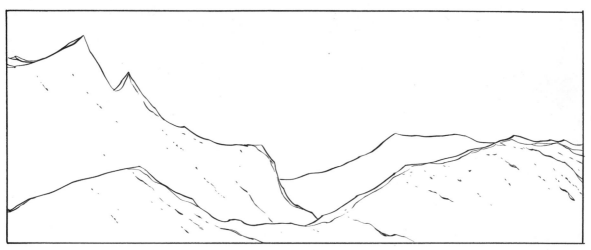

MASTER . . .

THE PAWAN GENERALS HAVE ARRIVED.

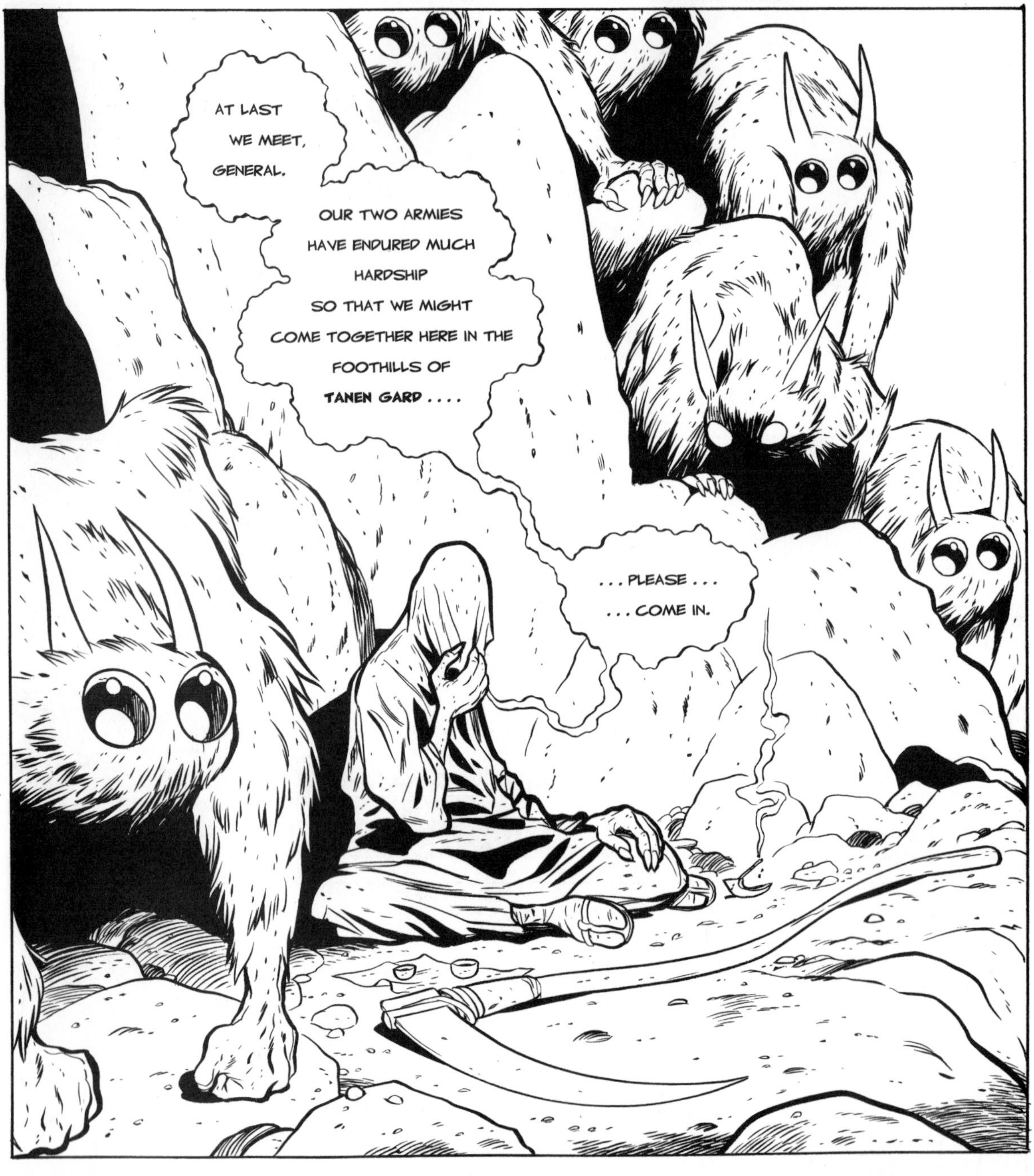
AT LAST WE MEET, GENERAL.
OUR TWO ARMIES HAVE ENDURED MUCH HARDSHIP SO THAT WE MIGHT COME TOGETHER HERE IN THE FOOTHILLS OF **TANEN GARD** . . . .
. . . PLEASE . . .
. . . COME IN.

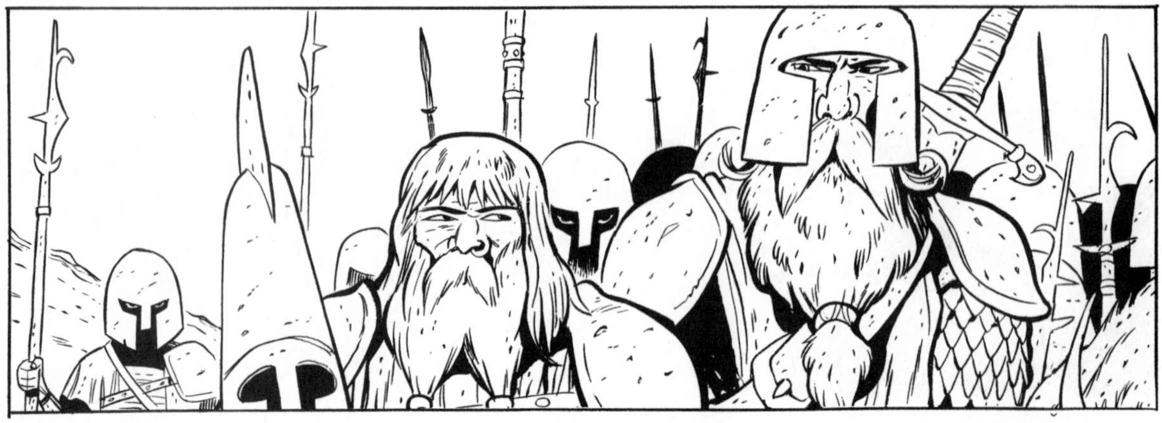

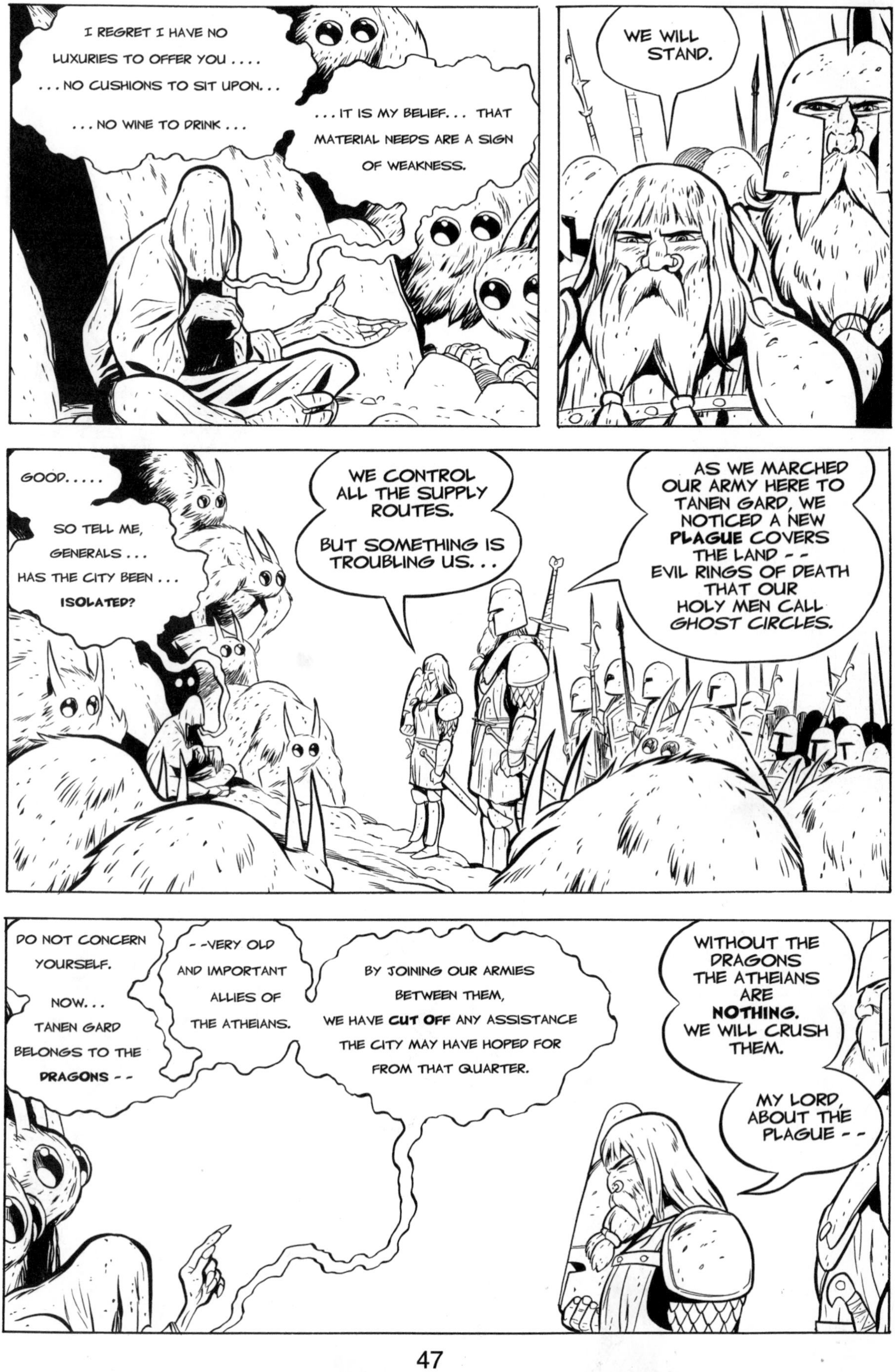

I REGRET I HAVE NO LUXURIES TO OFFER YOU . . . . NO CUSHIONS TO SIT UPON. . . . . . NO WINE TO DRINK . . .
. . . IT IS MY BELIEF. . . THAT MATERIAL NEEDS ARE A SIGN OF WEAKNESS.
WE WILL STAND.
GOOD. . . . .
SO TELL ME, GENERALS . . . HAS THE CITY BEEN . . . ISOLATED?
WE CONTROL ALL THE SUPPLY ROUTES.
BUT SOMETHING IS TROUBLING US. . .
AS WE MARCHED OUR ARMY HERE TO TANEN GARD, WE NOTICED A NEW PLAGUE COVERS THE LAND - - EVIL RINGS OF DEATH THAT OUR HOLY MEN CALL GHOST CIRCLES.
DO NOT CONCERN YOURSELF.
NOW. . . TANEN GARD BELONGS TO THE DRAGONS - -
- -VERY OLD AND IMPORTANT ALLIES OF THE ATHEIANS.
BY JOINING OUR ARMIES BETWEEN THEM, WE HAVE CUT OFF ANY ASSISTANCE THE CITY MAY HAVE HOPED FOR FROM THAT QUARTER.
WITHOUT THE DRAGONS THE ATHEIANS ARE NOTHING. WE WILL CRUSH THEM.
MY LORD, ABOUT THE PLAGUE - -

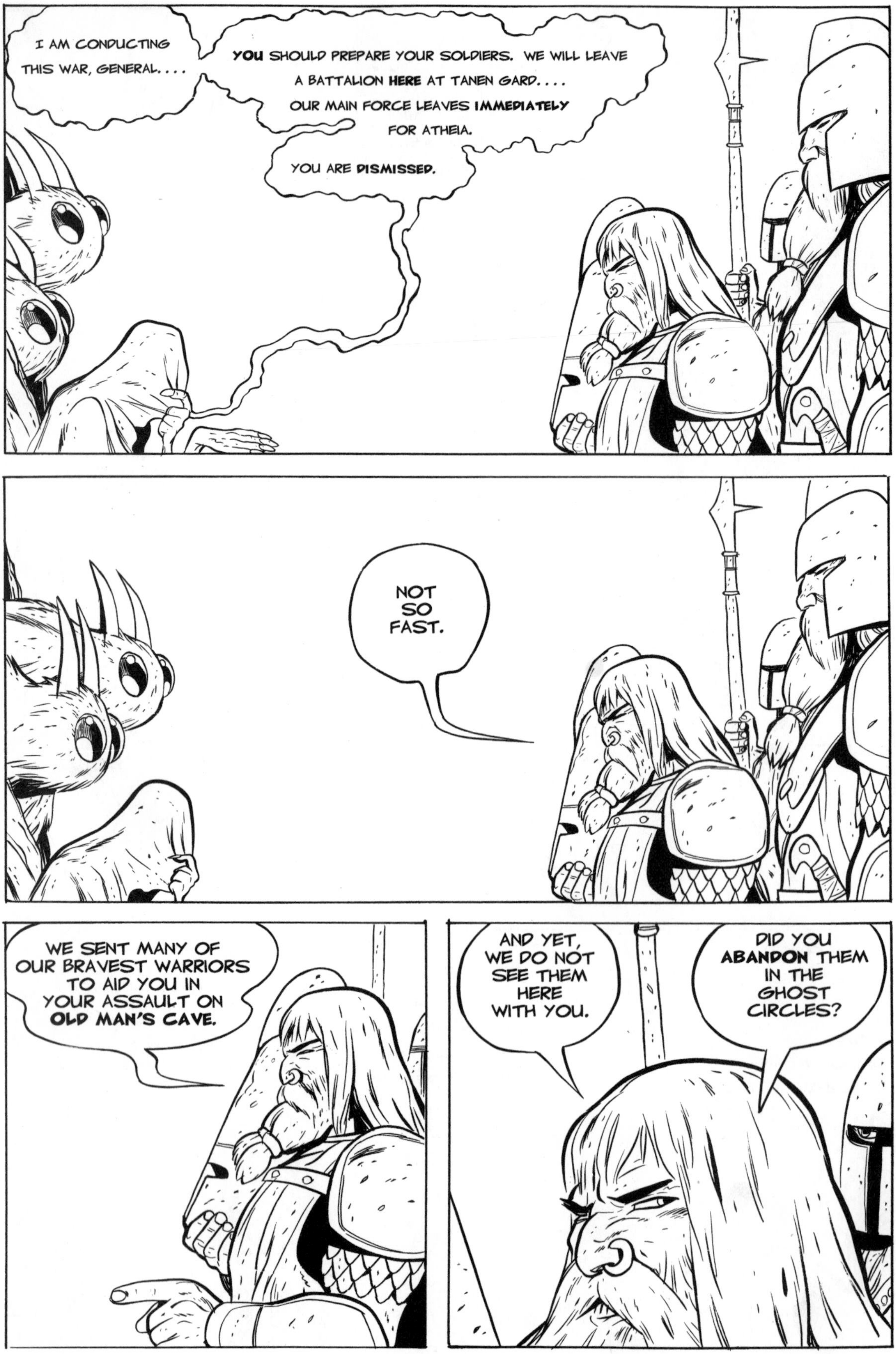
I AM CONDUCTING THIS WAR, GENERAL. . . .
YOU SHOULD PREPARE YOUR SOLDIERS. WE WILL LEAVE A BATTALION HERE AT TANEN GARD. . . . OUR MAIN FORCE LEAVES IMMEDIATELY FOR ATHEIA.
YOU ARE DISMISSED.
NOT SO FAST.
WE SENT MANY OF OUR BRAVEST WARRIORS TO AID YOU IN YOUR ASSAULT ON OLD MAN'S CAVE.
AND YET, WE DO NOT SEE THEM HERE WITH YOU.
DID YOU ABANDON THEM IN THE GHOST CIRCLES?

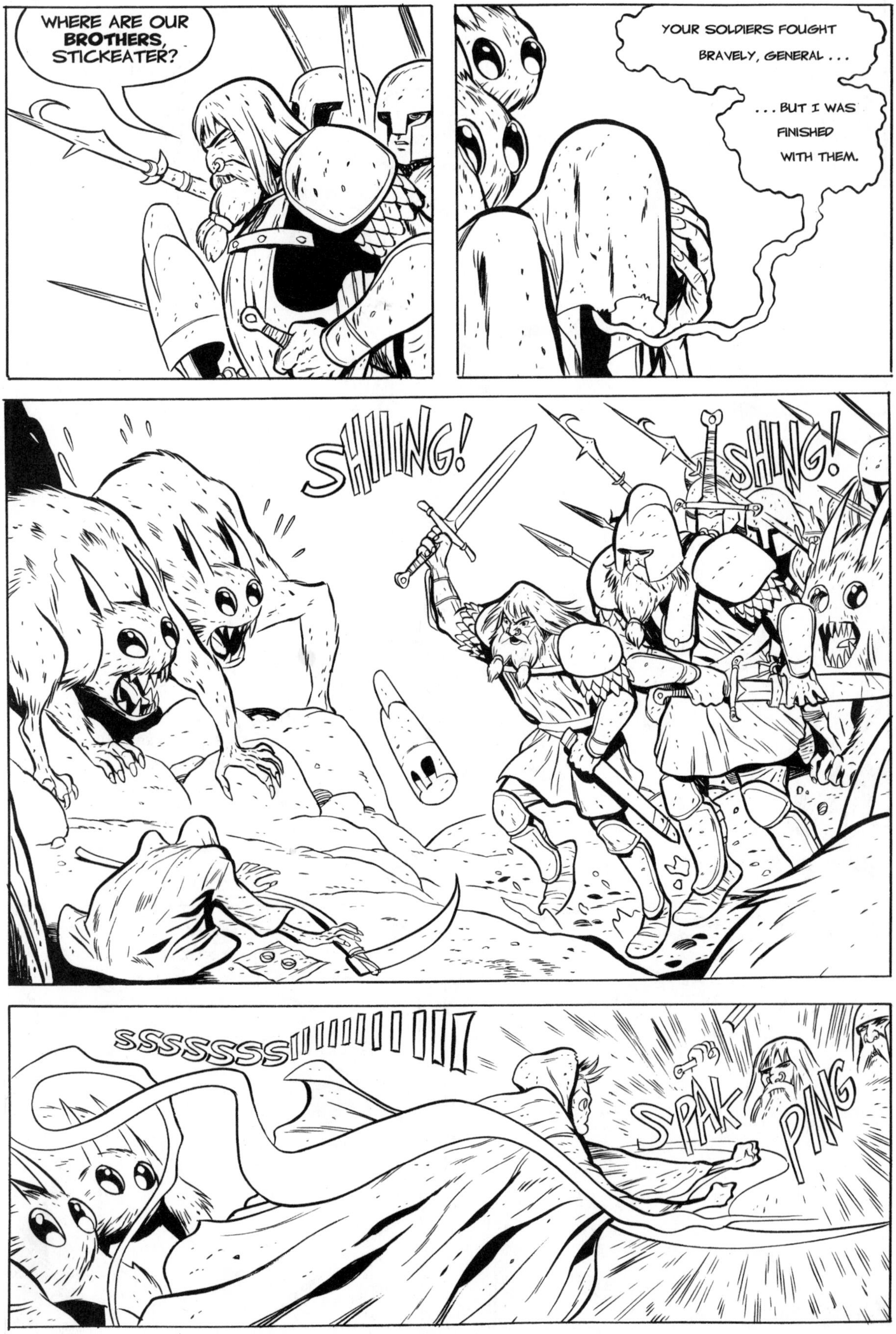
WHERE ARE OUR BROTHERS, STICKEATER?
YOUR SOLDIERS FOUGHT BRAVELY, GENERAL . . .
. . . BUT I WAS FINISHED WITH THEM.
SHIIING!
SHING!
SSSSSSSIIIIIIIIIIII
SPAK
PING

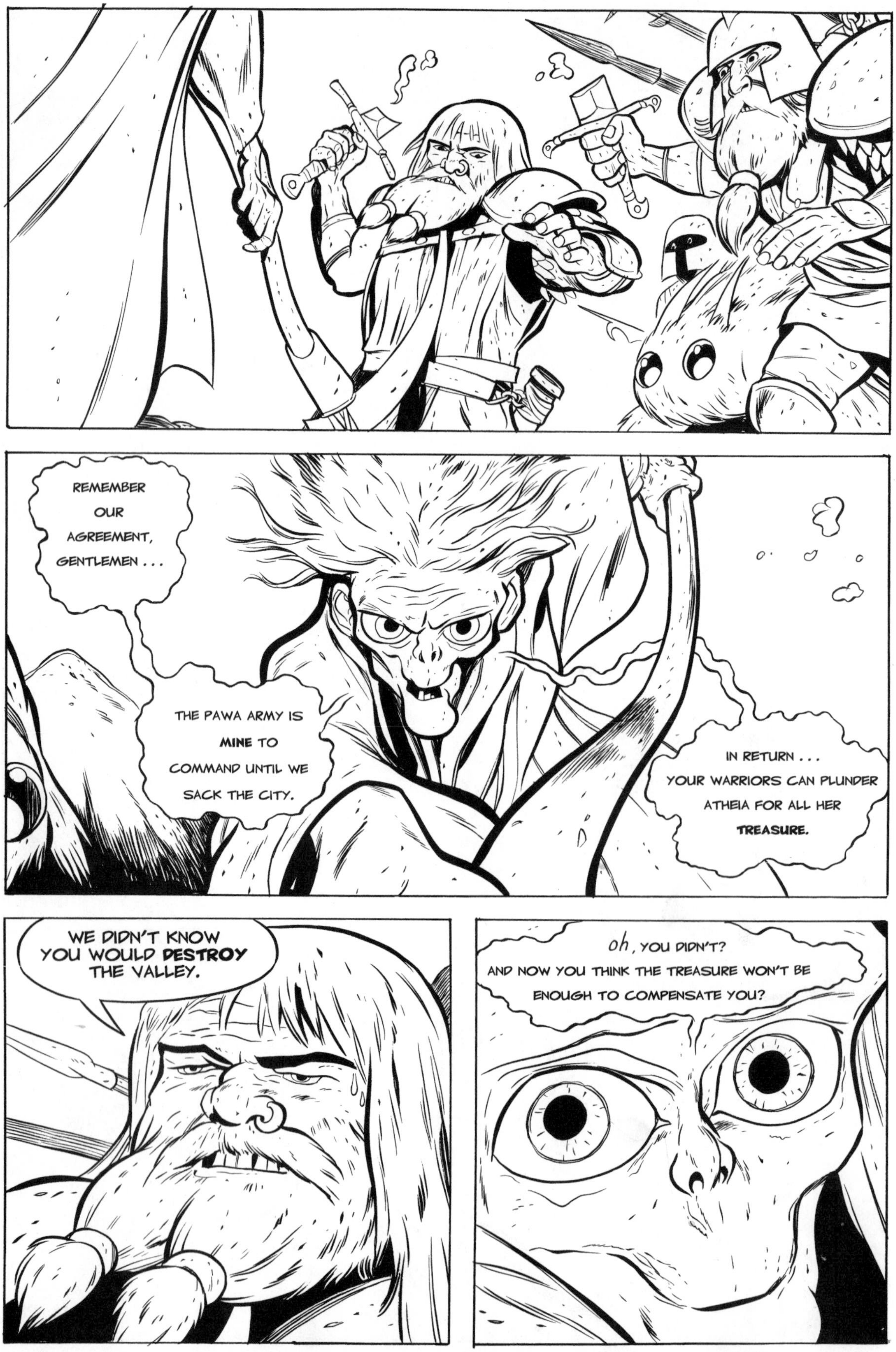
REMEMBER OUR AGREEMENT, GENTLEMEN . . .
THE PAWA ARMY IS MINE TO COMMAND UNTIL WE SACK THE CITY.
IN RETURN . . . YOUR WARRIORS CAN PLUNDER ATHEIA FOR ALL HER TREASURE.
WE DIDN'T KNOW YOU WOULD DESTROY THE VALLEY.
oh, YOU DIDN'T? AND NOW YOU THINK THE TREASURE WON'T BE ENOUGH TO COMPENSATE YOU?

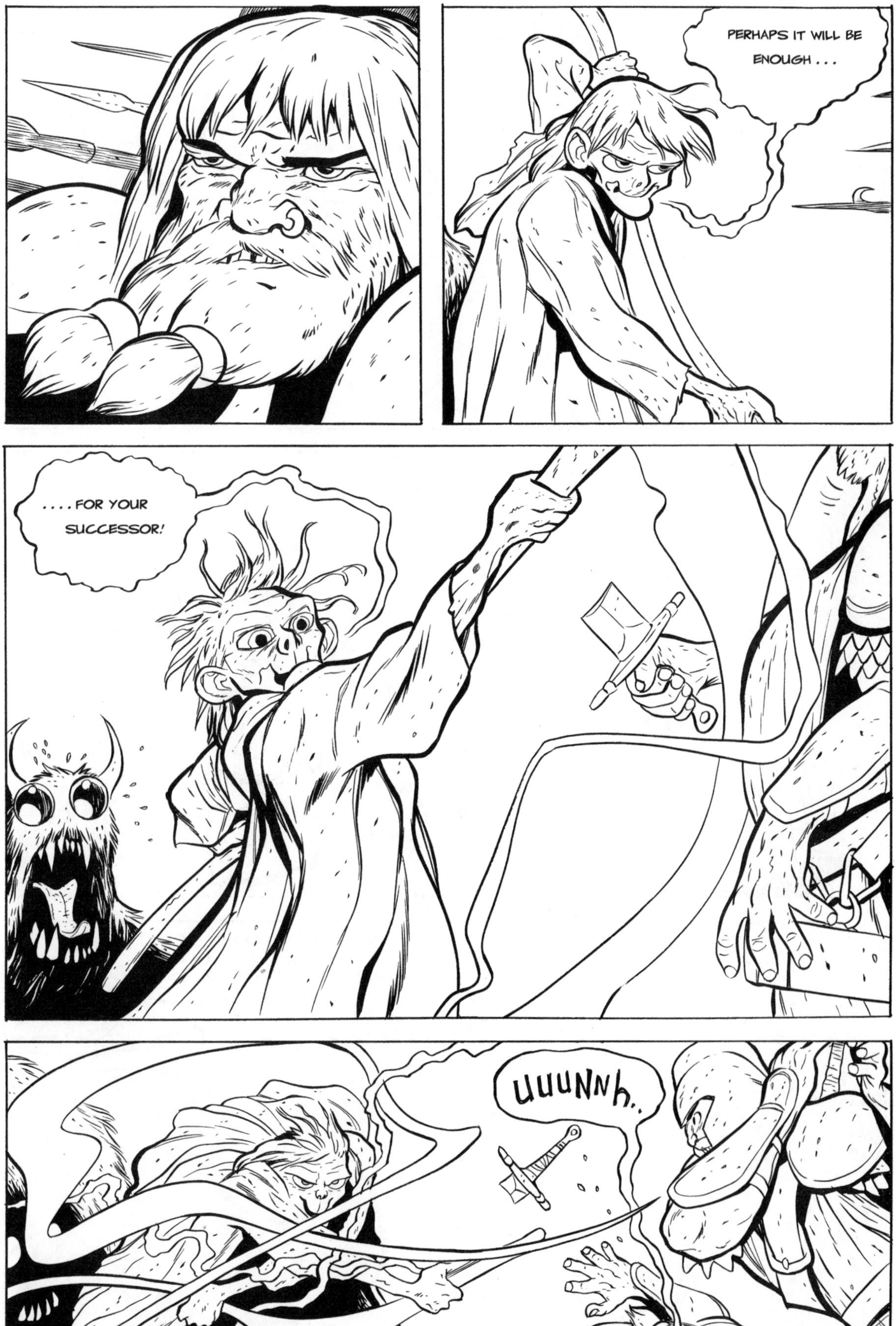
PERHAPS IT WILL BE ENOUGH . . .
. . . . FOR YOUR SUCCESSOR!
UUUNNh..

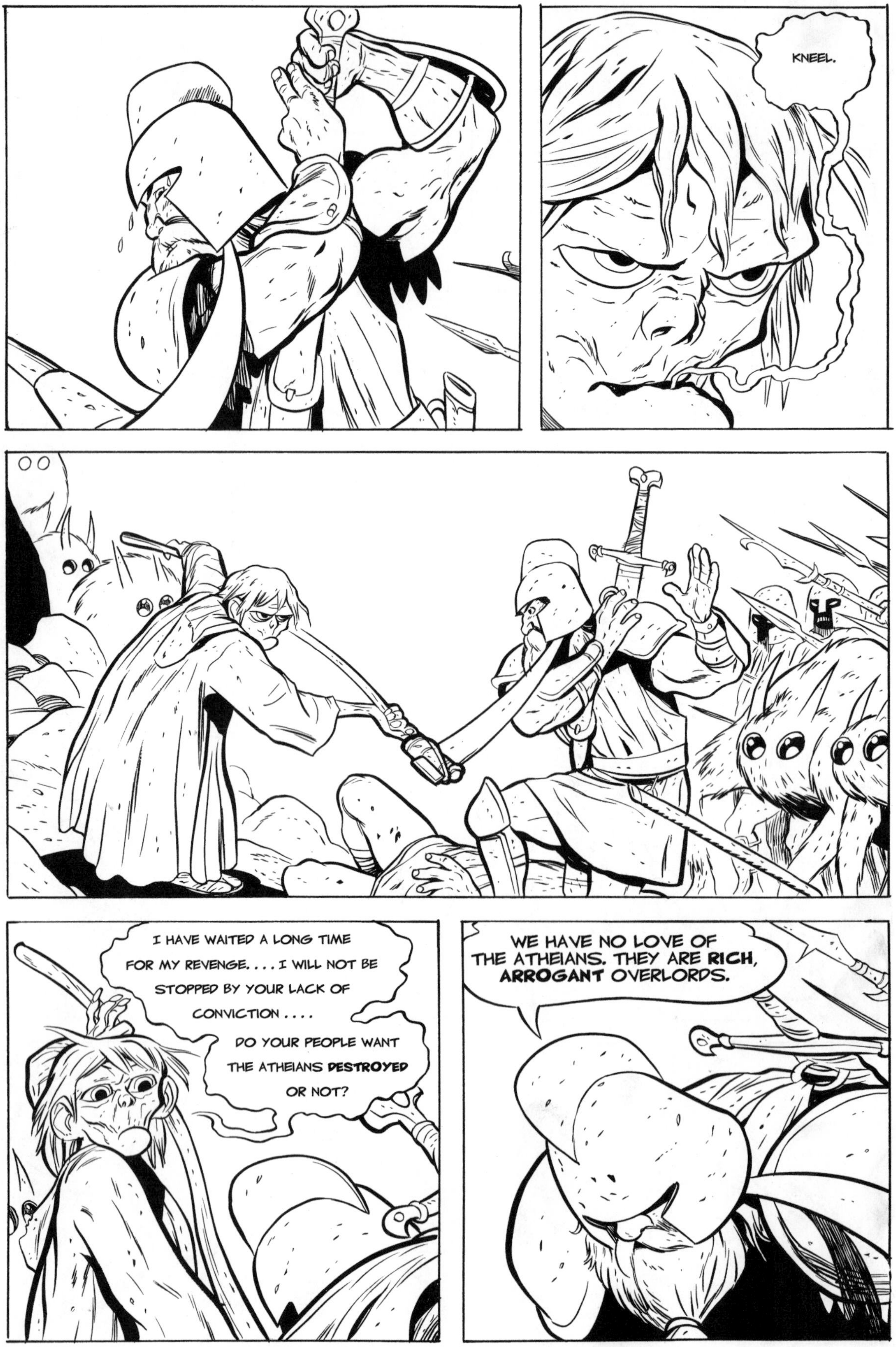
KNEEL.
I HAVE WAITED A LONG TIME FOR MY REVENGE. . . . I WILL NOT BE STOPPED BY YOUR LACK OF CONVICTION . . . .
DO YOUR PEOPLE WANT THE ATHEIANS **DESTROYED** OR NOT?
WE HAVE NO LOVE OF THE ATHEIANS. THEY ARE **RICH, ARROGANT** OVERLORDS.

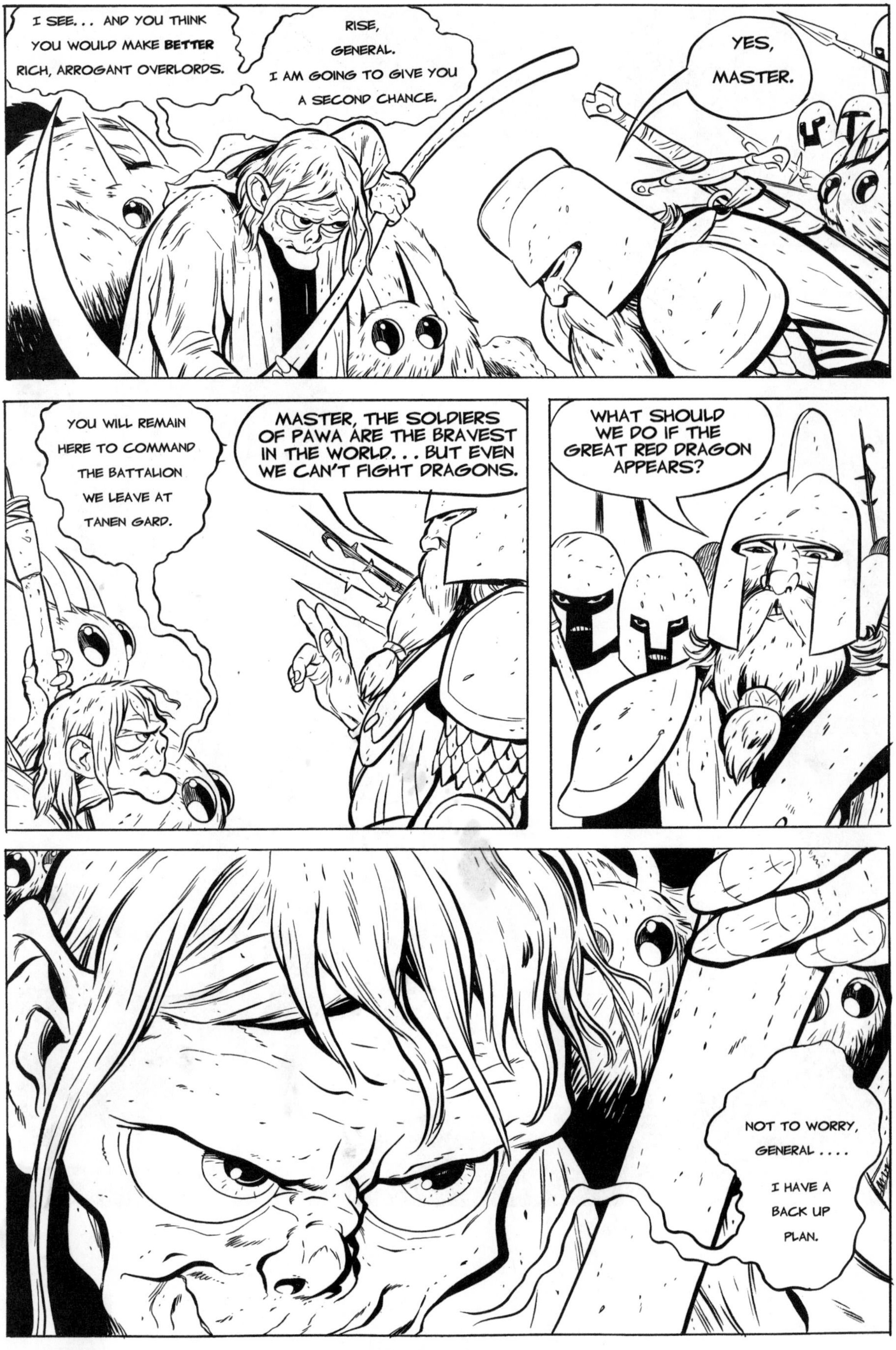
I SEE... AND YOU THINK YOU WOULD MAKE **BETTER** RICH, ARROGANT OVERLORDS.
RISE, GENERAL. I AM GOING TO GIVE YOU A SECOND CHANCE.
YES, MASTER.
YOU WILL REMAIN HERE TO COMMAND THE BATTALION WE LEAVE AT TANEN GARD.
MASTER, THE SOLDIERS OF PAWA ARE THE BRAVEST IN THE WORLD... BUT EVEN WE CAN'T FIGHT DRAGONS.
WHAT SHOULD WE DO IF THE GREAT RED DRAGON APPEARS?
NOT TO WORRY, GENERAL.... I HAVE A BACK UP PLAN.

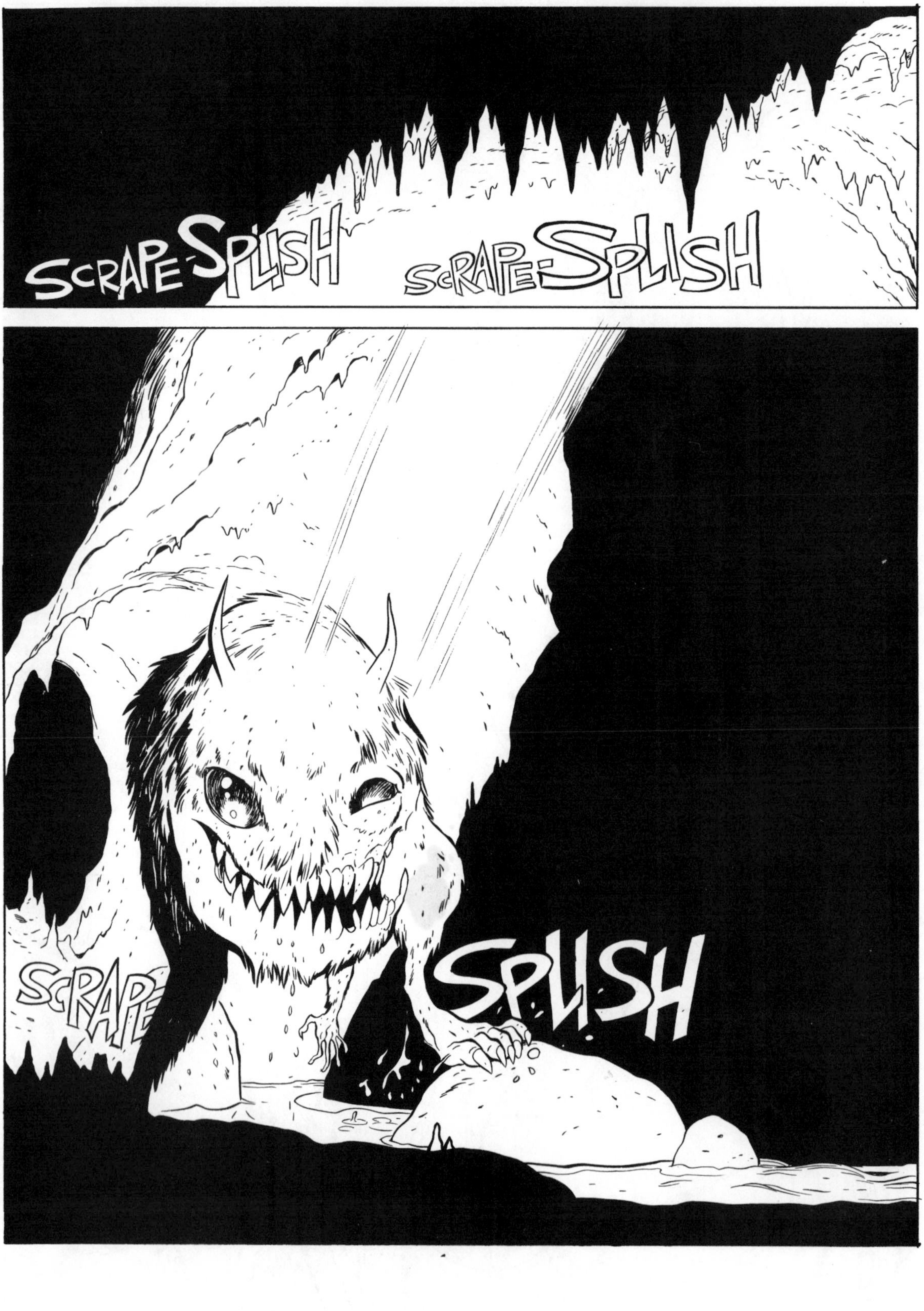
SCRAPE-SPLISH
SCRAPE-SPLISH
SCRAPE
SPLISH

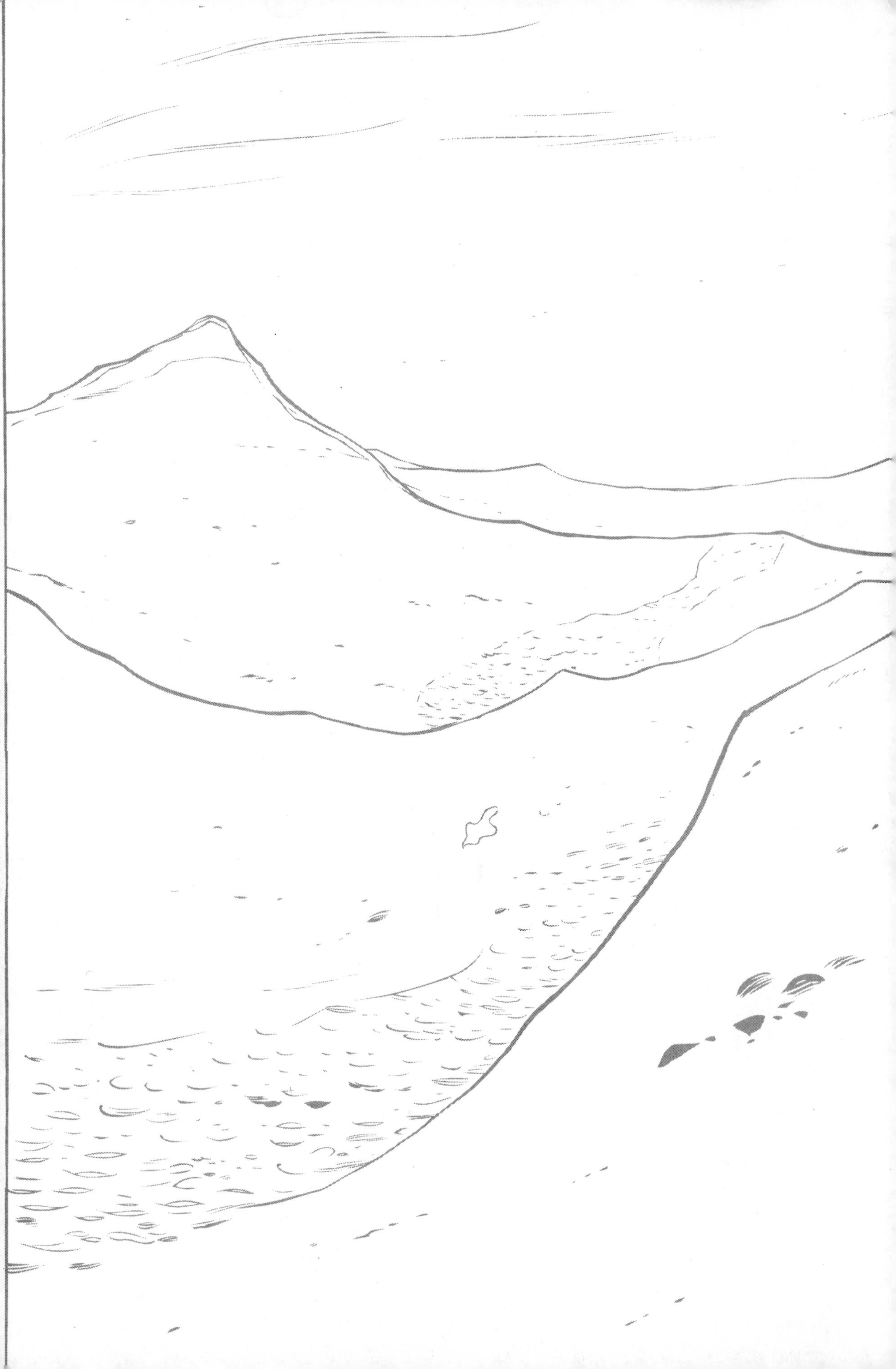

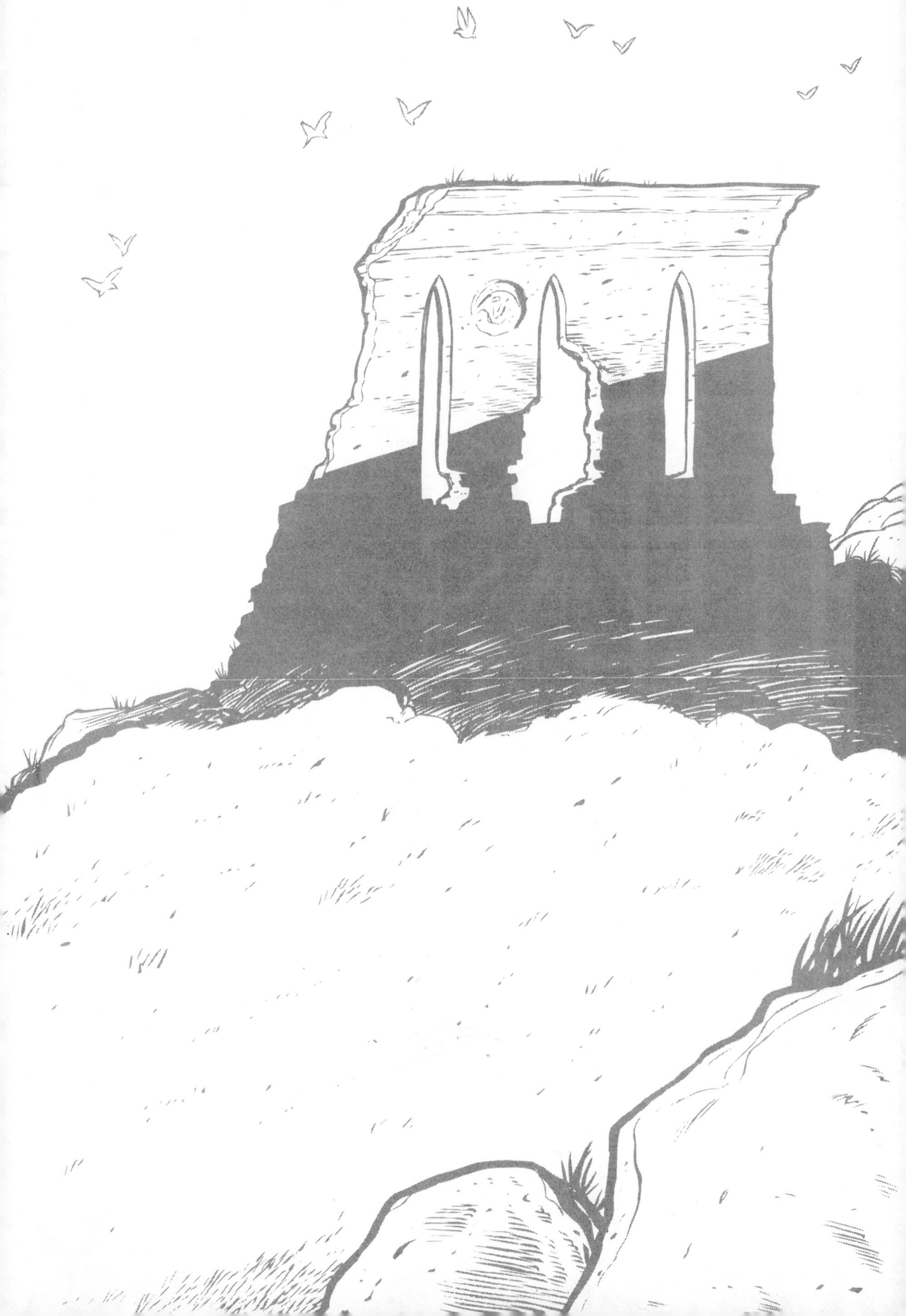

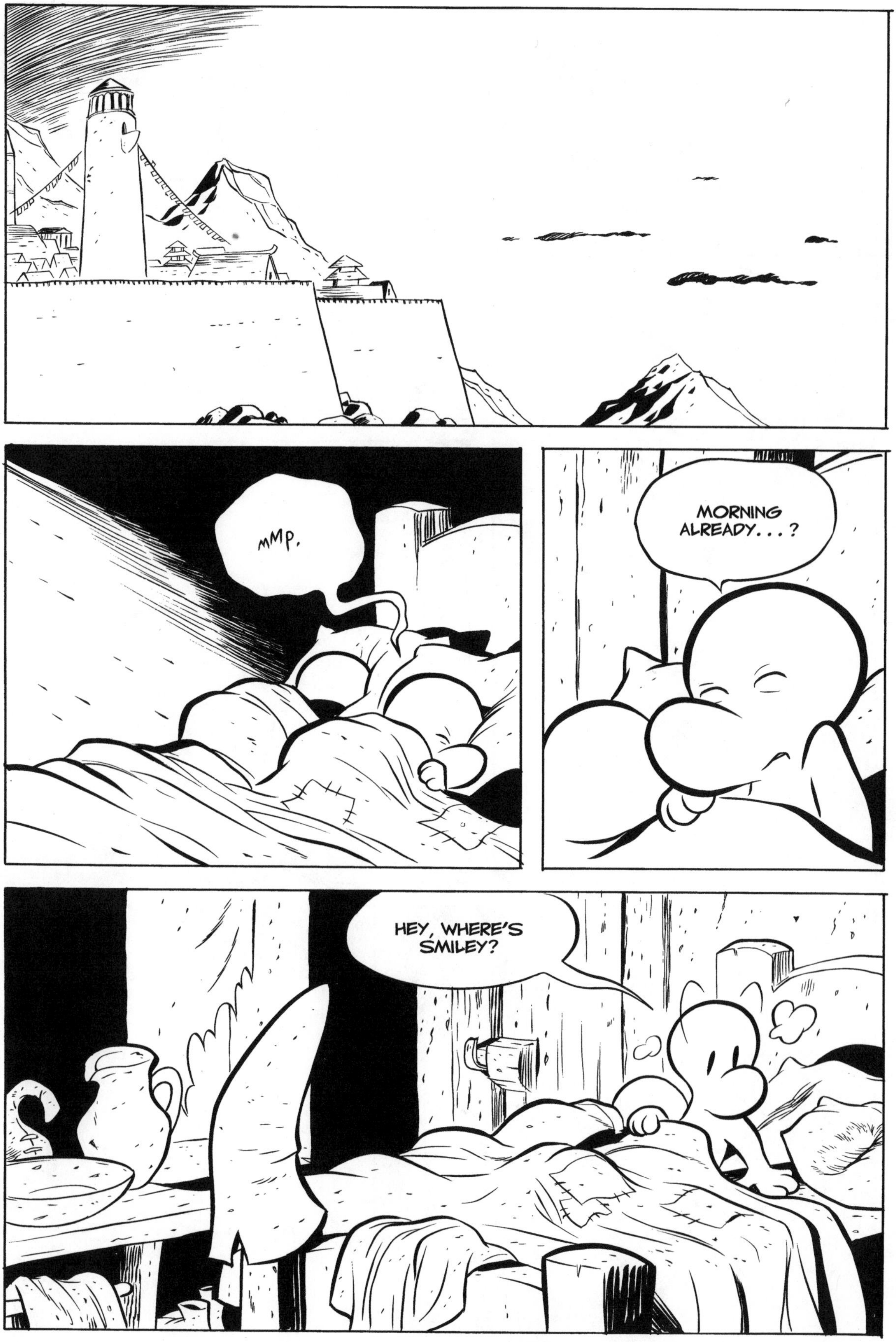
MMP.
MORNING ALREADY...?
HEY, WHERE'S SMILEY?

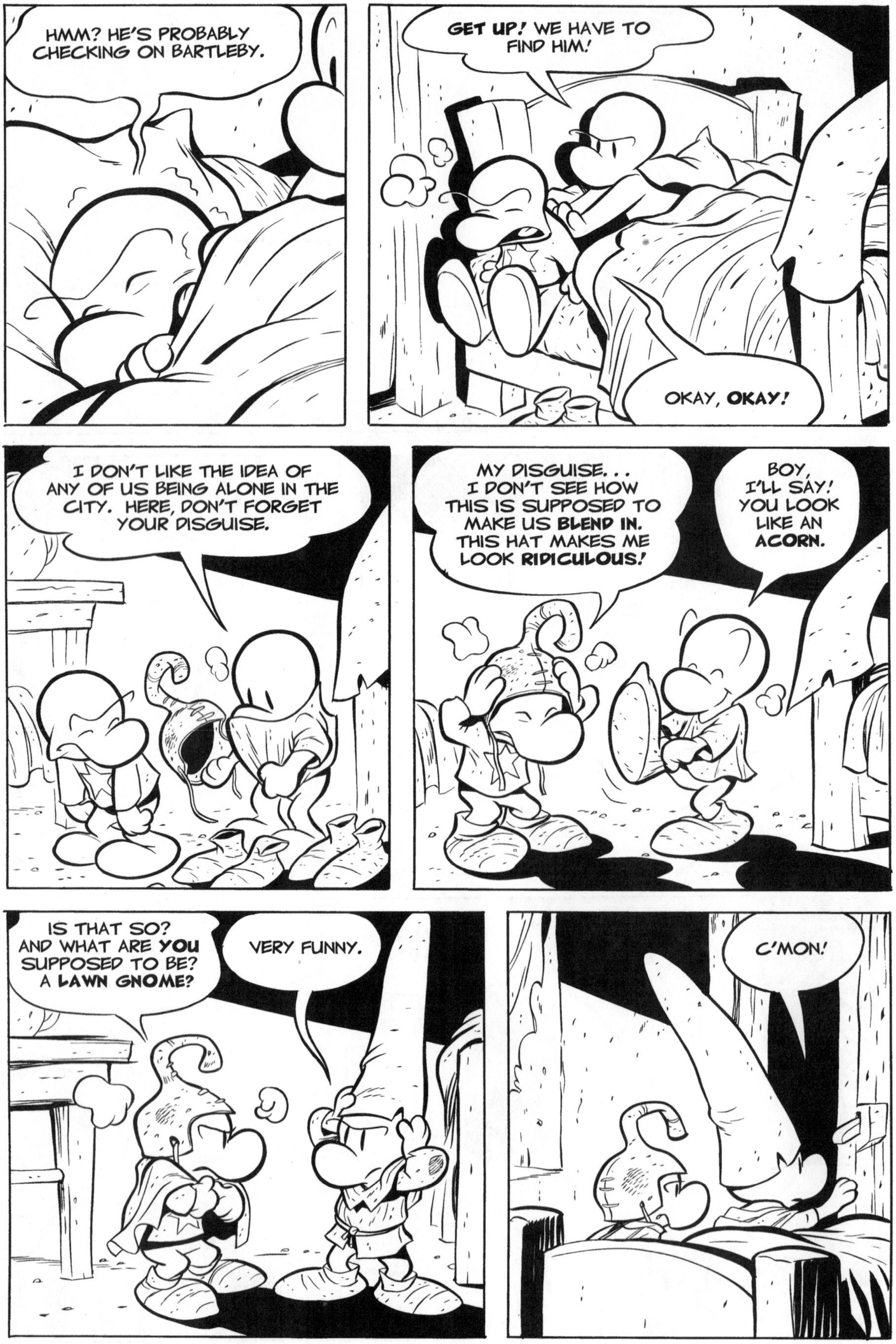
HMM? HE'S PROBABLY CHECKING ON BARTLEBY.
GET UP! WE HAVE TO FIND HIM!
OKAY, OKAY!
I DON'T LIKE THE IDEA OF ANY OF US BEING ALONE IN THE CITY. HERE, DON'T FORGET YOUR DISGUISE.
MY DISGUISE. . . I DON'T SEE HOW THIS IS SUPPOSED TO MAKE US BLEND IN. THIS HAT MAKES ME LOOK RIDICULOUS!
BOY, I'LL SAY! YOU LOOK LIKE AN ACORN.
IS THAT SO? AND WHAT ARE YOU SUPPOSED TO BE? A LAWN GNOME?
VERY FUNNY.
C'MON!

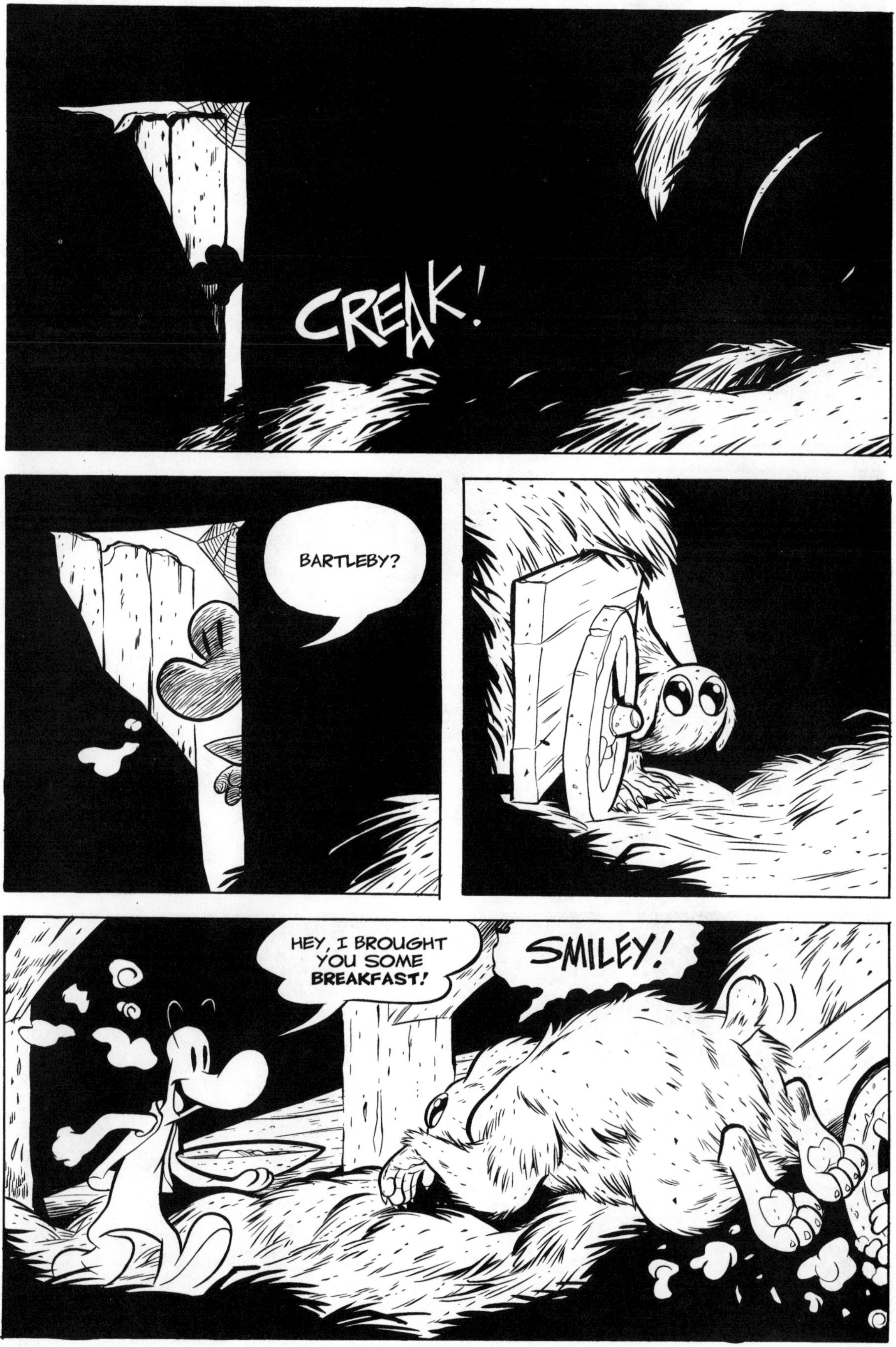
CREAK!
BARTLEBY?
HEY, I BROUGHT YOU SOME BREAKFAST!
SMILEY!

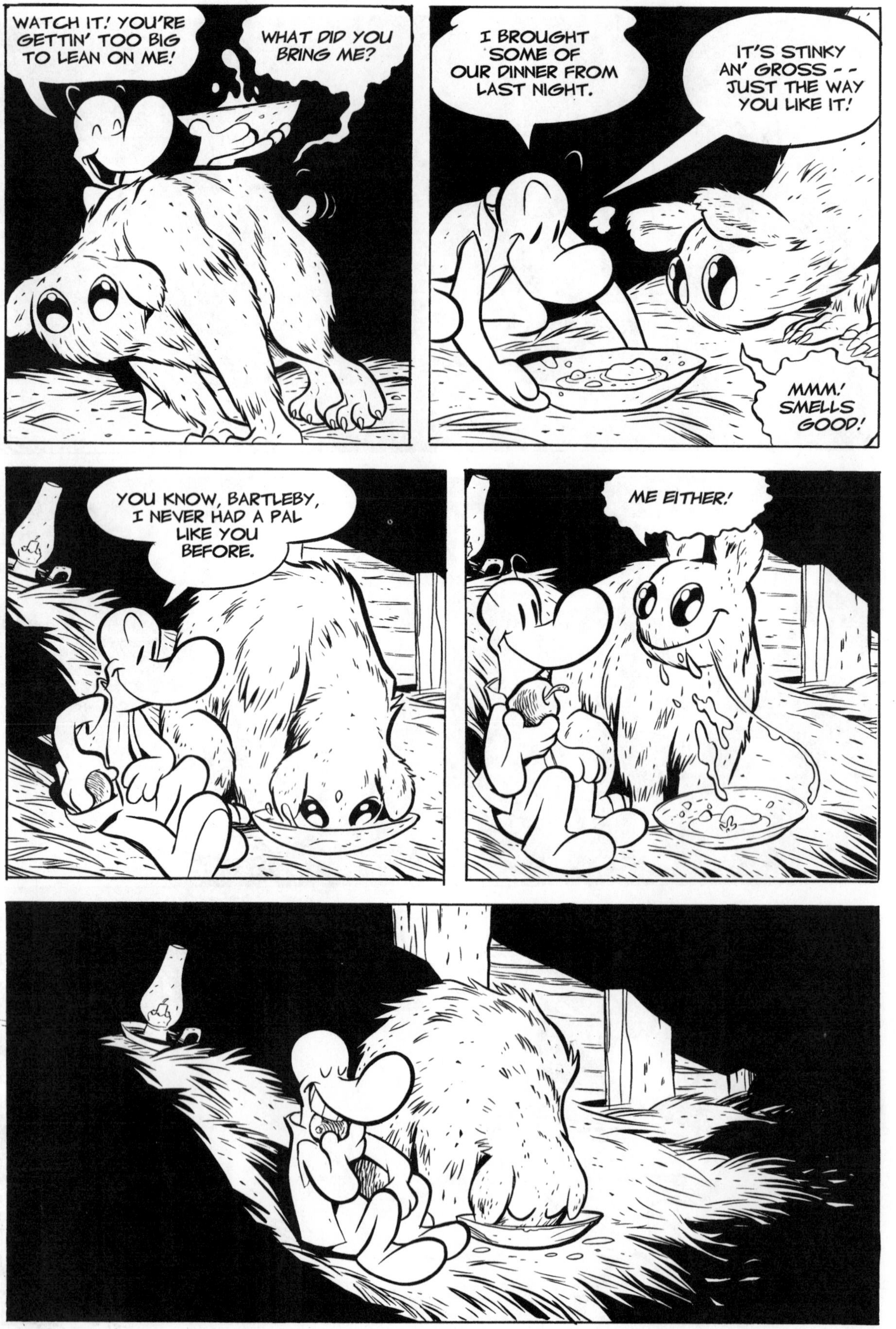
WATCH IT! YOU'RE GETTIN' TOO BIG TO LEAN ON ME!
WHAT DID YOU BRING ME?
I BROUGHT SOME OF OUR DINNER FROM LAST NIGHT.
IT'S STINKY AN' GROSS - - JUST THE WAY YOU LIKE IT!
MMM! SMELLS GOOD!
YOU KNOW, BARTLEBY, I NEVER HAD A PAL LIKE YOU BEFORE.
ME EITHER!

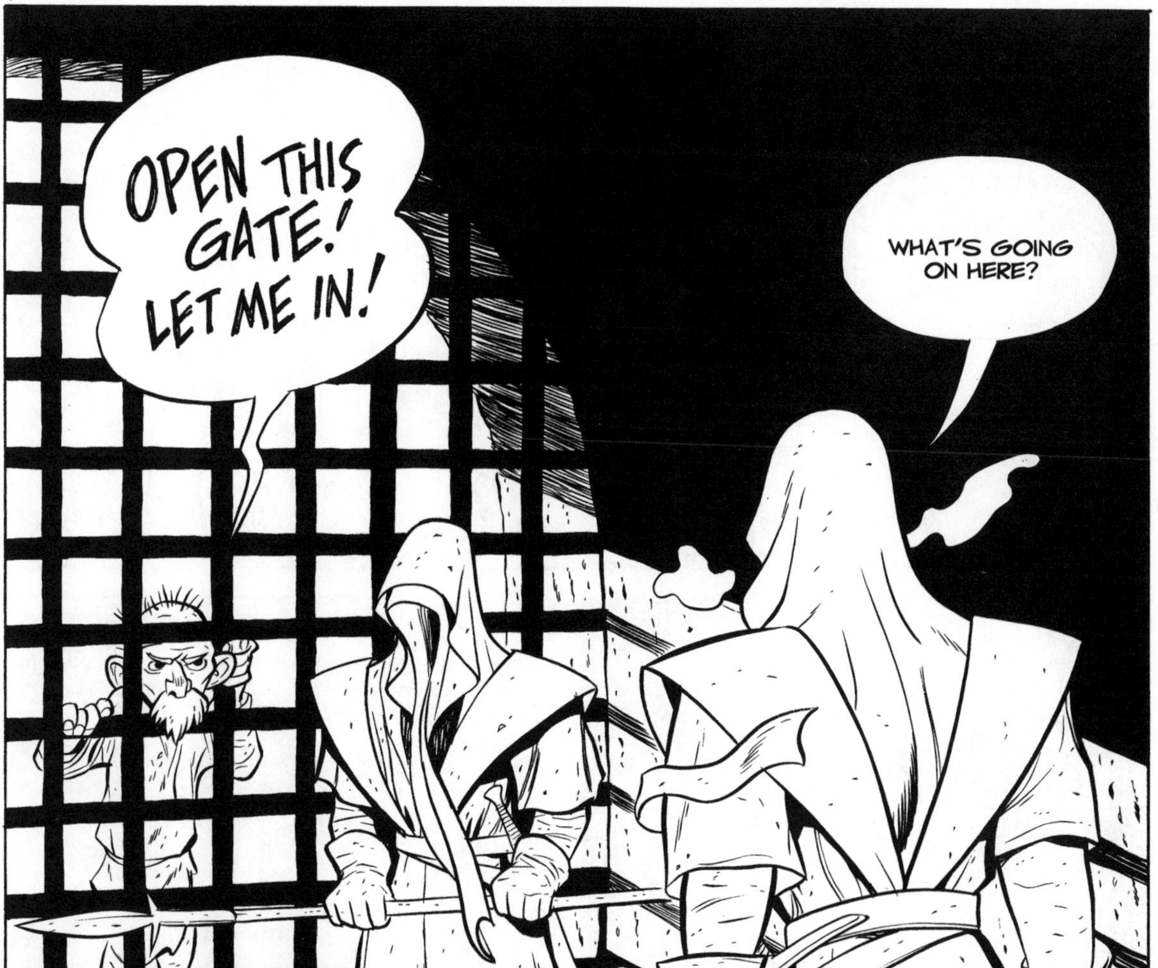
OPEN THIS GATE! LET ME IN!
WHAT'S GOING ON HERE?

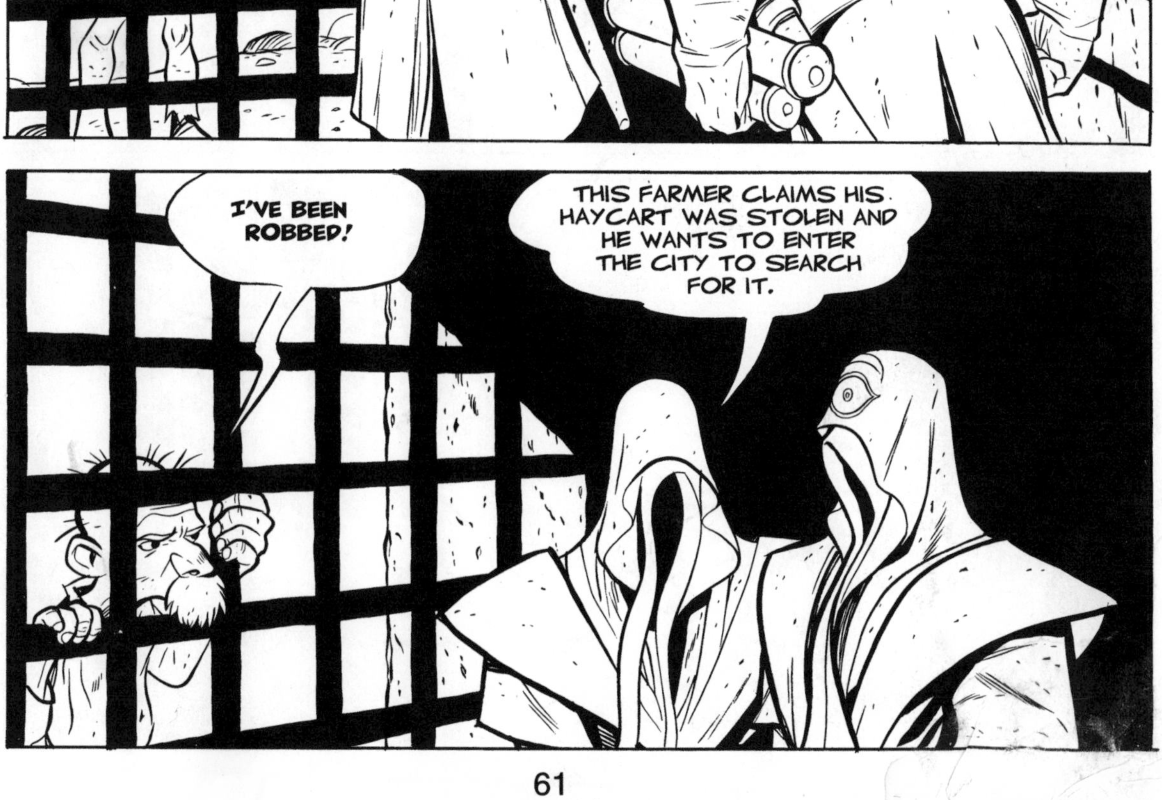
I'VE BEEN ROBBED!
THIS FARMER CLAIMS HIS HAYCART WAS STOLEN AND HE WANTS TO ENTER THE CITY TO SEARCH FOR IT.

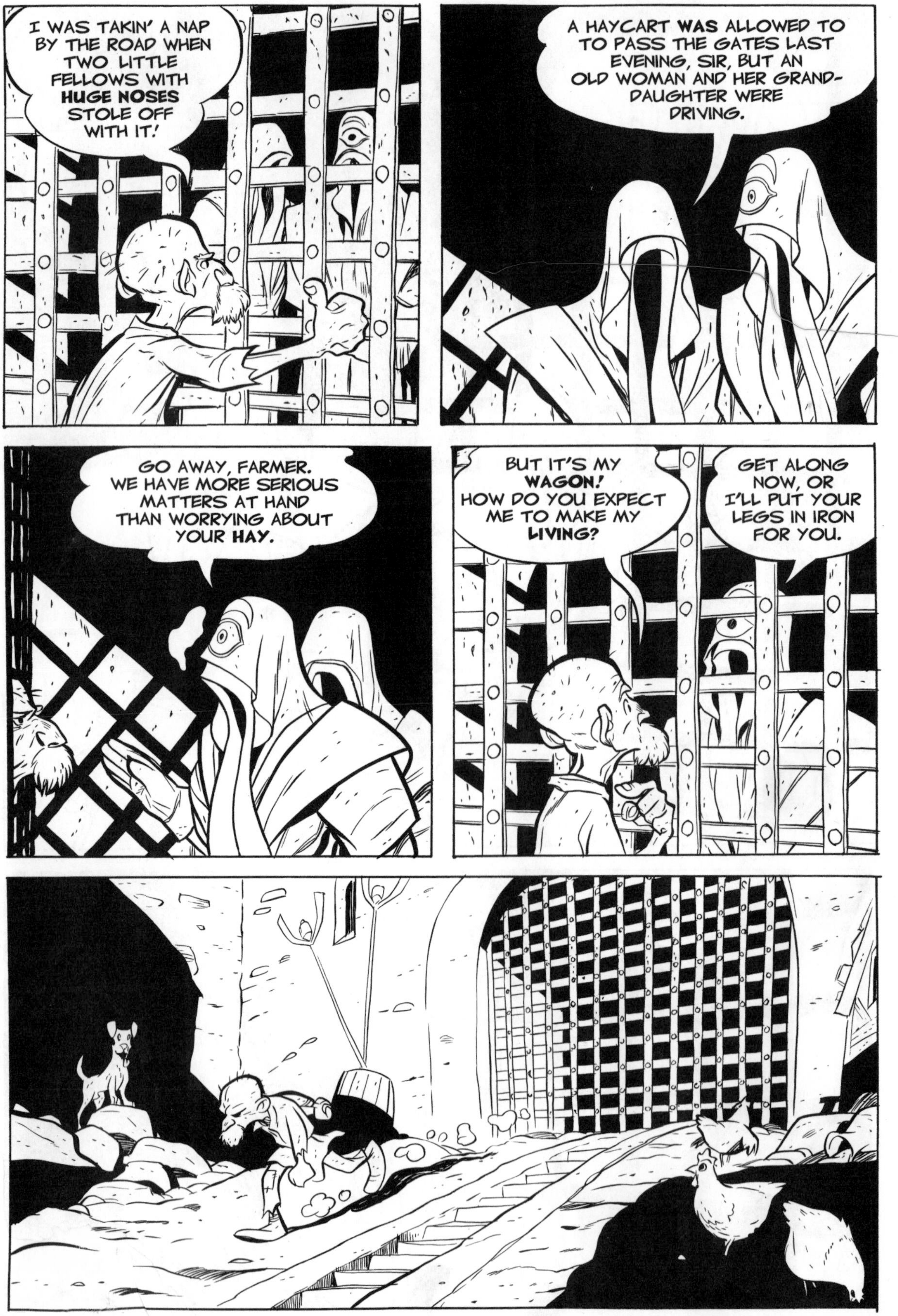
I WAS TAKIN' A NAP BY THE ROAD WHEN TWO LITTLE FELLOWS WITH **HUGE NOSES** STOLE OFF WITH IT!
A HAYCART **WAS** ALLOWED TO TO PASS THE GATES LAST EVENING, SIR, BUT AN OLD WOMAN AND HER GRAND-DAUGHTER WERE DRIVING.
GO AWAY, FARMER. WE HAVE MORE SERIOUS MATTERS AT HAND THAN WORRYING ABOUT YOUR **HAY**.
BUT IT'S MY **WAGON**! HOW DO YOU EXPECT ME TO MAKE MY **LIVING**?
GET ALONG NOW, OR I'LL PUT YOUR LEGS IN IRON FOR YOU.

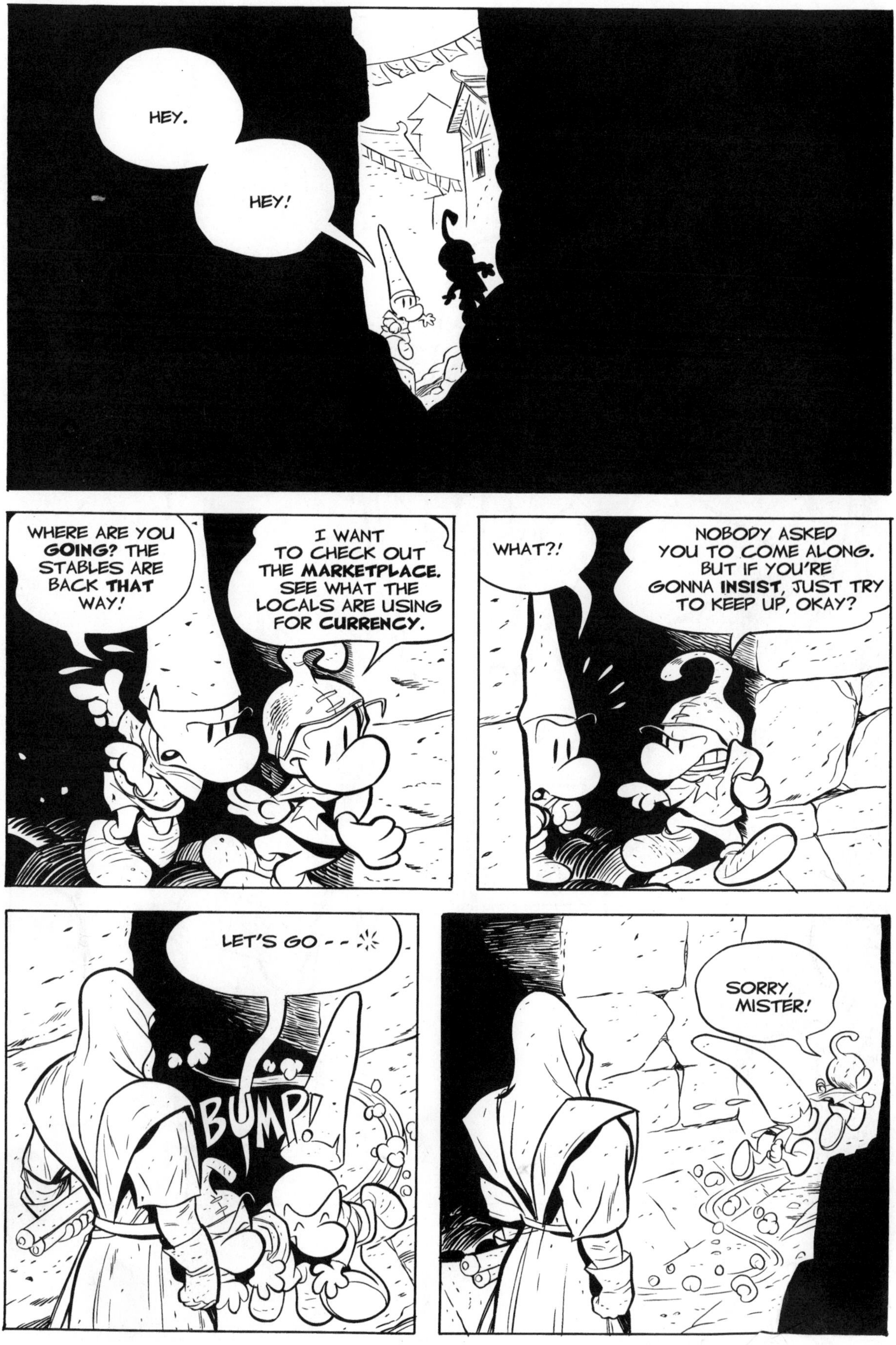
HEY.
HEY!
WHERE ARE YOU GOING? THE STABLES ARE BACK THAT WAY!
I WANT TO CHECK OUT THE MARKETPLACE. SEE WHAT THE LOCALS ARE USING FOR CURRENCY.
WHAT?!
NOBODY ASKED YOU TO COME ALONG. BUT IF YOU'RE GONNA INSIST, JUST TRY TO KEEP UP, OKAY?
LET'S GO - -
BUMP!
SORRY, MISTER!

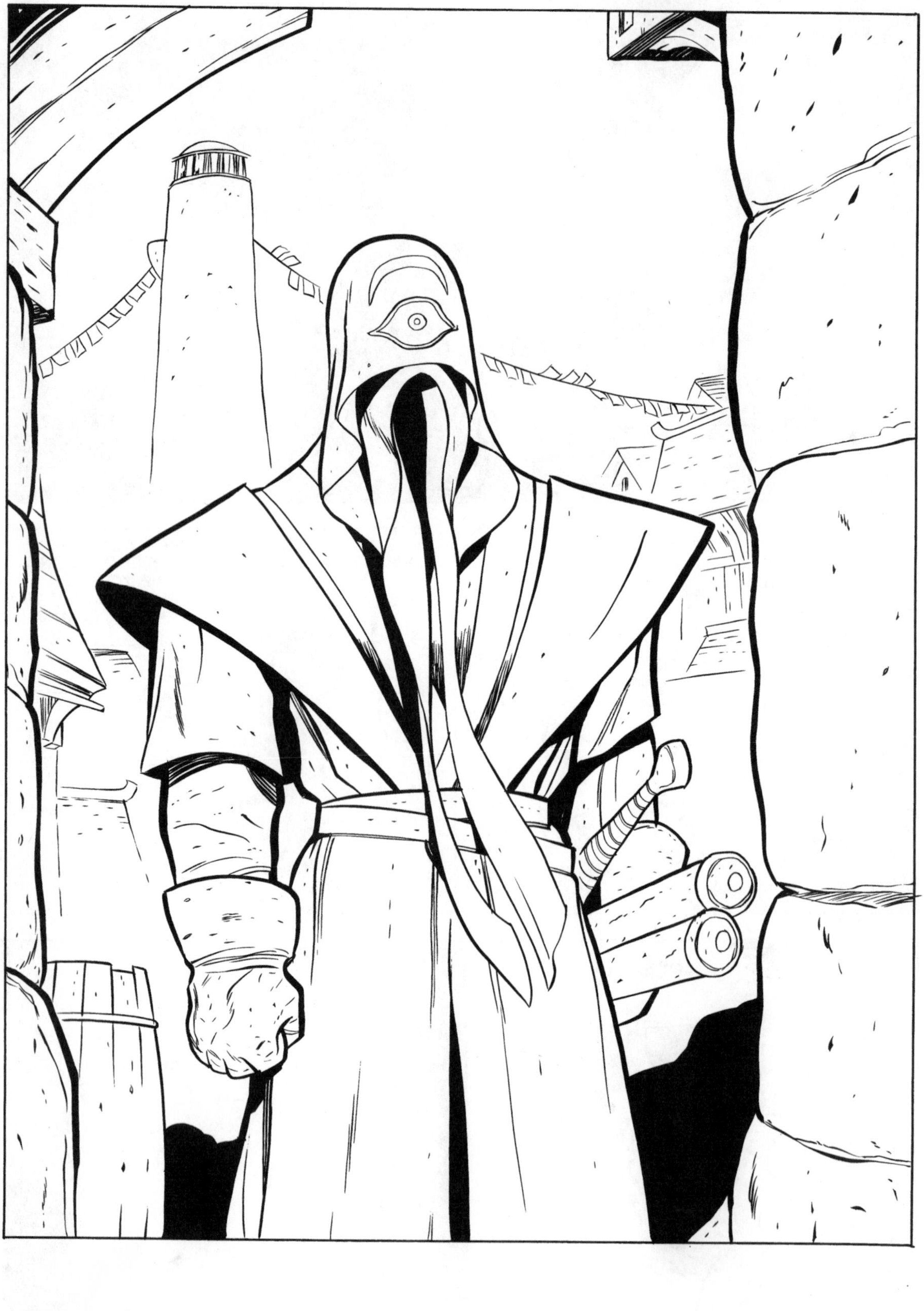

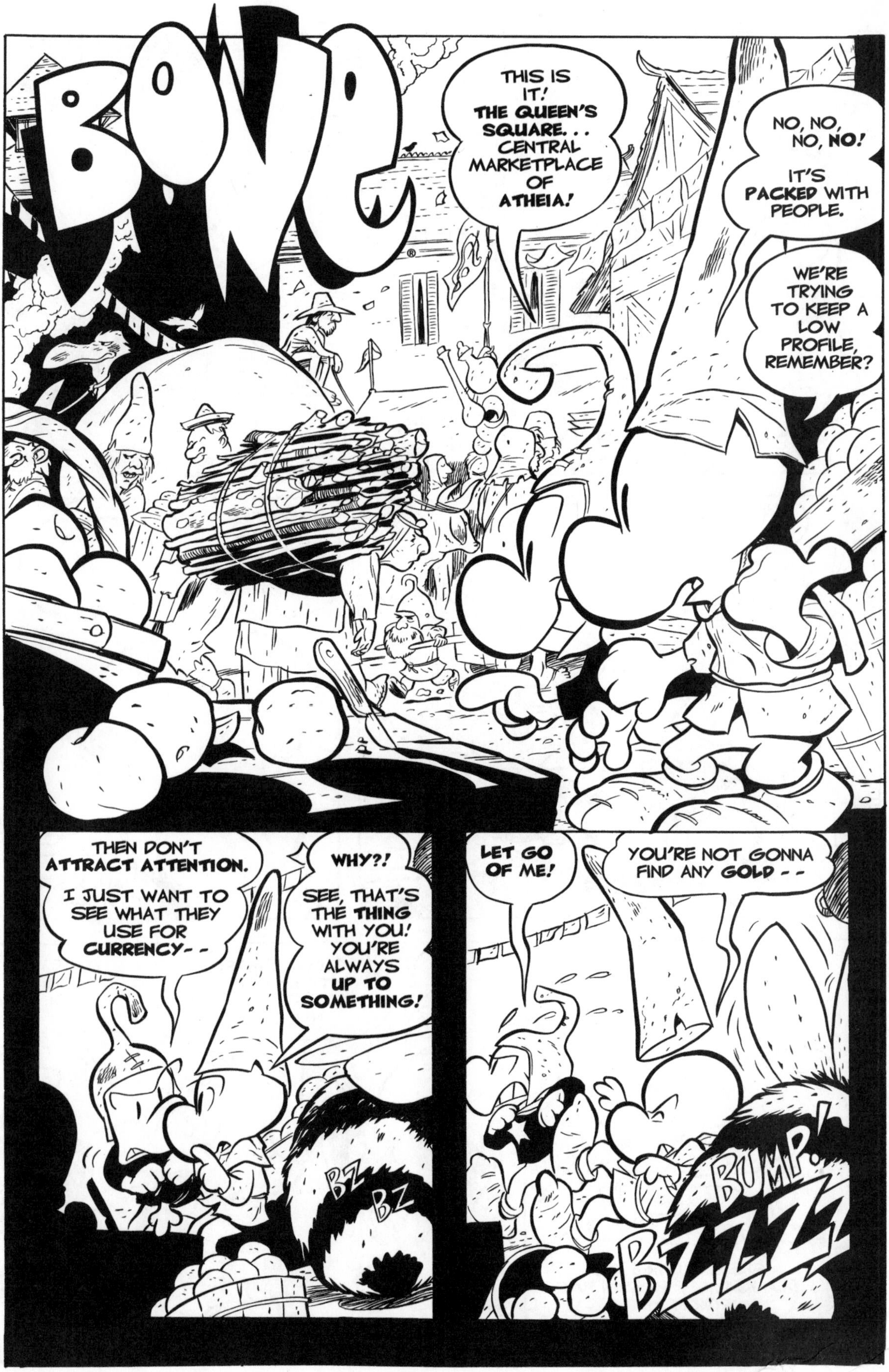
BONE®
THIS IS IT! THE QUEEN'S SQUARE... CENTRAL MARKETPLACE OF ATHEIA!
NO, NO, NO, NO! IT'S PACKED WITH PEOPLE.
WE'RE TRYING TO KEEP A LOW PROFILE, REMEMBER?
THEN DON'T ATTRACT ATTENTION.
I JUST WANT TO SEE WHAT THEY USE FOR CURRENCY- -
WHY?!
SEE, THAT'S THE THING WITH YOU! YOU'RE ALWAYS UP TO SOMETHING!
BZ BZ
LET GO OF ME!
YOU'RE NOT GONNA FIND ANY GOLD - -
BUMP!
BZZZZ

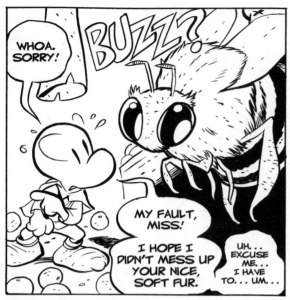

WHOA. SORRY!

BUZZ??

MY FAULT, MISS!

I HOPE I DIDN'T MESS UP YOUR NICE, SOFT FUR.

UH... EXCUSE ME... I HAVE TO... UM...

PHONEY! WAIT UP!

THIS ISN'T WORTH THE RISK. THEY DON'T **USE** MONEY HERE!

OH, YEAH?

WELL, THE **TINGLING SENSATION** IN MY SCALP SAYS THEY **DO!**

LOOK! THERE'S A TRANSACTION TAKING PLACE **RIGHT NOW.**

ALL I SEE IS A BLANKET.

SHE'S **BUYING** THE BLANKET. SHE HASN'T PAID FOR IT YET. LET'S JUST **WATCH!**

SHE'LL PAY FOR IT WITH AN **EGG,** JUST LIKE EVERYWHERE **ELSE** IN THE VALLEY.

O, YE OF **LITTLE** FAITH...

ZZZZZ

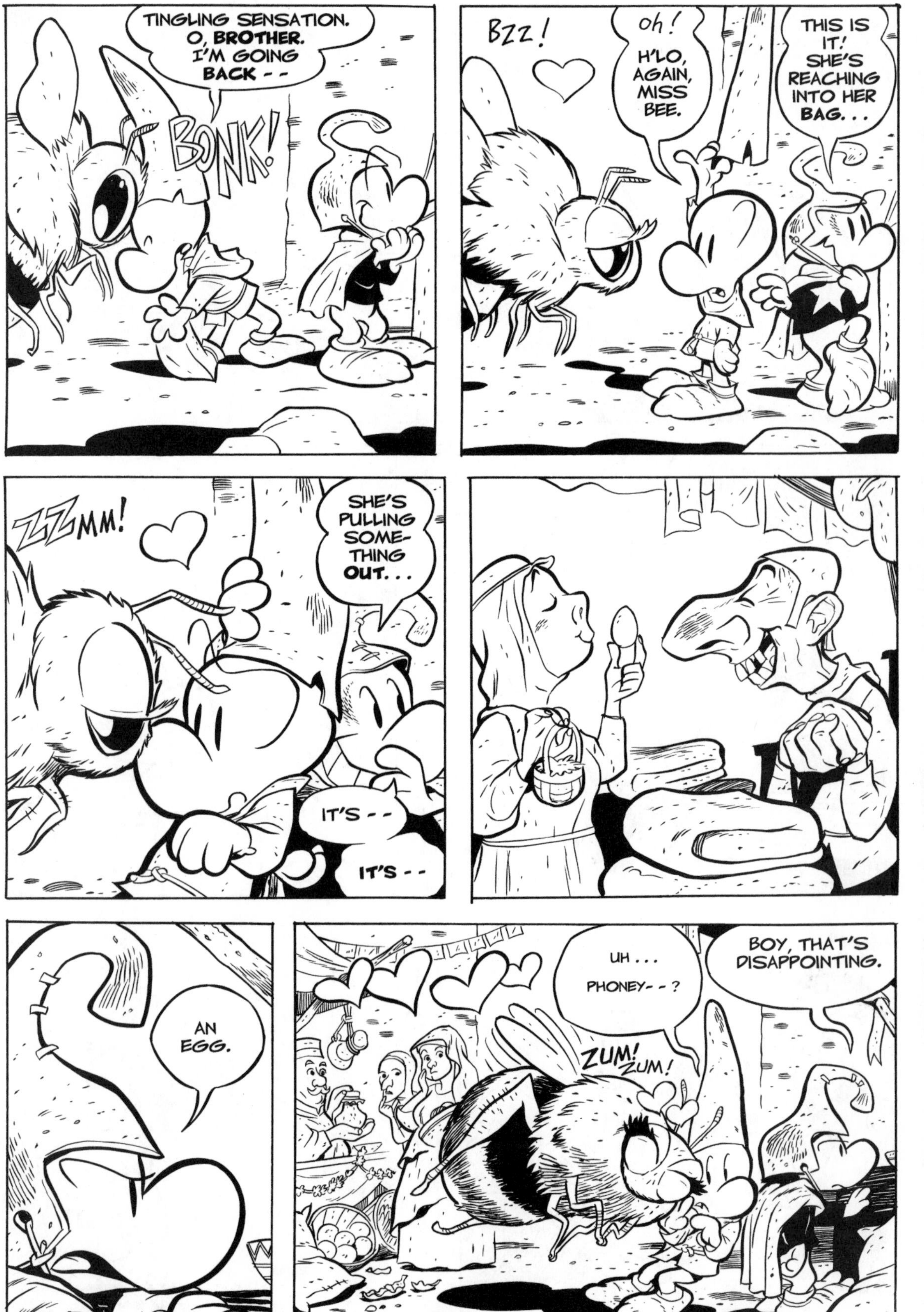
TINGLING SENSATION. O, BROTHER. I'M GOING BACK - -
BONK!
BZZ!
oh!
H'LO, AGAIN, MISS BEE.
THIS IS IT! SHE'S REACHING INTO HER BAG . . .
ZZMM!
SHE'S PULLING SOME-THING OUT . . .
IT'S - -
IT'S - -
AN EGG.
UH . . .
PHONEY- - ?
BOY, THAT'S DISAPPOINTING.
ZUM! ZUM!

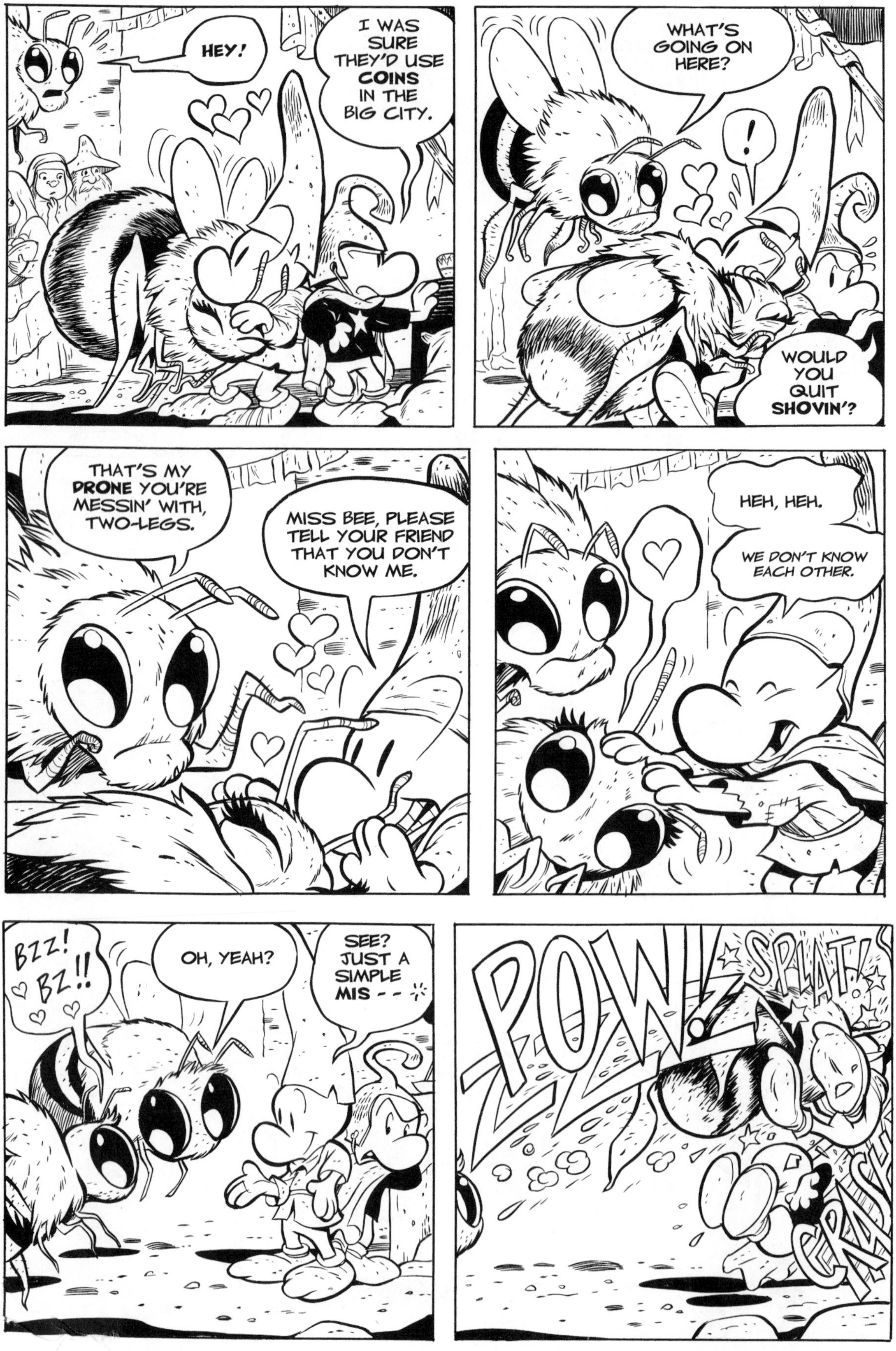
HEY!
I WAS SURE THEY'D USE **COINS** IN THE BIG CITY.
WHAT'S GOING ON HERE?
!
WOULD YOU QUIT **SHOVIN'**?
THAT'S MY **DRONE** YOU'RE MESSIN' WITH, TWO-LEGS.
MISS BEE, PLEASE TELL YOUR FRIEND THAT YOU DON'T KNOW ME.
HEH, HEH.
WE DON'T KNOW EACH OTHER.
BZZ! BZ!!
OH, YEAH?
SEE? JUST A SIMPLE **MIS** - -
POW!
SPLAT!
CRASH

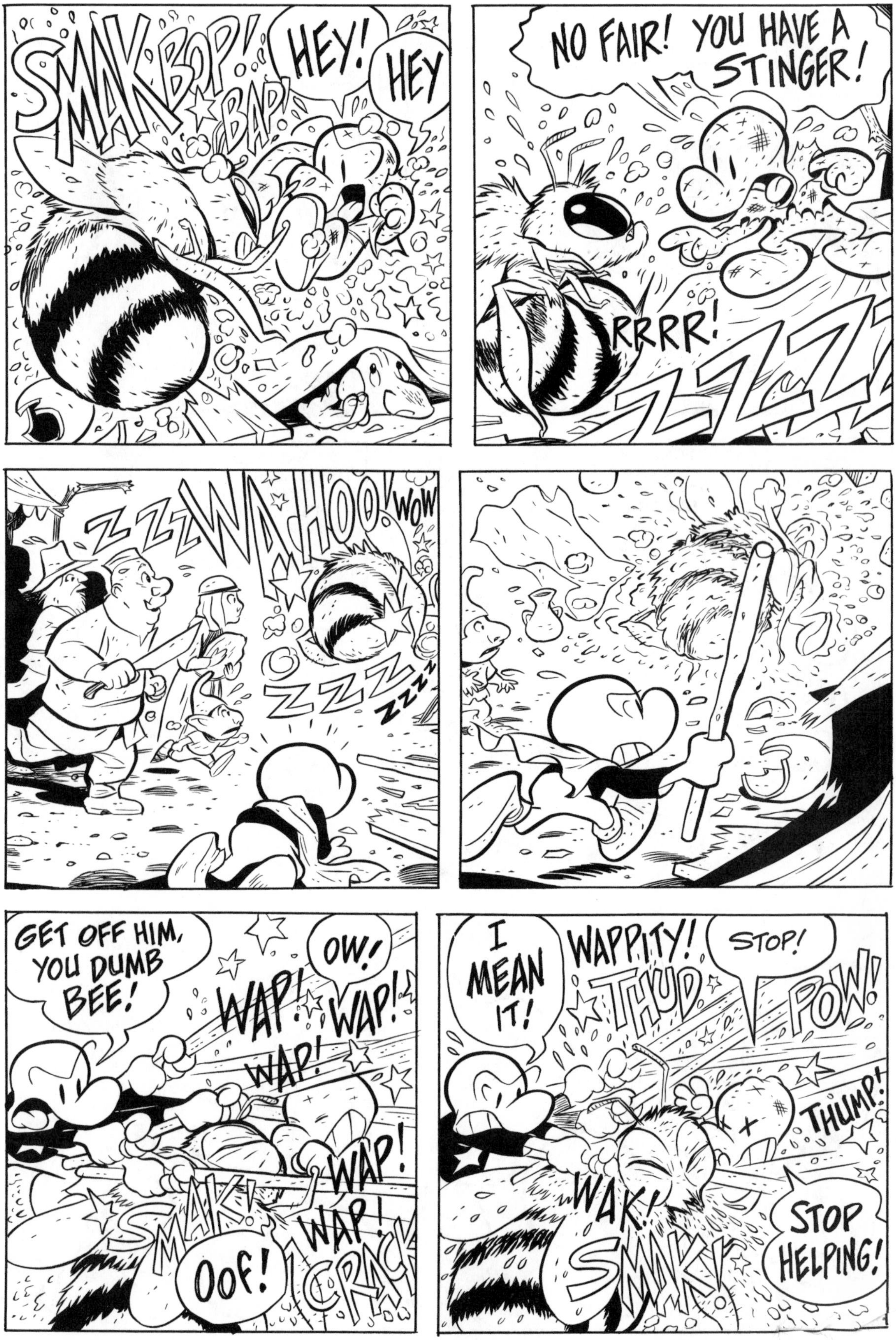
SMAK BOP!
BAP!
HEY!
HEY
NO FAIR! YOU HAVE A STINGER!
RRRR!
ZZZZ
ZZZWA HOO!
WOW
ZZZ
ZZZZ
GET OFF HIM, YOU DUMB BEE!
OW!
WAP!
WAP!
WAP!
WAP!
SMAK!
OOF!
WAP!
CRACK
I MEAN IT!
WAPPITY!
THUD
STOP!
POW!
THUMP!
WAK!
SMAK!
STOP HELPING!

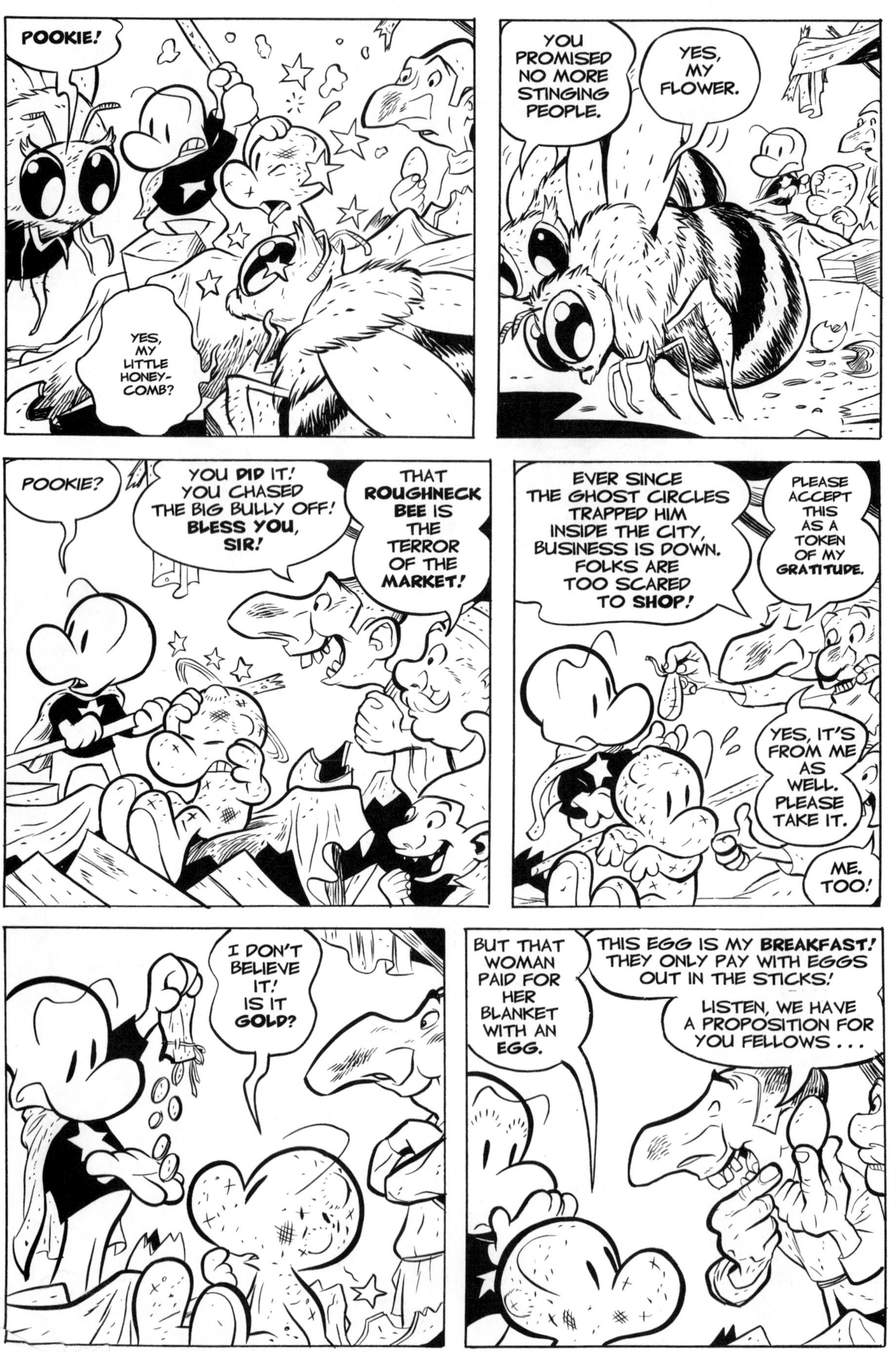
POOKIE!
YES, MY LITTLE HONEY-COMB?
YOU PROMISED NO MORE STINGING PEOPLE.
YES, MY FLOWER.
POOKIE?
YOU DID IT! YOU CHASED THE BIG BULLY OFF! BLESS YOU, SIR!
THAT ROUGHNECK BEE IS THE TERROR OF THE MARKET!
EVER SINCE THE GHOST CIRCLES TRAPPED HIM INSIDE THE CITY, BUSINESS IS DOWN. FOLKS ARE TOO SCARED TO SHOP!
PLEASE ACCEPT THIS AS A TOKEN OF MY GRATITUDE.
YES, IT'S FROM ME AS WELL. PLEASE TAKE IT.
ME. TOO!
I DON'T BELIEVE IT! IS IT GOLD?
BUT THAT WOMAN PAID FOR HER BLANKET WITH AN EGG.
THIS EGG IS MY BREAKFAST! THEY ONLY PAY WITH EGGS OUT IN THE STICKS!
LISTEN, WE HAVE A PROPOSITION FOR YOU FELLOWS . . .

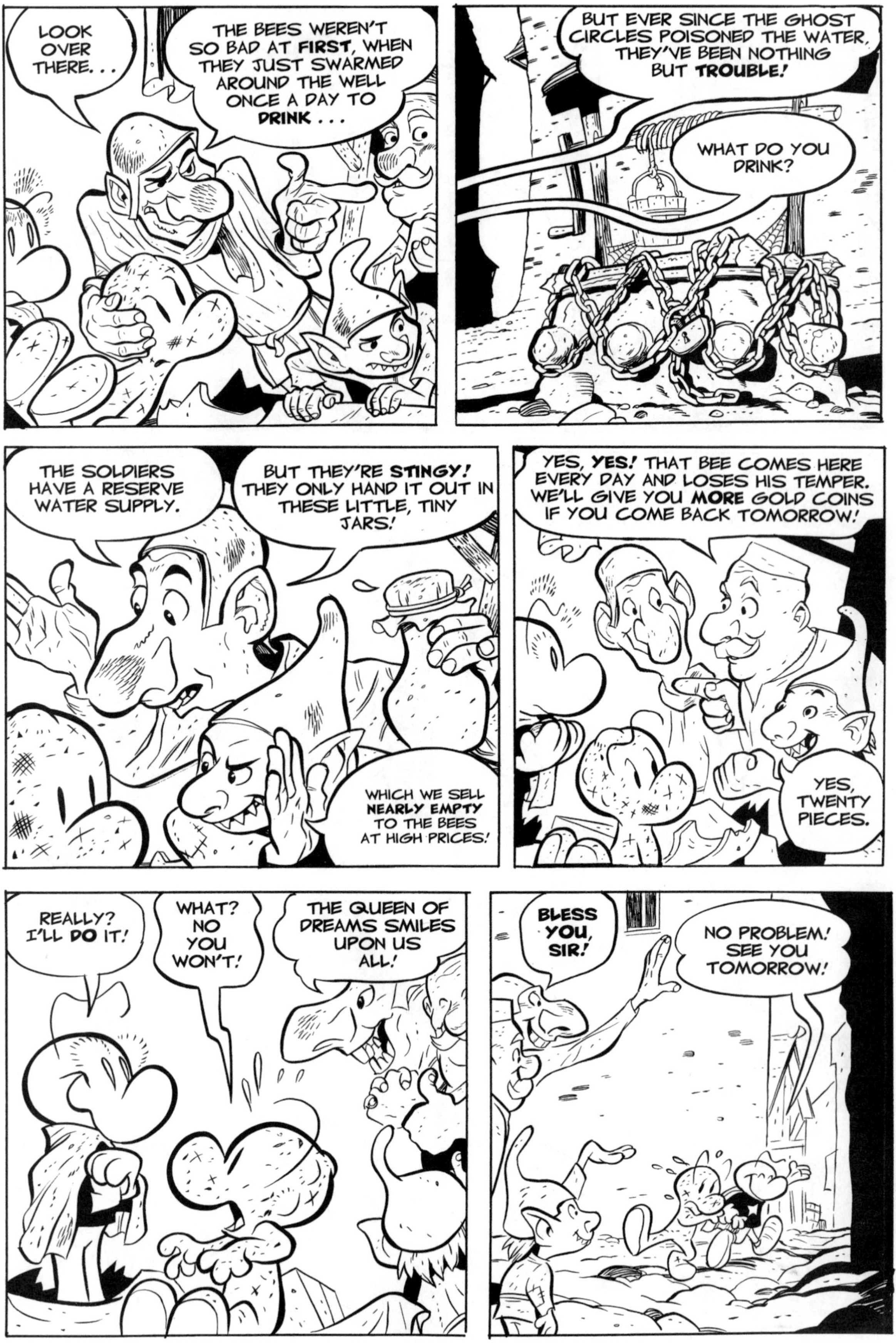
LOOK OVER THERE. . .
THE BEES WEREN'T SO BAD AT **FIRST**, WHEN THEY JUST SWARMED AROUND THE WELL ONCE A DAY TO **DRINK** . . .
BUT EVER SINCE THE GHOST CIRCLES POISONED THE WATER, THEY'VE BEEN NOTHING BUT **TROUBLE!**
WHAT DO YOU DRINK?
THE SOLDIERS HAVE A RESERVE WATER SUPPLY.
BUT THEY'RE **STINGY!** THEY ONLY HAND IT OUT IN THESE LITTLE, TINY JARS!
WHICH WE SELL **NEARLY EMPTY** TO THE BEES AT HIGH PRICES!
YES, **YES!** THAT BEE COMES HERE EVERY DAY AND LOSES HIS TEMPER. WE'LL GIVE YOU **MORE** GOLD COINS IF YOU COME BACK TOMORROW!
YES, TWENTY PIECES.
REALLY? I'LL **DO** IT!
WHAT? NO YOU WON'T!
THE QUEEN OF DREAMS SMILES UPON US ALL!
BLESS YOU, SIR!
NO PROBLEM! SEE YOU TOMORROW!

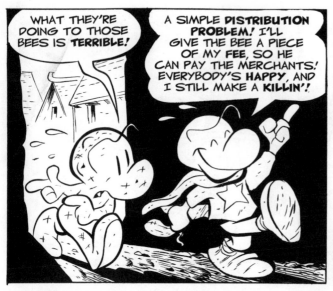

WHAT THEY'RE DOING TO THOSE BEES IS **TERRIBLE!**

A SIMPLE **DISTRIBUTION PROBLEM!** I'LL GIVE THE BEE A PIECE OF MY **FEE**, SO HE CAN PAY THE MERCHANTS! EVERYBODY'S **HAPPY**, AND I STILL MAKE A **KILLIN'!**

ON TOP OF **THAT**, MY SCALP IS **BIG** TINGLIN', FONE BONE!

THAT ONLY HAPPENS WHEN I'M ABOUT TO **SCORE BIG!**

FORGET THE **GOLD.** I'M NOT GONNA LET YOU JEOPARDIZE **THORN'S** SAFETY.

THIS HAS NOTHIN' TO DO WITH HER. I'LL HANDLE THE DEAL SO **EVERYBODY'S** HAPPY. I **PROMISE** NOTHIN'LL GO WRONG.

OF COURSE IT'S GONNA GO **WRONG!**

WHOA. WHOA, WAIT. IS THIS THE WAY WE CAME IN?

UH ...

C'MON, WE'LL GO UP AND GET OUR BEARINGS.

ANYWAY, NOBODY'S GOING TO FIND OUT THAT THORN IS A PRINCESS IN DISGUISE --

PHONEY!!

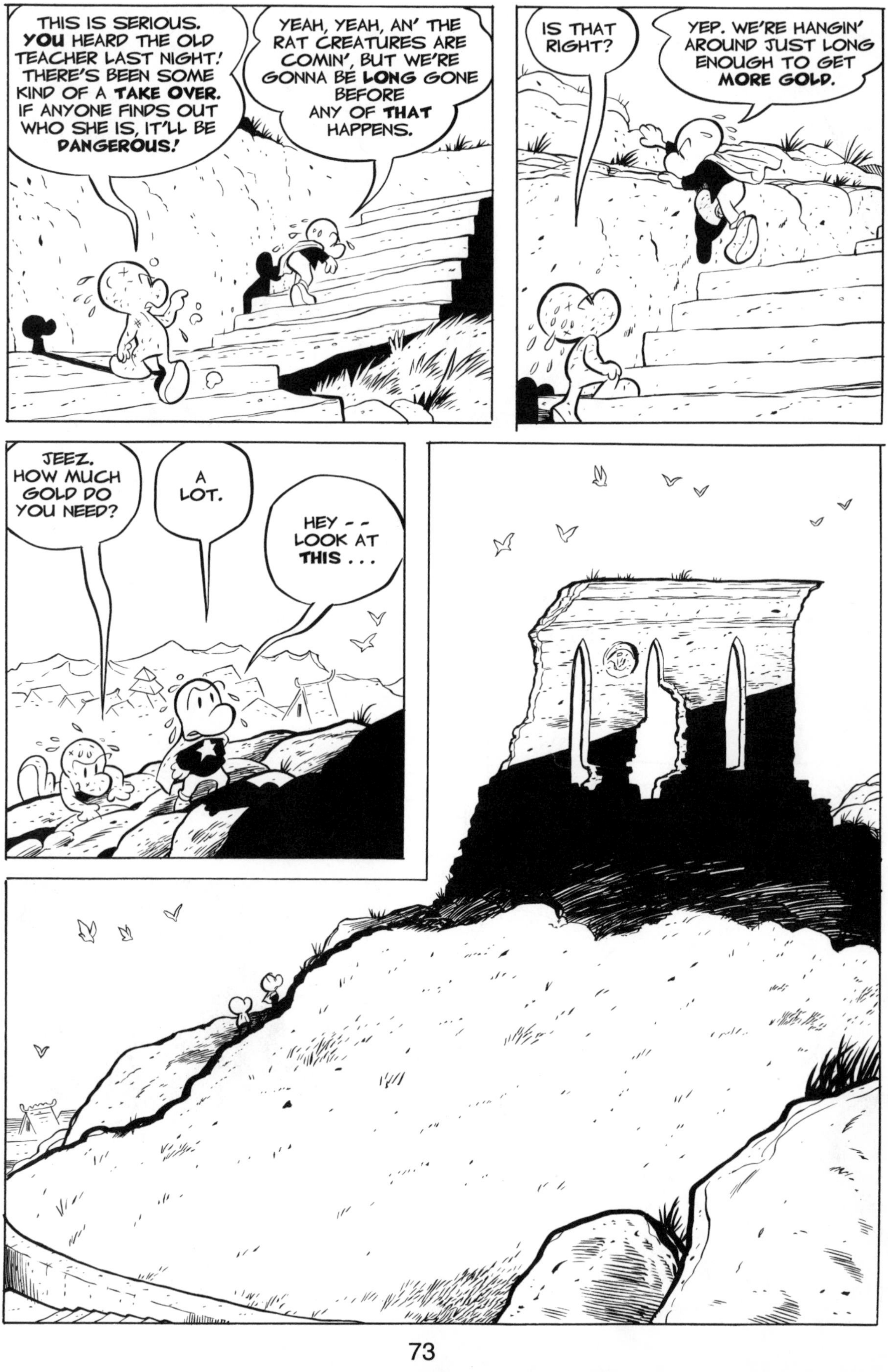
THIS IS SERIOUS. YOU HEARD THE OLD TEACHER LAST NIGHT! THERE'S BEEN SOME KIND OF A TAKE OVER. IF ANYONE FINDS OUT WHO SHE IS, IT'LL BE DANGEROUS!
YEAH, YEAH, AN' THE RAT CREATURES ARE COMIN', BUT WE'RE GONNA BE LONG GONE BEFORE ANY OF THAT HAPPENS.
IS THAT RIGHT?
YEP. WE'RE HANGIN' AROUND JUST LONG ENOUGH TO GET MORE GOLD.
JEEZ. HOW MUCH GOLD DO YOU NEED?
A LOT.
HEY - - LOOK AT THIS . . .

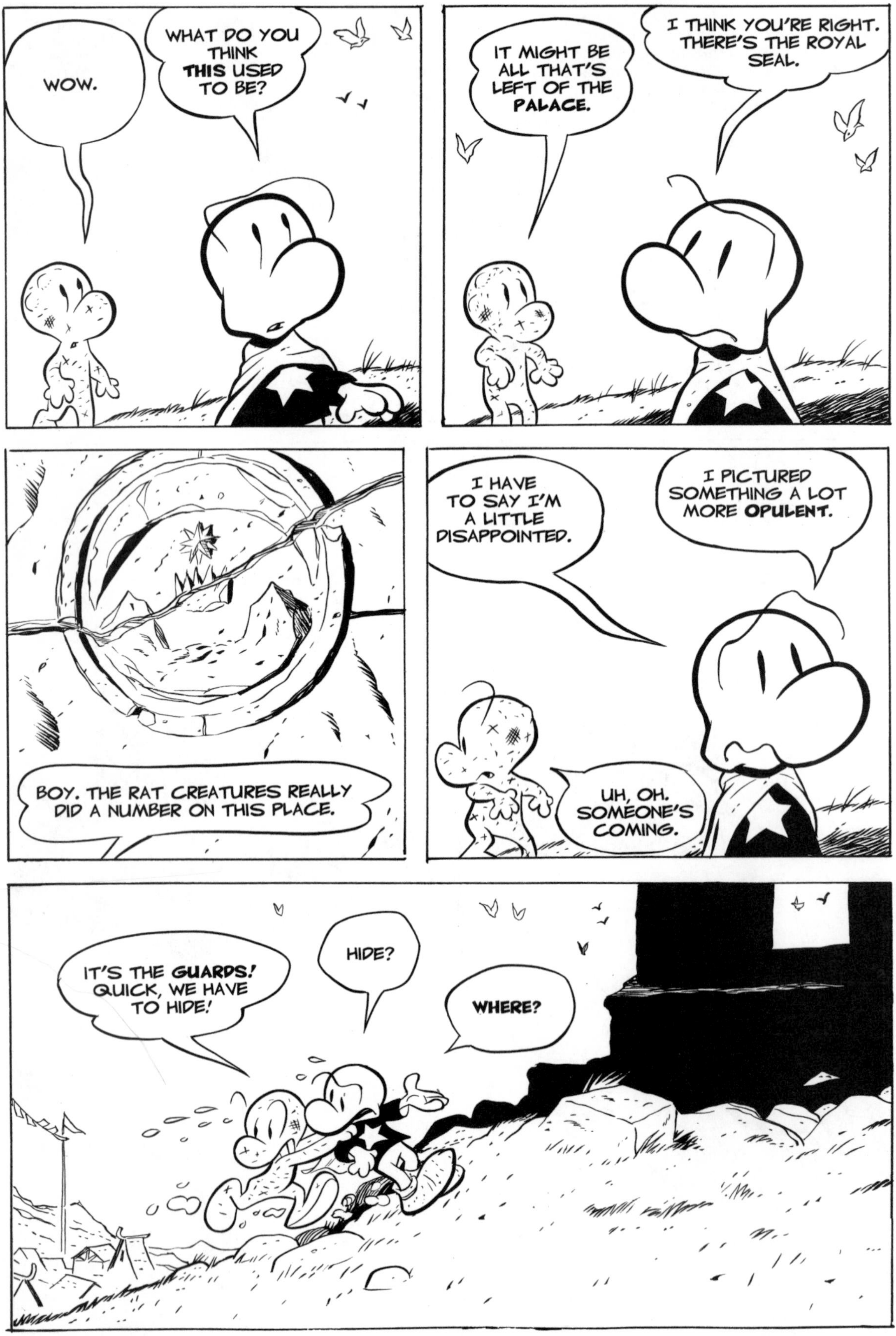
WOW.
WHAT DO YOU THINK THIS USED TO BE?
IT MIGHT BE ALL THAT'S LEFT OF THE PALACE.
I THINK YOU'RE RIGHT. THERE'S THE ROYAL SEAL.
BOY. THE RAT CREATURES REALLY DID A NUMBER ON THIS PLACE.
I HAVE TO SAY I'M A LITTLE DISAPPOINTED.
I PICTURED SOMETHING A LOT MORE OPULENT.
UH, OH. SOMEONE'S COMING.
IT'S THE GUARDS! QUICK, WE HAVE TO HIDE!
HIDE?
WHERE?

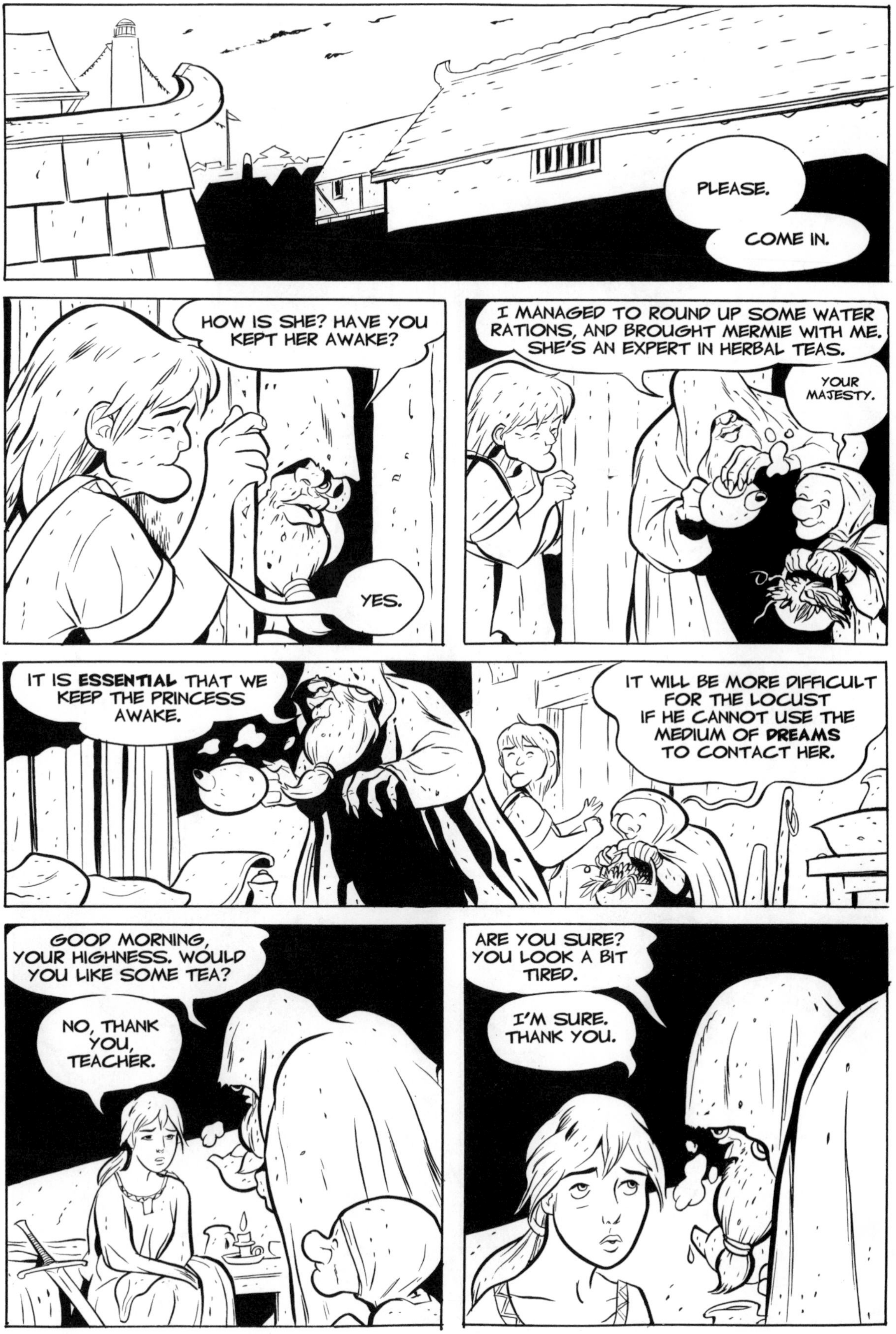
PLEASE.
COME IN.
HOW IS SHE? HAVE YOU KEPT HER AWAKE?
YES.
I MANAGED TO ROUND UP SOME WATER RATIONS, AND BROUGHT MERMIE WITH ME. SHE'S AN EXPERT IN HERBAL TEAS.
YOUR MAJESTY.
IT IS **ESSENTIAL** THAT WE KEEP THE PRINCESS AWAKE.
IT WILL BE MORE DIFFICULT FOR THE LOCUST IF HE CANNOT USE THE MEDIUM OF **DREAMS** TO CONTACT HER.
GOOD MORNING, YOUR HIGHNESS. WOULD YOU LIKE SOME TEA?
NO, THANK YOU, TEACHER.
ARE YOU SURE? YOU LOOK A BIT TIRED.
I'M SURE. THANK YOU.

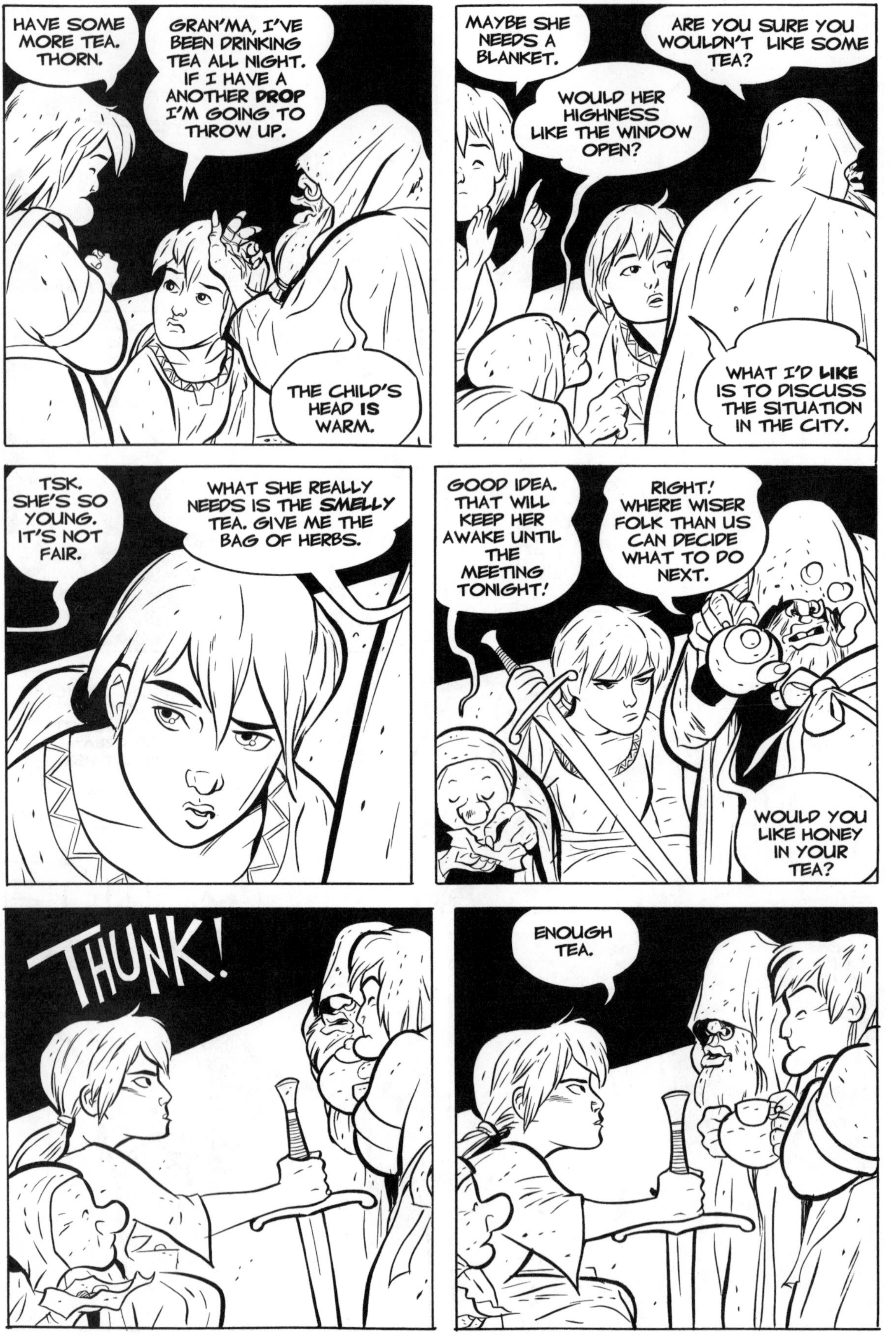
HAVE SOME MORE TEA. THORN.
GRAN'MA, I'VE BEEN DRINKING TEA ALL NIGHT. IF I HAVE A ANOTHER DROP I'M GOING TO THROW UP.
THE CHILD'S HEAD IS WARM.
MAYBE SHE NEEDS A BLANKET.
ARE YOU SURE YOU WOULDN'T LIKE SOME TEA?
WOULD HER HIGHNESS LIKE THE WINDOW OPEN?
WHAT I'D LIKE IS TO DISCUSS THE SITUATION IN THE CITY.
TSK. SHE'S SO YOUNG. IT'S NOT FAIR.
WHAT SHE REALLY NEEDS IS THE SMELLY TEA. GIVE ME THE BAG OF HERBS.
GOOD IDEA. THAT WILL KEEP HER AWAKE UNTIL THE MEETING TONIGHT!
RIGHT! WHERE WISER FOLK THAN US CAN DECIDE WHAT TO DO NEXT.
WOULD YOU LIKE HONEY IN YOUR TEA?
THUNK!
ENOUGH TEA.

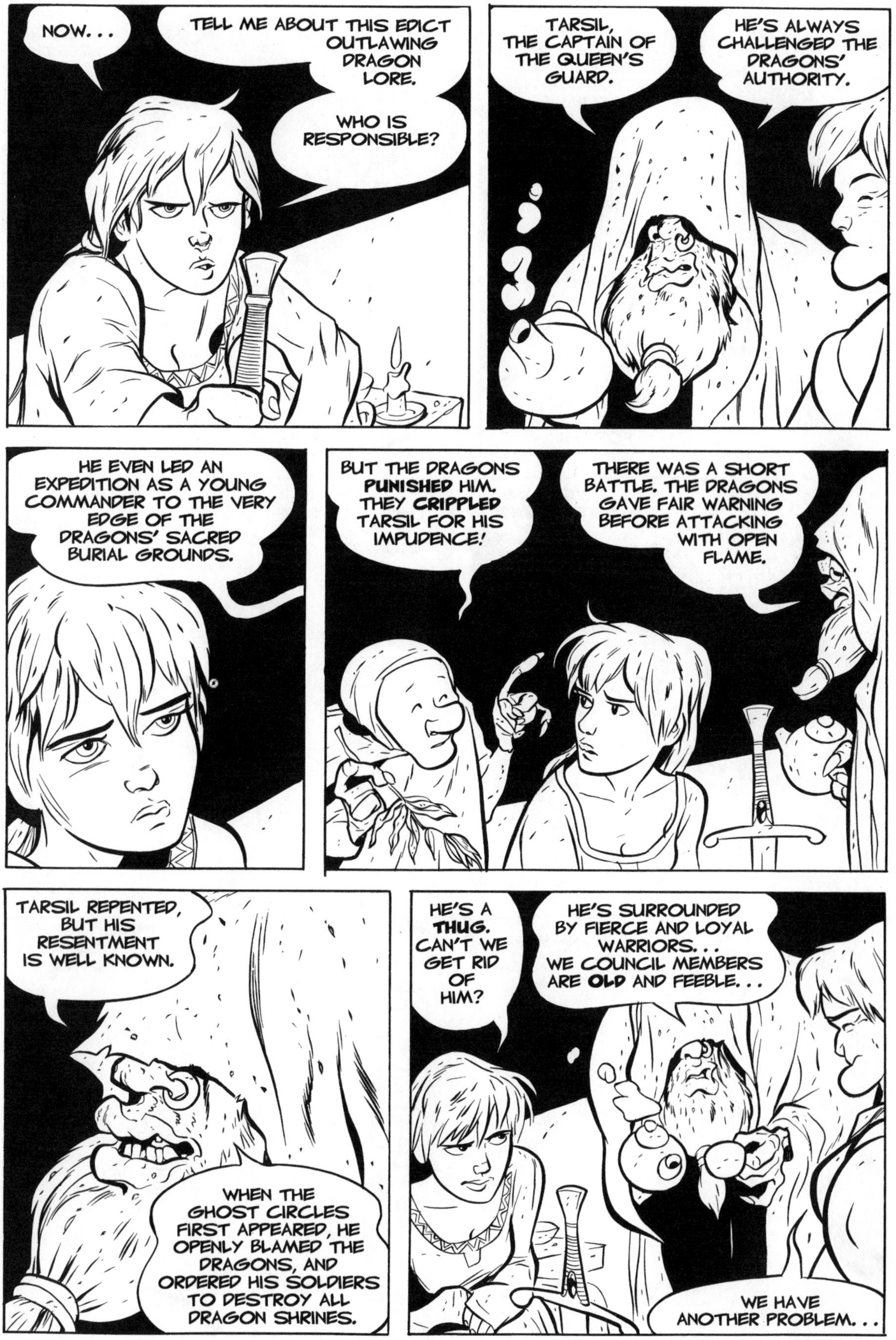

NOW...
TELL ME ABOUT THIS EDICT OUTLAWING DRAGON LORE.
WHO IS RESPONSIBLE?
TARSIL, THE CAPTAIN OF THE QUEEN'S GUARD.
HE'S ALWAYS CHALLENGED THE DRAGONS' AUTHORITY.
HE EVEN LED AN EXPEDITION AS A YOUNG COMMANDER TO THE VERY EDGE OF THE DRAGONS' SACRED BURIAL GROUNDS.
BUT THE DRAGONS **PUNISHED** HIM. THEY **CRIPPLED** TARSIL FOR HIS IMPUDENCE!
THERE WAS A SHORT BATTLE. THE DRAGONS GAVE FAIR WARNING BEFORE ATTACKING WITH OPEN FLAME.
TARSIL REPENTED, BUT HIS RESENTMENT IS WELL KNOWN.
WHEN THE GHOST CIRCLES FIRST APPEARED, HE OPENLY BLAMED THE DRAGONS, AND ORDERED HIS SOLDIERS TO DESTROY ALL DRAGON SHRINES.
HE'S A **THUG**. CAN'T WE GET RID OF HIM?
HE'S SURROUNDED BY FIERCE AND LOYAL WARRIORS... WE COUNCIL MEMBERS ARE **OLD** AND FEEBLE...
WE HAVE ANOTHER PROBLEM...

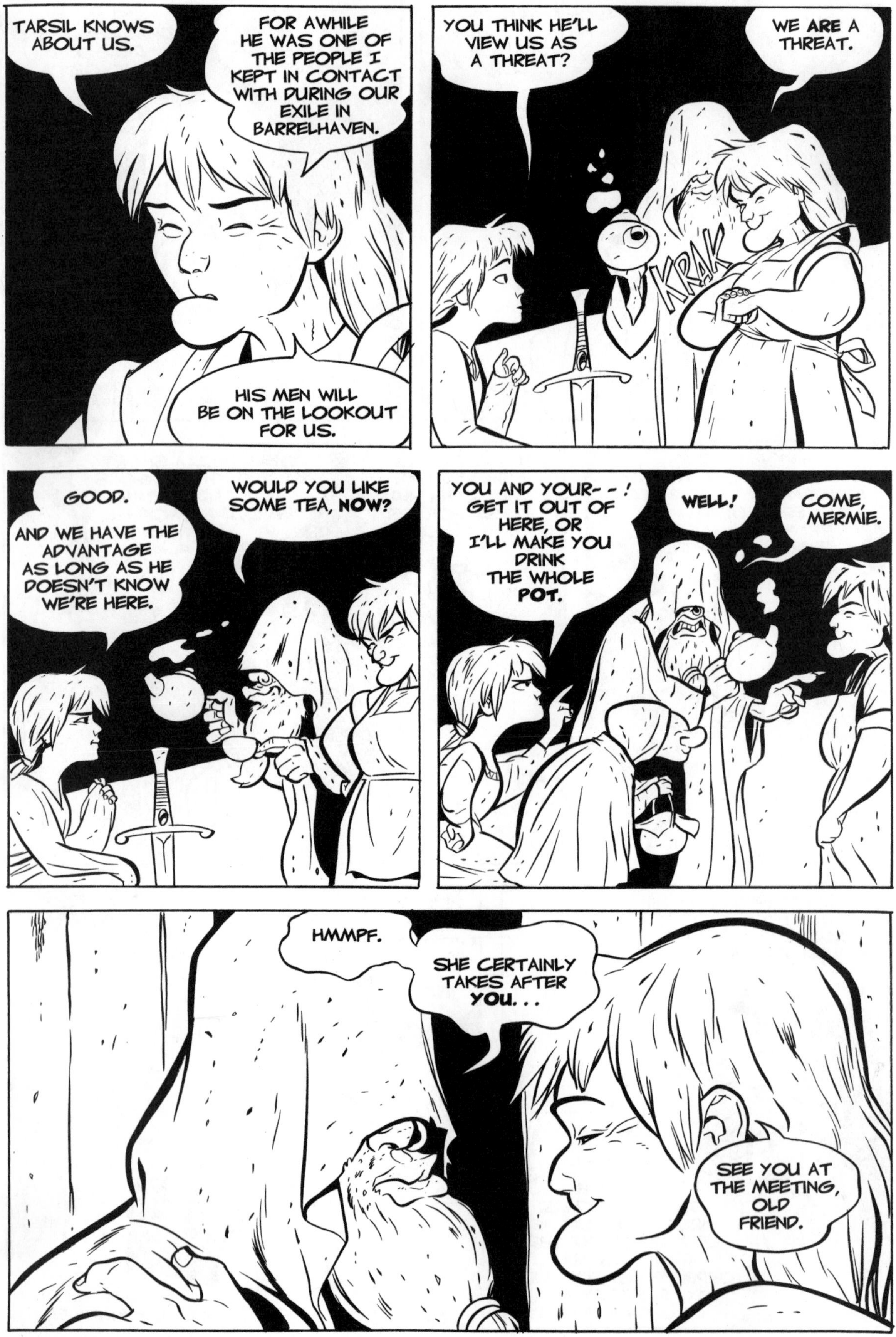
TARSIL KNOWS ABOUT US.
FOR AWHILE HE WAS ONE OF THE PEOPLE I KEPT IN CONTACT WITH DURING OUR EXILE IN BARRELHAVEN.
HIS MEN WILL BE ON THE LOOKOUT FOR US.
YOU THINK HE'LL VIEW US AS A THREAT?
WE ARE A THREAT.
KRAK
GOOD.
AND WE HAVE THE ADVANTAGE AS LONG AS HE DOESN'T KNOW WE'RE HERE.
WOULD YOU LIKE SOME TEA, NOW?
YOU AND YOUR- - ! GET IT OUT OF HERE, OR I'LL MAKE YOU DRINK THE WHOLE POT.
WELL!
COME, MERMIE.
HMMPF.
SHE CERTAINLY TAKES AFTER YOU. . .
SEE YOU AT THE MEETING, OLD FRIEND.

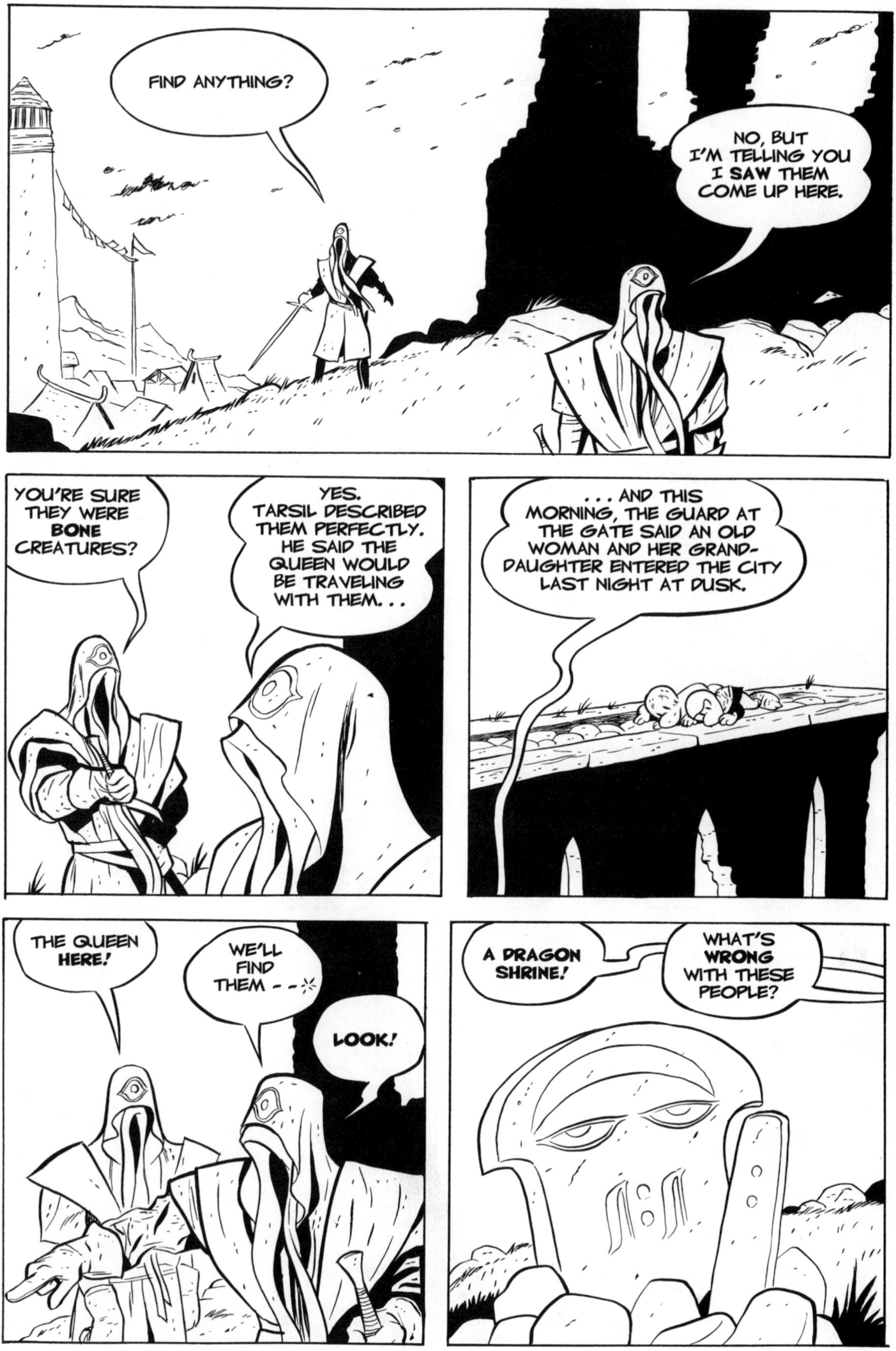
FIND ANYTHING?
NO, BUT I'M TELLING YOU I SAW THEM COME UP HERE.
YOU'RE SURE THEY WERE BONE CREATURES?
YES. TARSIL DESCRIBED THEM PERFECTLY. HE SAID THE QUEEN WOULD BE TRAVELING WITH THEM...
...AND THIS MORNING, THE GUARD AT THE GATE SAID AN OLD WOMAN AND HER GRAND-DAUGHTER ENTERED THE CITY LAST NIGHT AT DUSK.
THE QUEEN HERE!
WE'LL FIND THEM --
LOOK!
A DRAGON SHRINE!
WHAT'S WRONG WITH THESE PEOPLE?

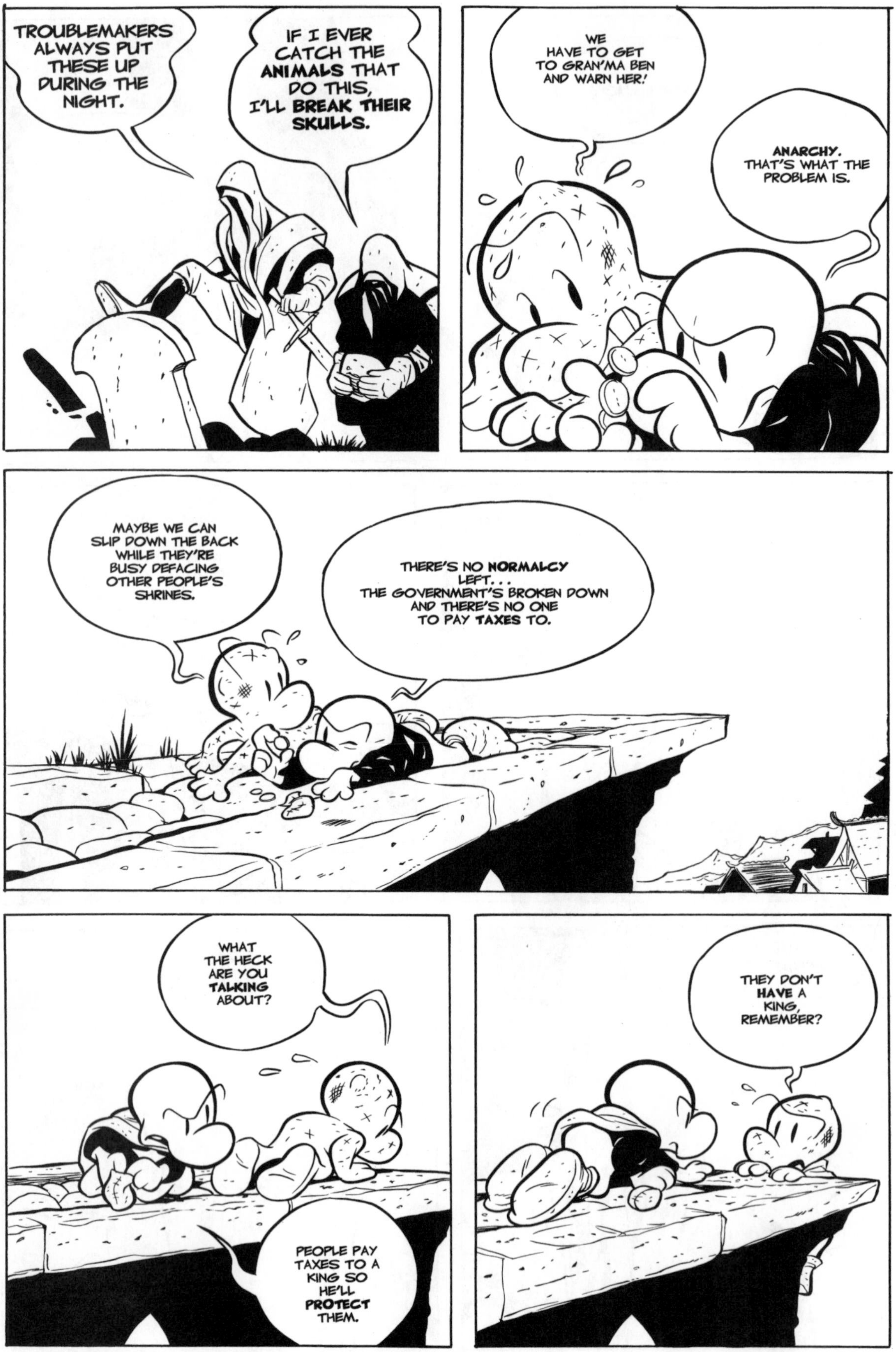
TROUBLEMAKERS ALWAYS PUT THESE UP DURING THE NIGHT.
IF I EVER CATCH THE ANIMALS THAT DO THIS, I'LL BREAK THEIR SKULLS.
WE HAVE TO GET TO GRAN'MA BEN AND WARN HER!
ANARCHY. THAT'S WHAT THE PROBLEM IS.
MAYBE WE CAN SLIP DOWN THE BACK WHILE THEY'RE BUSY DEFACING OTHER PEOPLE'S SHRINES.
THERE'S NO NORMALCY LEFT... THE GOVERNMENT'S BROKEN DOWN AND THERE'S NO ONE TO PAY TAXES TO.
WHAT THE HECK ARE YOU TALKING ABOUT?
PEOPLE PAY TAXES TO A KING SO HE'LL PROTECT THEM.
THEY DON'T HAVE A KING, REMEMBER?

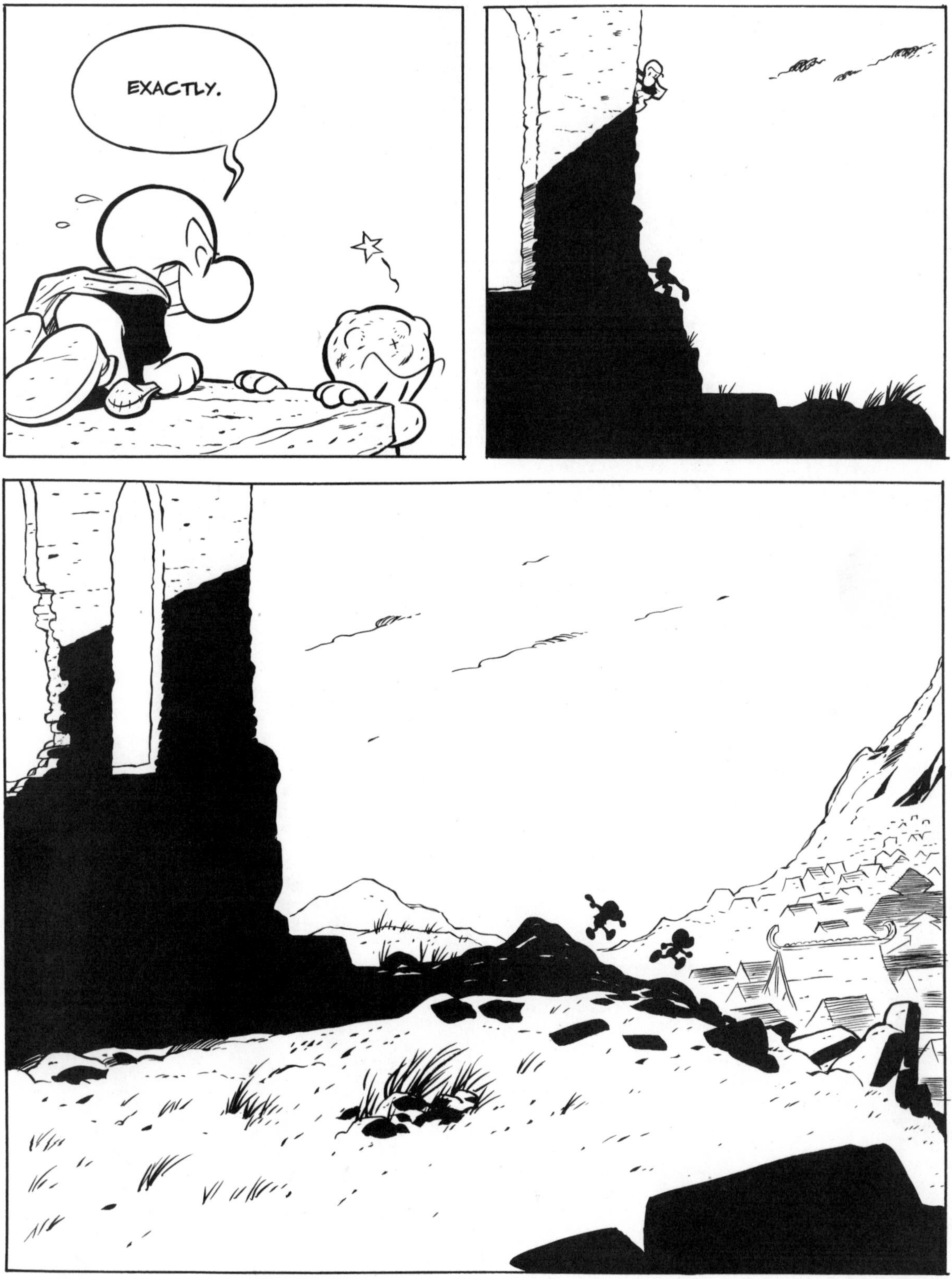
EXACTLY.

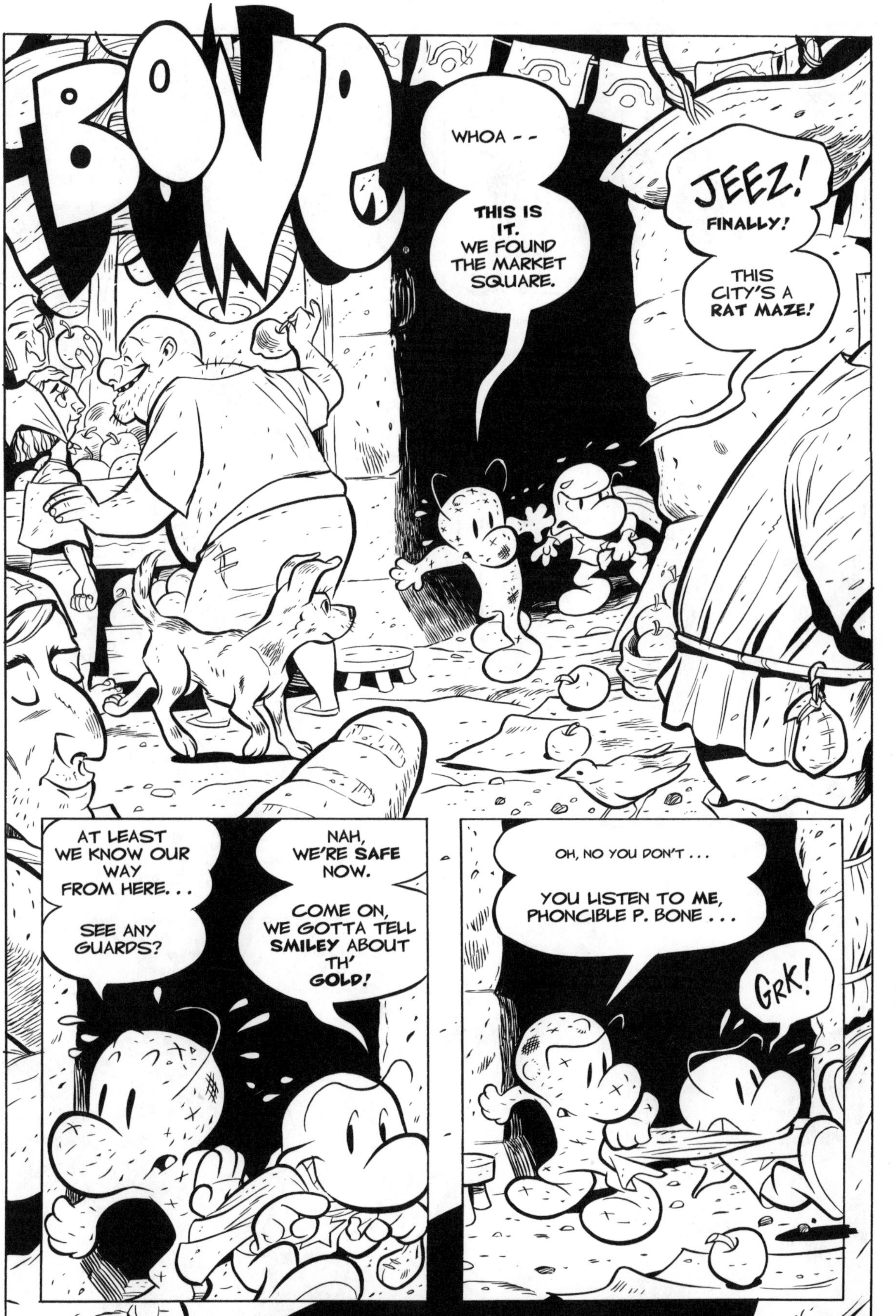
BONE®
WHOA --
THIS IS IT. WE FOUND THE MARKET SQUARE.
JEEZ! FINALLY!
THIS CITY'S A RAT MAZE!
AT LEAST WE KNOW OUR WAY FROM HERE...
SEE ANY GUARDS?
NAH, WE'RE SAFE NOW.
COME ON, WE GOTTA TELL SMILEY ABOUT TH' GOLD!
OH, NO YOU DON'T ...
YOU LISTEN TO ME, PHONCIBLE P. BONE ...
GRK!

BECAUSE OF US, TARSIL KNOWS GRAN'MA BEN AND THORN ARE IN THE CITY. WE HAVE TO **WARN** THEM!

WHAT ABOUT THE GIANT **BEE?** WE'RE GONNA NEED SMILEY'S HELP TO PROTECT THE PEDDLERS.

FORGET THE BEE! I TOLD YOU THAT PLAN IS GONNA **BACKFIRE!**

OKAY, FORGET THE BEE --

LET'S FIGURE OUT WHERE THE PEDDLERS GOT ALL THIS **GOLD** TO PAY US FROM!

WHO CARES?

IT'S **GOLD,** FONE BONE! **GOLD!** WHERE DID THEY GET SO **MUCH** OF IT?!

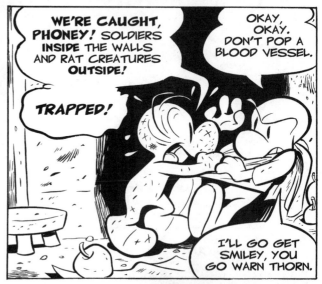

WE'RE CAUGHT, PHONEY! SOLDIERS INSIDE THE WALLS AND RAT CREATURES **OUTSIDE!**

TRAPPED!

OKAY, OKAY. DON'T POP A BLOOD VESSEL.

I'LL GO GET SMILEY, YOU GO WARN THORN.

RIGHT. WE'LL RENDEZVOUS AT GRAN'MA BEN'S ROOM BEFORE THE UNDERGROUND MEETING.

AND **BE CAREFUL!** THERE'S STILL A LOT OF GUARDS LURKING ABOUT.

YES, MOTHER.

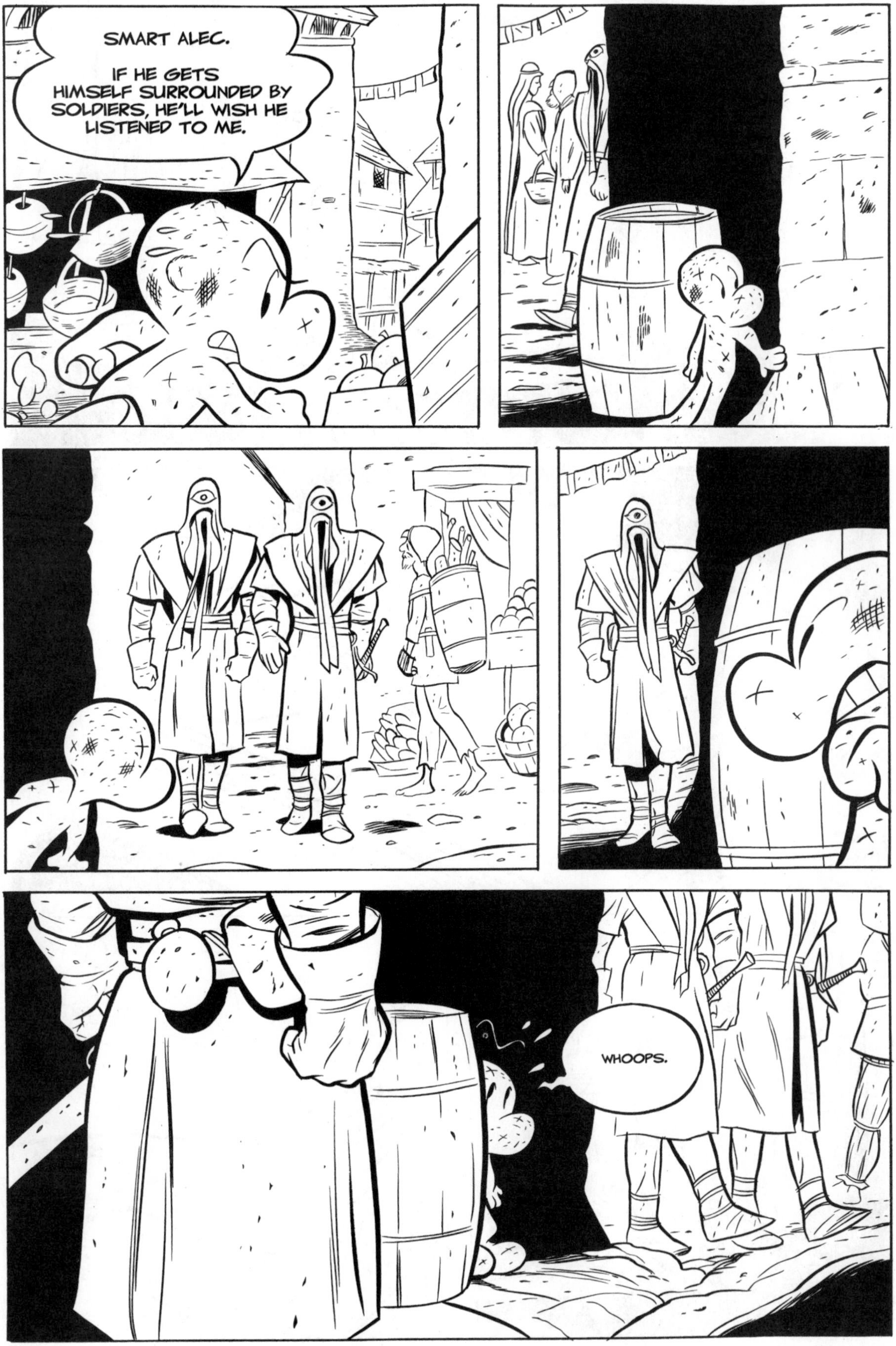
SMART ALEC.
IF HE GETS HIMSELF SURROUNDED BY SOLDIERS, HE'LL WISH HE LISTENED TO ME.
WHOOPS.

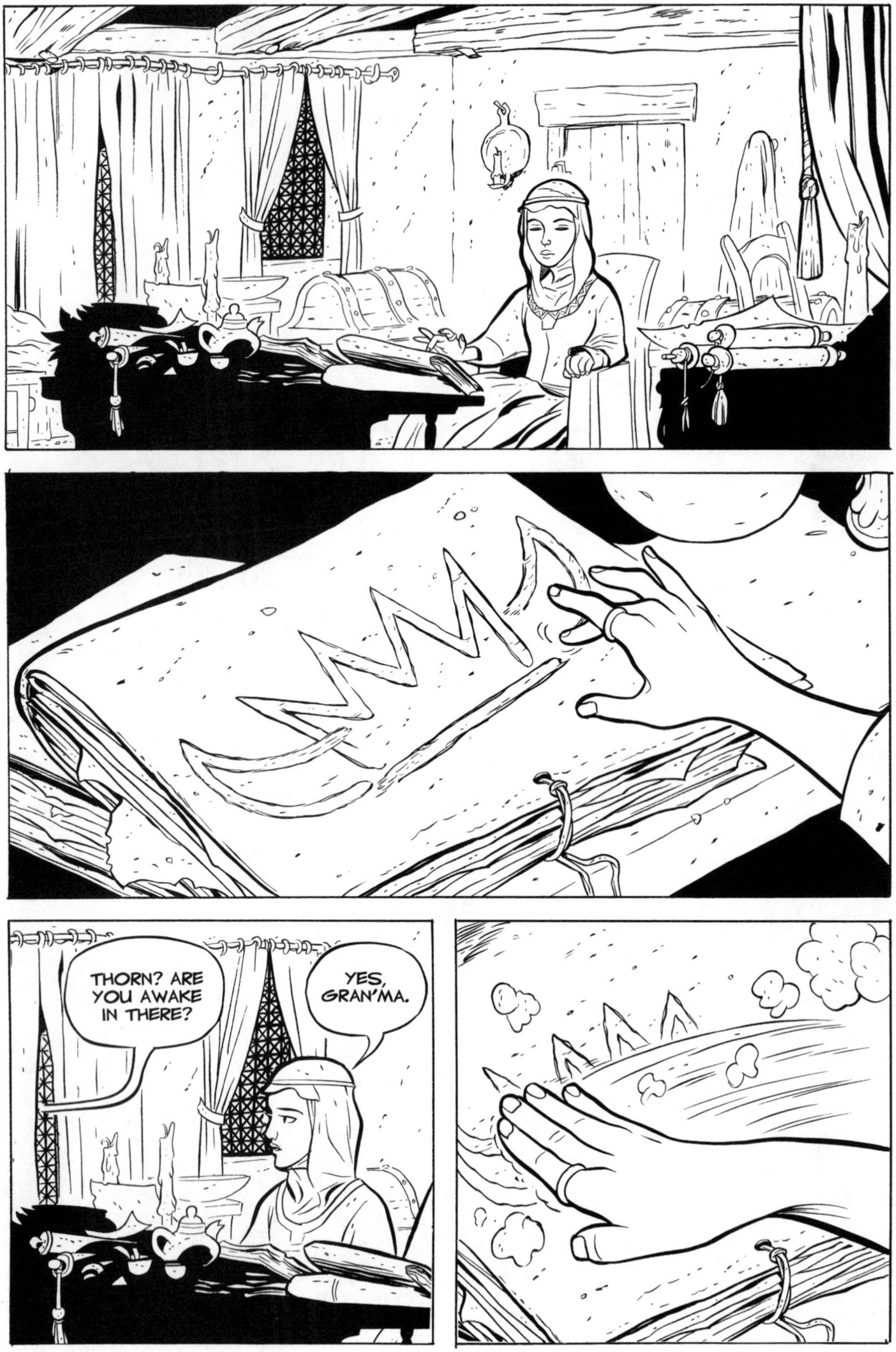
THORN? ARE YOU AWAKE IN THERE?
YES, GRAN'MA.

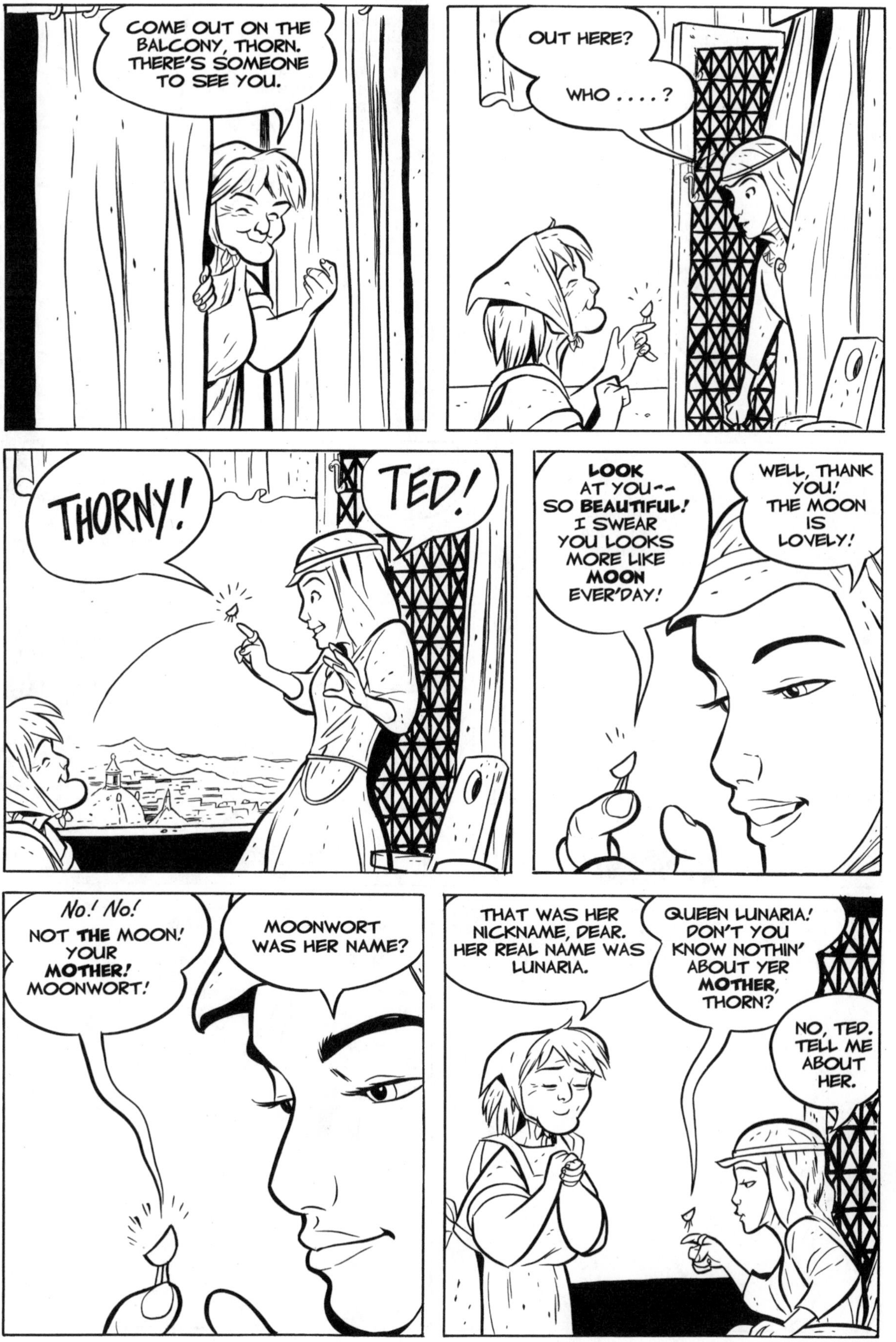
COME OUT ON THE BALCONY, THORN. THERE'S SOMEONE TO SEE YOU.
OUT HERE?
WHO . . . . ?
THORNY!
TED!
LOOK AT YOU-- SO BEAUTIFUL! I SWEAR YOU LOOKS MORE LIKE MOON EVER'DAY!
WELL, THANK YOU! THE MOON IS LOVELY!
No! No! NOT THE MOON! YOUR MOTHER! MOONWORT!
MOONWORT WAS HER NAME?
THAT WAS HER NICKNAME, DEAR. HER REAL NAME WAS LUNARIA.
QUEEN LUNARIA! DON'T YOU KNOW NOTHIN' ABOUT YER MOTHER, THORN?
NO, TED. TELL ME ABOUT HER.

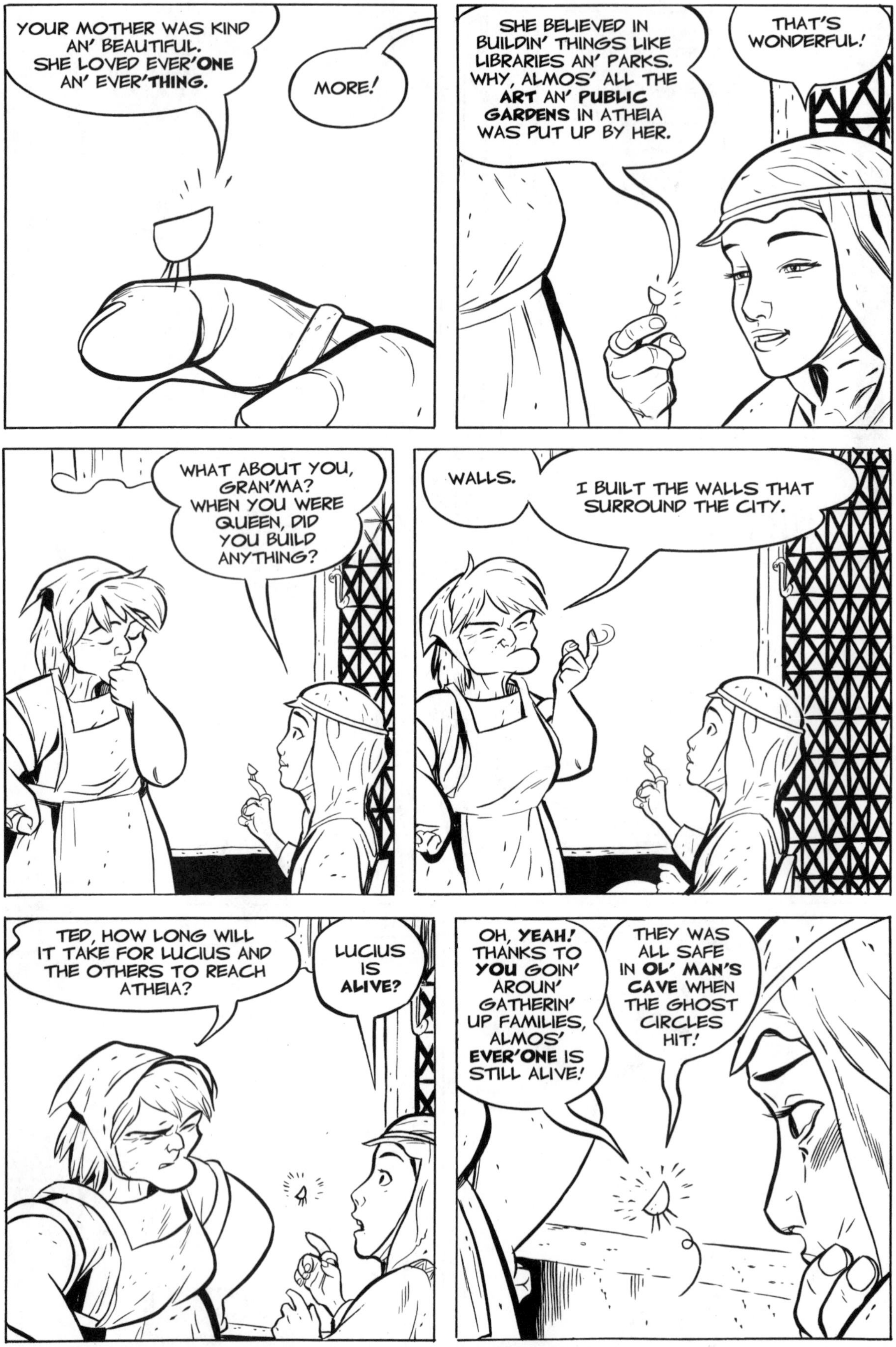

YOUR MOTHER WAS KIND AN' BEAUTIFUL. SHE LOVED EVER'ONE AN' EVER'THING.
MORE!
SHE BELIEVED IN BUILDIN' THINGS LIKE LIBRARIES AN' PARKS. WHY, ALMOS' ALL THE ART AN' PUBLIC GARDENS IN ATHEIA WAS PUT UP BY HER.
THAT'S WONDERFUL!
WHAT ABOUT YOU, GRAN'MA? WHEN YOU WERE QUEEN, DID YOU BUILD ANYTHING?
WALLS.
I BUILT THE WALLS THAT SURROUND THE CITY.
TED, HOW LONG WILL IT TAKE FOR LUCIUS AND THE OTHERS TO REACH ATHEIA?
LUCIUS IS ALIVE?
OH, YEAH! THANKS TO YOU GOIN' AROUN' GATHERIN' UP FAMILIES, ALMOS' EVER'ONE IS STILL ALIVE!
THEY WAS ALL SAFE IN OL' MAN'S CAVE WHEN THE GHOST CIRCLES HIT!

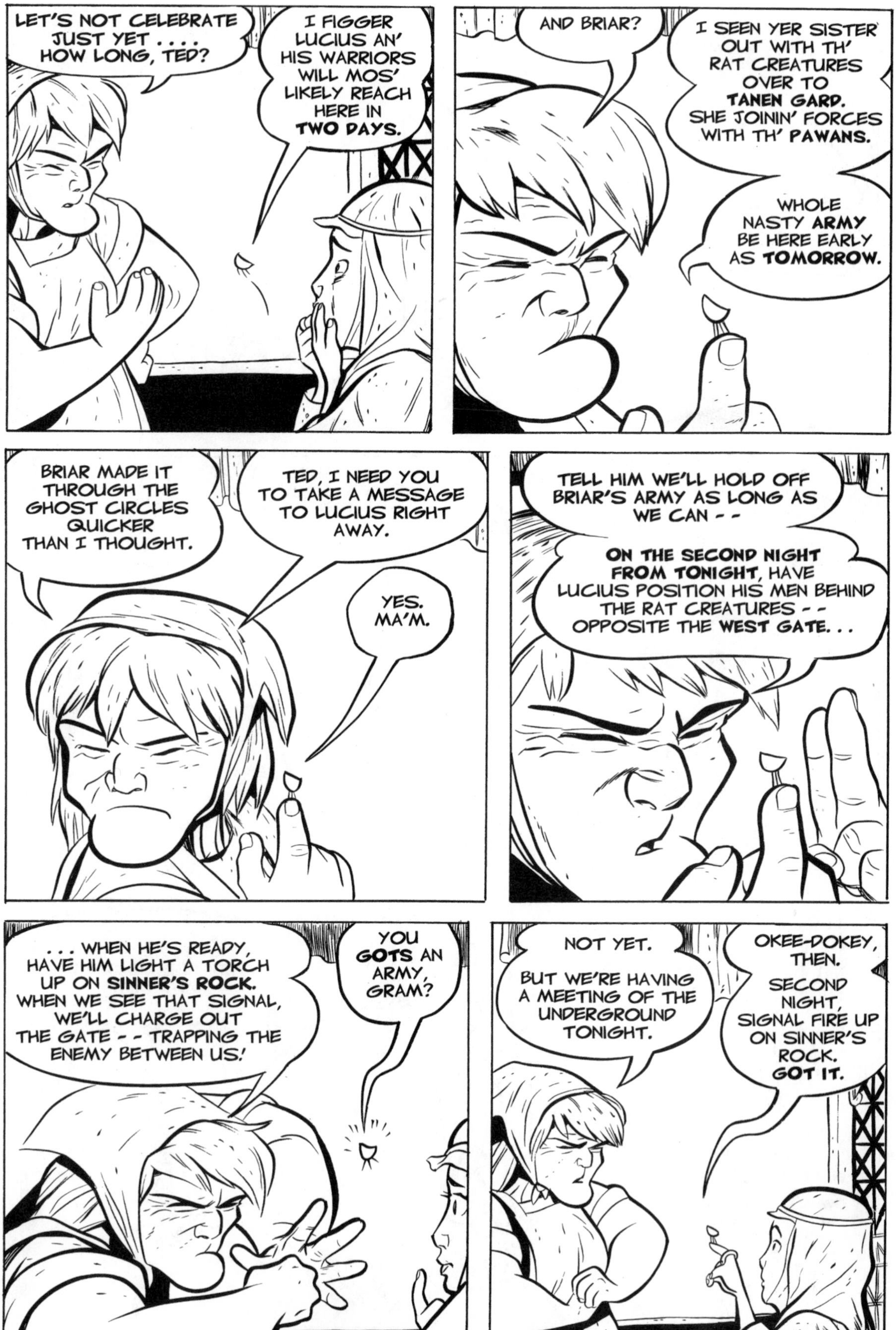
LET'S NOT CELEBRATE JUST YET . . . . HOW LONG, TED?
I FIGGER LUCIUS AN' HIS WARRIORS WILL MOS' LIKELY REACH HERE IN **TWO DAYS.**
AND BRIAR?
I SEEN YER SISTER OUT WITH TH' RAT CREATURES OVER TO **TANEN GARD.** SHE JOININ' FORCES WITH TH' **PAWANS.**
WHOLE NASTY **ARMY** BE HERE EARLY AS **TOMORROW.**
BRIAR MADE IT THROUGH THE GHOST CIRCLES QUICKER THAN I THOUGHT.
TED, I NEED YOU TO TAKE A MESSAGE TO LUCIUS RIGHT AWAY.
YES. MA'M.
TELL HIM WE'LL HOLD OFF BRIAR'S ARMY AS LONG AS WE CAN - -
ON THE SECOND NIGHT FROM TONIGHT, HAVE LUCIUS POSITION HIS MEN BEHIND THE RAT CREATURES - - OPPOSITE THE **WEST GATE**. . .
. . . WHEN HE'S READY, HAVE HIM LIGHT A TORCH UP ON **SINNER'S ROCK.** WHEN WE SEE THAT SIGNAL, WE'LL CHARGE OUT THE GATE - - TRAPPING THE ENEMY BETWEEN US!
YOU **GOTS** AN ARMY, GRAM?
NOT YET.
BUT WE'RE HAVING A MEETING OF THE UNDERGROUND TONIGHT.
OKEE-DOKEY, THEN.
SECOND NIGHT, SIGNAL FIRE UP ON SINNER'S ROCK. **GOT IT.**

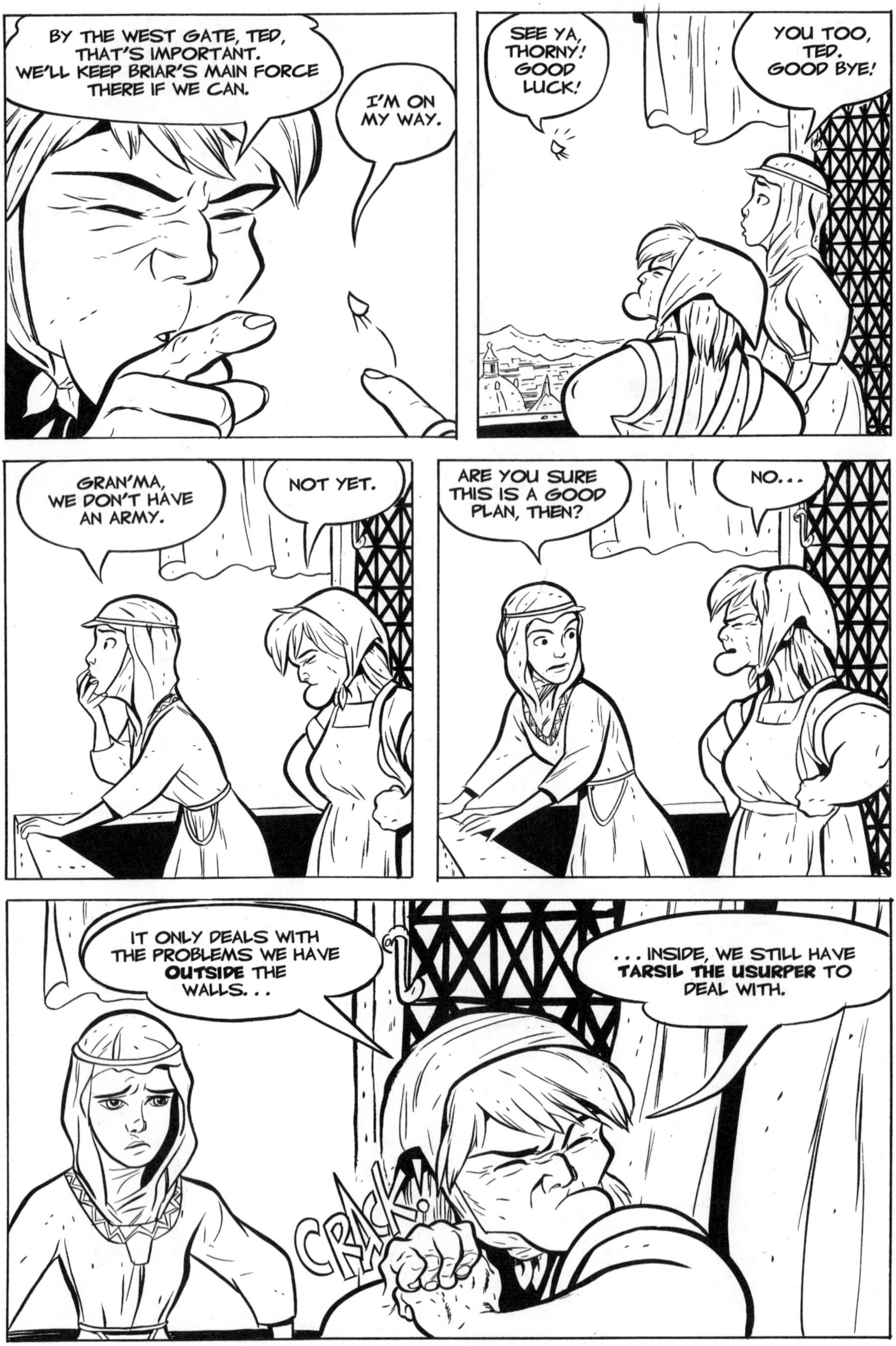
BY THE WEST GATE, TED, THAT'S IMPORTANT. WE'LL KEEP BRIAR'S MAIN FORCE THERE IF WE CAN.
I'M ON MY WAY.
SEE YA, THORNY! GOOD LUCK!
YOU TOO, TED. GOOD BYE!
GRAN'MA, WE DON'T HAVE AN ARMY.
NOT YET.
ARE YOU SURE THIS IS A GOOD PLAN, THEN?
NO...
IT ONLY DEALS WITH THE PROBLEMS WE HAVE **OUTSIDE** THE WALLS...
...INSIDE, WE STILL HAVE **TARSIL THE USURPER** TO DEAL WITH.
CRACK!

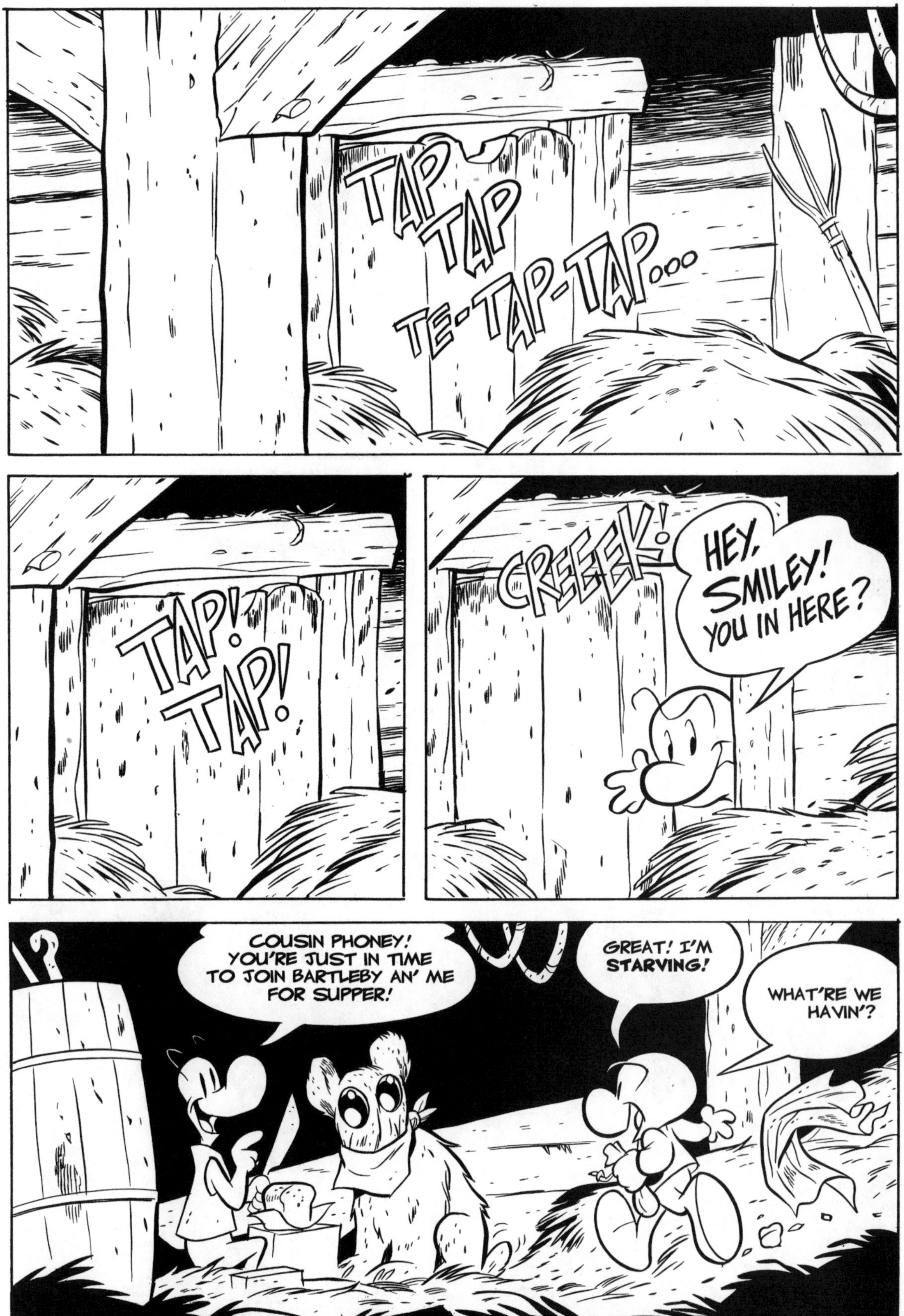
TAP TAP TE-TAP-TAP...
TAP! TAP!
CREEEK!
HEY, SMILEY! YOU IN HERE?
COUSIN PHONEY! YOU'RE JUST IN TIME TO JOIN BARTLEBY AN' ME FOR SUPPER!
GREAT! I'M STARVING!
WHAT'RE WE HAVIN'?

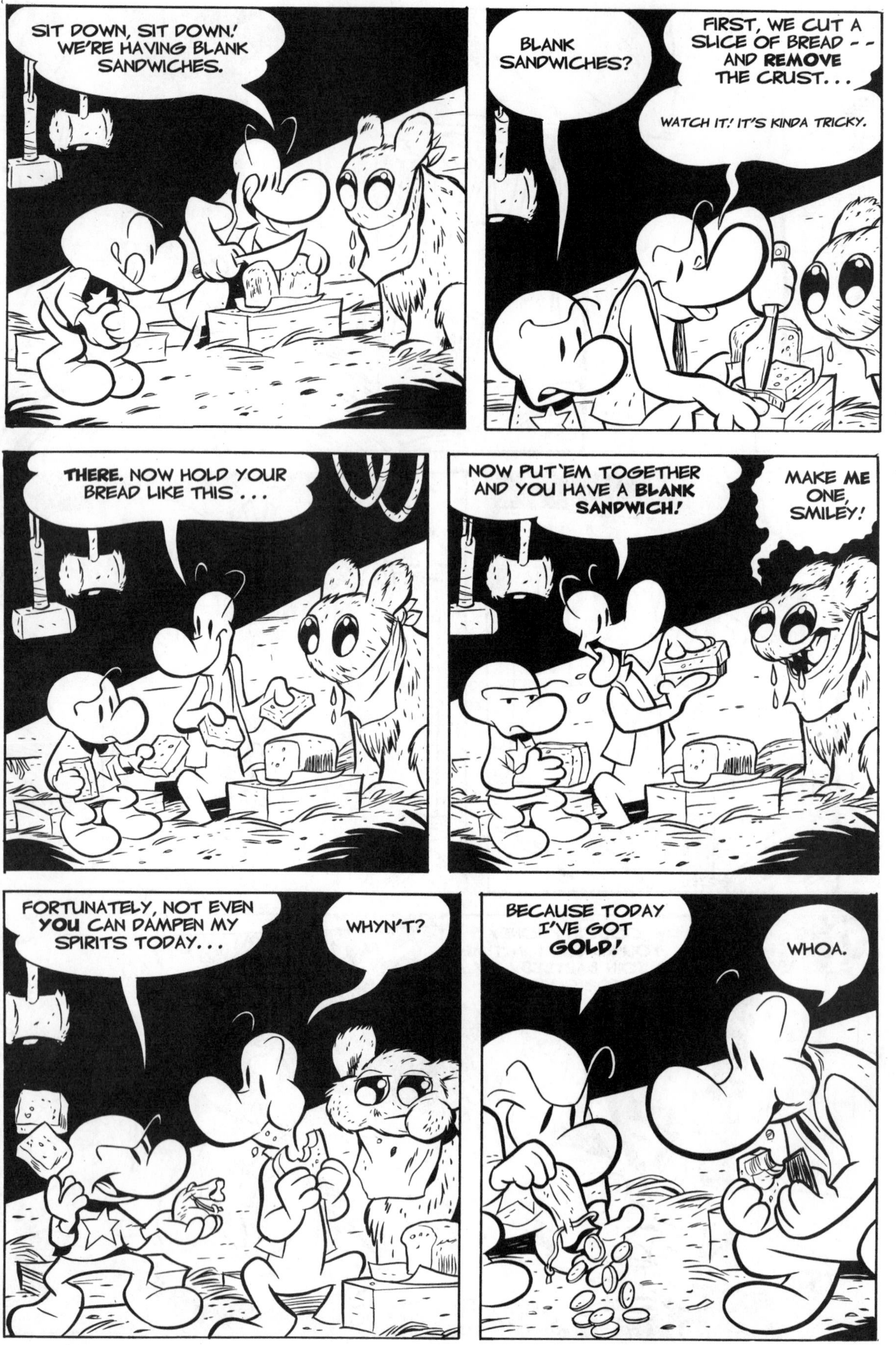
SIT DOWN, SIT DOWN! WE'RE HAVING BLANK SANDWICHES.
BLANK SANDWICHES?
FIRST, WE CUT A SLICE OF BREAD - - AND **REMOVE** THE CRUST. . .
WATCH IT! IT'S KINDA TRICKY.
THERE. NOW HOLD YOUR BREAD LIKE THIS . . .
NOW PUT 'EM TOGETHER AND YOU HAVE A **BLANK SANDWICH!**
MAKE **ME** ONE, SMILEY!
FORTUNATELY, NOT EVEN **YOU** CAN DAMPEN MY SPIRITS TODAY. . .
WHYN'T?
BECAUSE TODAY I'VE GOT **GOLD!**
WHOA.

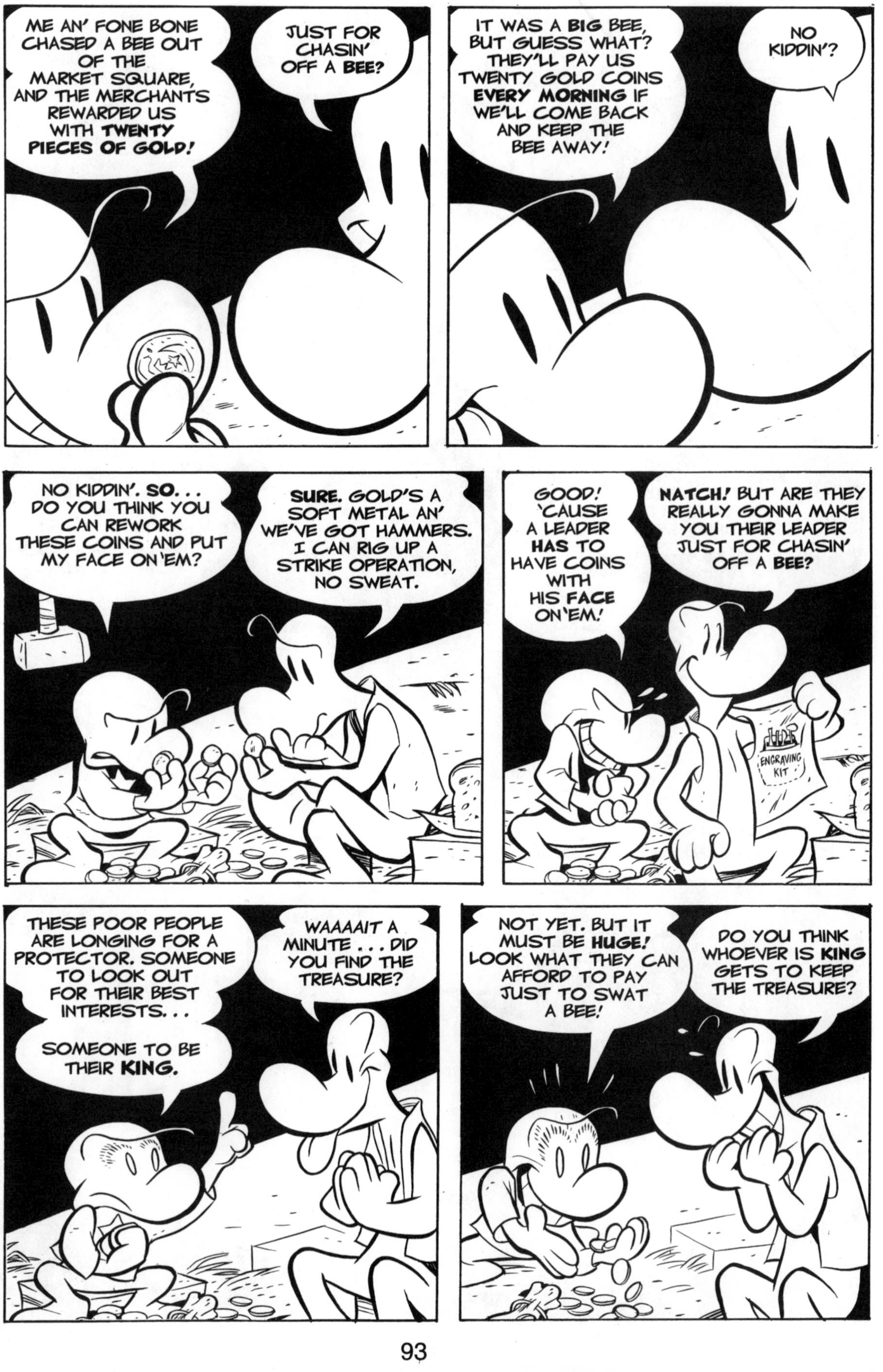
ME AN' FONE BONE CHASED A BEE OUT OF THE MARKET SQUARE, AND THE MERCHANTS REWARDED US WITH **TWENTY PIECES OF GOLD!**
JUST FOR CHASIN' OFF A **BEE?**
IT WAS A **BIG** BEE, BUT GUESS WHAT? THEY'LL PAY US TWENTY GOLD COINS **EVERY MORNING** IF WE'LL COME BACK AND KEEP THE BEE AWAY!
NO KIDDIN'?
NO KIDDIN'. **SO...** DO YOU THINK YOU CAN REWORK THESE COINS AND PUT MY FACE ON 'EM?
SURE. GOLD'S A SOFT METAL AN' WE'VE GOT HAMMERS. I CAN RIG UP A STRIKE OPERATION, NO SWEAT.
GOOD! 'CAUSE A LEADER **HAS** TO HAVE COINS WITH HIS **FACE** ON 'EM!
NATCH! BUT ARE THEY REALLY GONNA MAKE YOU THEIR LEADER JUST FOR CHASIN' OFF A **BEE?**
ENGRAVING KIT
THESE POOR PEOPLE ARE LONGING FOR A PROTECTOR. SOMEONE TO LOOK OUT FOR THEIR BEST INTERESTS...
SOMEONE TO BE THEIR **KING.**
WAAAAIT A MINUTE... DID YOU FIND THE TREASURE?
NOT YET. BUT IT MUST BE **HUGE!** LOOK WHAT THEY CAN AFFORD TO PAY JUST TO SWAT A BEE!
DO YOU THINK WHOEVER IS **KING** GETS TO KEEP THE TREASURE?

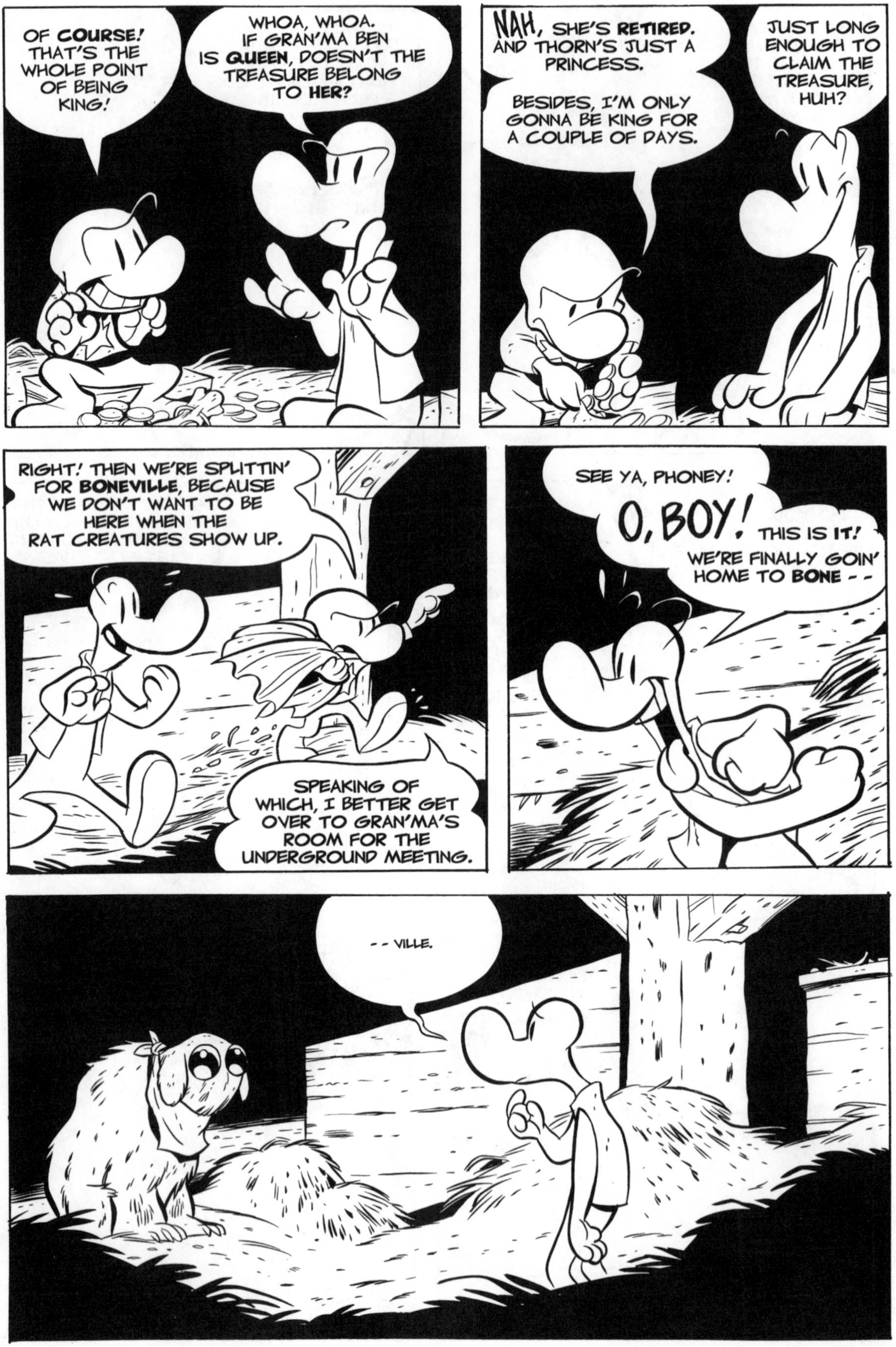
OF COURSE! THAT'S THE WHOLE POINT OF BEING KING!
WHOA, WHOA. IF GRAN'MA BEN IS QUEEN, DOESN'T THE TREASURE BELONG TO HER?
NAH, SHE'S RETIRED. AND THORN'S JUST A PRINCESS.
BESIDES, I'M ONLY GONNA BE KING FOR A COUPLE OF DAYS.
JUST LONG ENOUGH TO CLAIM THE TREASURE, HUH?
RIGHT! THEN WE'RE SPLITTIN' FOR BONEVILLE, BECAUSE WE DON'T WANT TO BE HERE WHEN THE RAT CREATURES SHOW UP.
SPEAKING OF WHICH, I BETTER GET OVER TO GRAN'MA'S ROOM FOR THE UNDERGROUND MEETING.
SEE YA, PHONEY!
O, BOY! THIS IS IT! WE'RE FINALLY GOIN' HOME TO BONE - -
- - VILLE.

THE PAWANS AND THE RAT CREATURES ARE WORKING **TOGETHER**...

...THIS IS NOT A TRADE EMBARGO, GUILD MASTER. THIS IS AN ACT OF **WAR**.

LORD TARSIL, IF I MAY SPEAK ON BEHALF OF THE MERCHANT HOUSES...

...THERE ARE MANY IN THE GUILD WHO BELIEVE THE PAWAN ARMY WOULD END ITS BLOCKADE OF OUR TRADE ROUTES IF YOU **RELAXED** YOUR BAN ON DRAGON LORE --

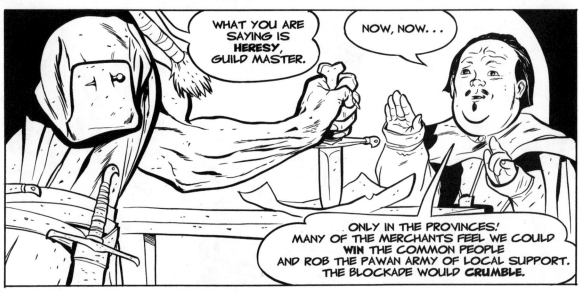

WHAT YOU ARE SAYING IS **HERESY**, GUILD MASTER.

NOW, NOW...

ONLY IN THE PROVINCES! MANY OF THE MERCHANTS FEEL WE COULD **WIN** THE COMMON PEOPLE AND ROB THE PAWAN ARMY OF LOCAL SUPPORT. THE BLOCKADE WOULD **CRUMBLE**.

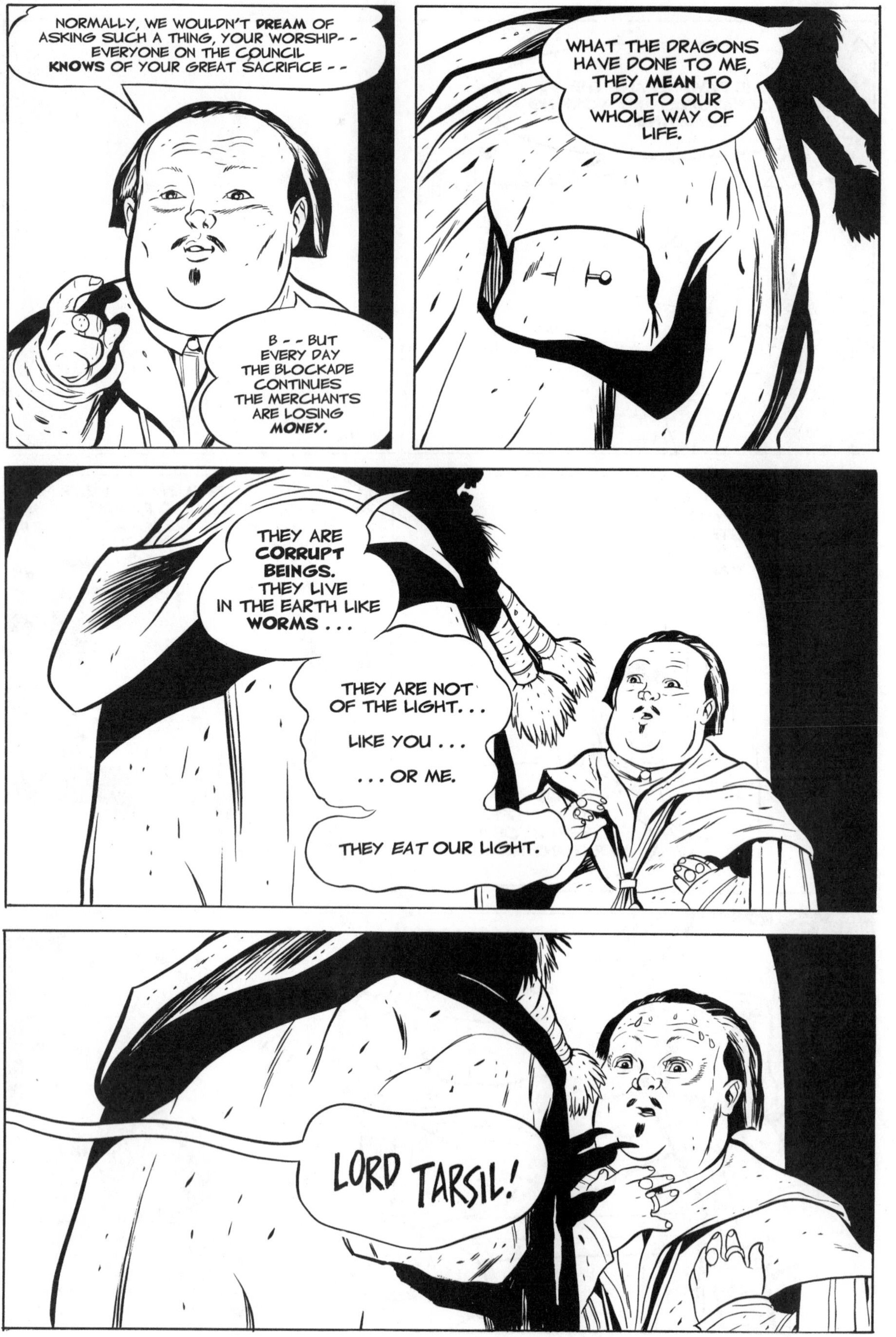
NORMALLY, WE WOULDN'T DREAM OF ASKING SUCH A THING, YOUR WORSHIP- - EVERYONE ON THE COUNCIL KNOWS OF YOUR GREAT SACRIFICE - -
B - - BUT EVERY DAY THE BLOCKADE CONTINUES THE MERCHANTS ARE LOSING MONEY.
WHAT THE DRAGONS HAVE DONE TO ME, THEY MEAN TO DO TO OUR WHOLE WAY OF LIFE.
THEY ARE CORRUPT BEINGS. THEY LIVE IN THE EARTH LIKE WORMS . . .
THEY ARE NOT OF THE LIGHT. . .
LIKE YOU . . .
. . . OR ME.
THEY EAT OUR LIGHT.
LORD TARSIL!

YES?

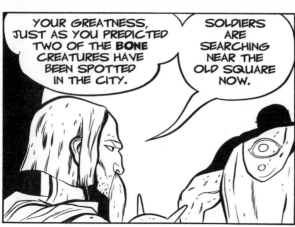

YOUR GREATNESS, JUST AS YOU PREDICTED TWO OF THE **BONE** CREATURES HAVE BEEN SPOTTED IN THE CITY.

SOLDIERS ARE SEARCHING NEAR THE OLD SQUARE NOW.

THE QUEEN.

WHAT OF THE QUEEN AND HER GRANDDAUGHTER . . ? THE HEIR TO THE THRONE?

AN OLD WOMAN AND HER GRANDDAUGHTER ENTERED THE WEST GATE LAST NIGHT, BUT THEIR WHEREABOUTS ARE UNKNOWN.

PUT MORE SOLDIERS ON THE STREET. . .

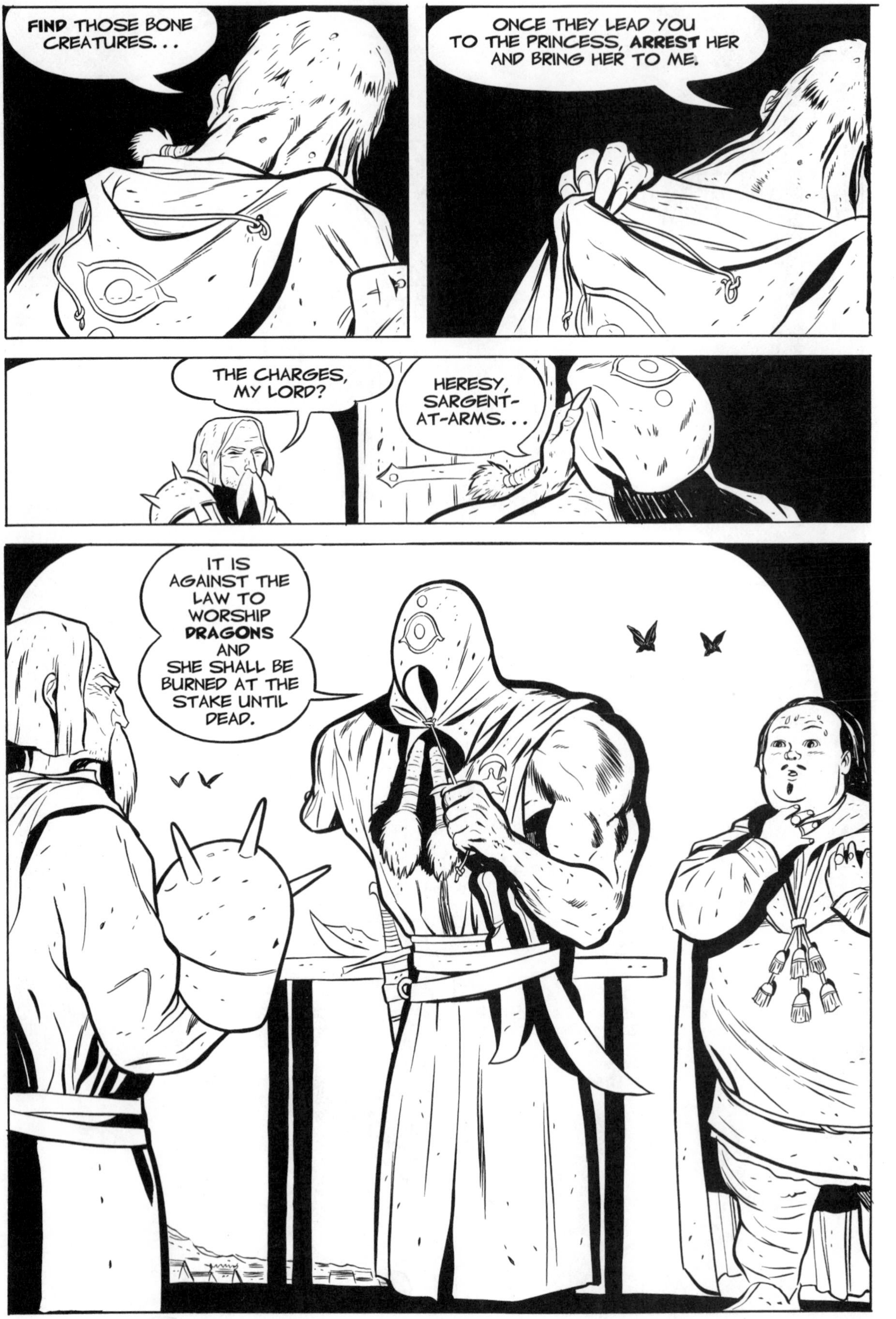
FIND THOSE BONE CREATURES. . .
ONCE THEY LEAD YOU TO THE PRINCESS, ARREST HER AND BRING HER TO ME.
THE CHARGES, MY LORD?
HERESY, SARGENT-AT-ARMS. . .
IT IS AGAINST THE LAW TO WORSHIP DRAGONS AND SHE SHALL BE BURNED AT THE STAKE UNTIL DEAD.

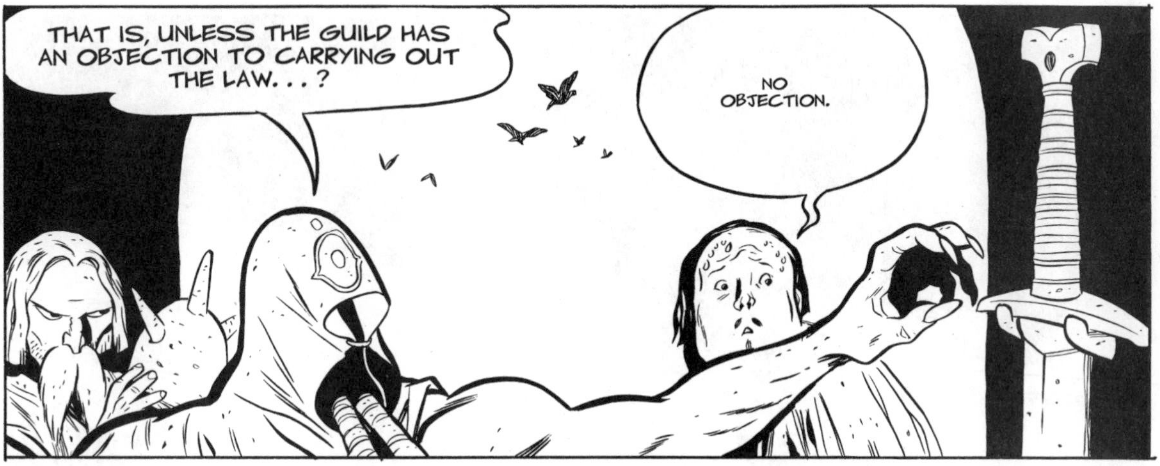
THAT IS, UNLESS THE GUILD HAS AN OBJECTION TO CARRYING OUT THE LAW. . . ?
NO OBJECTION.

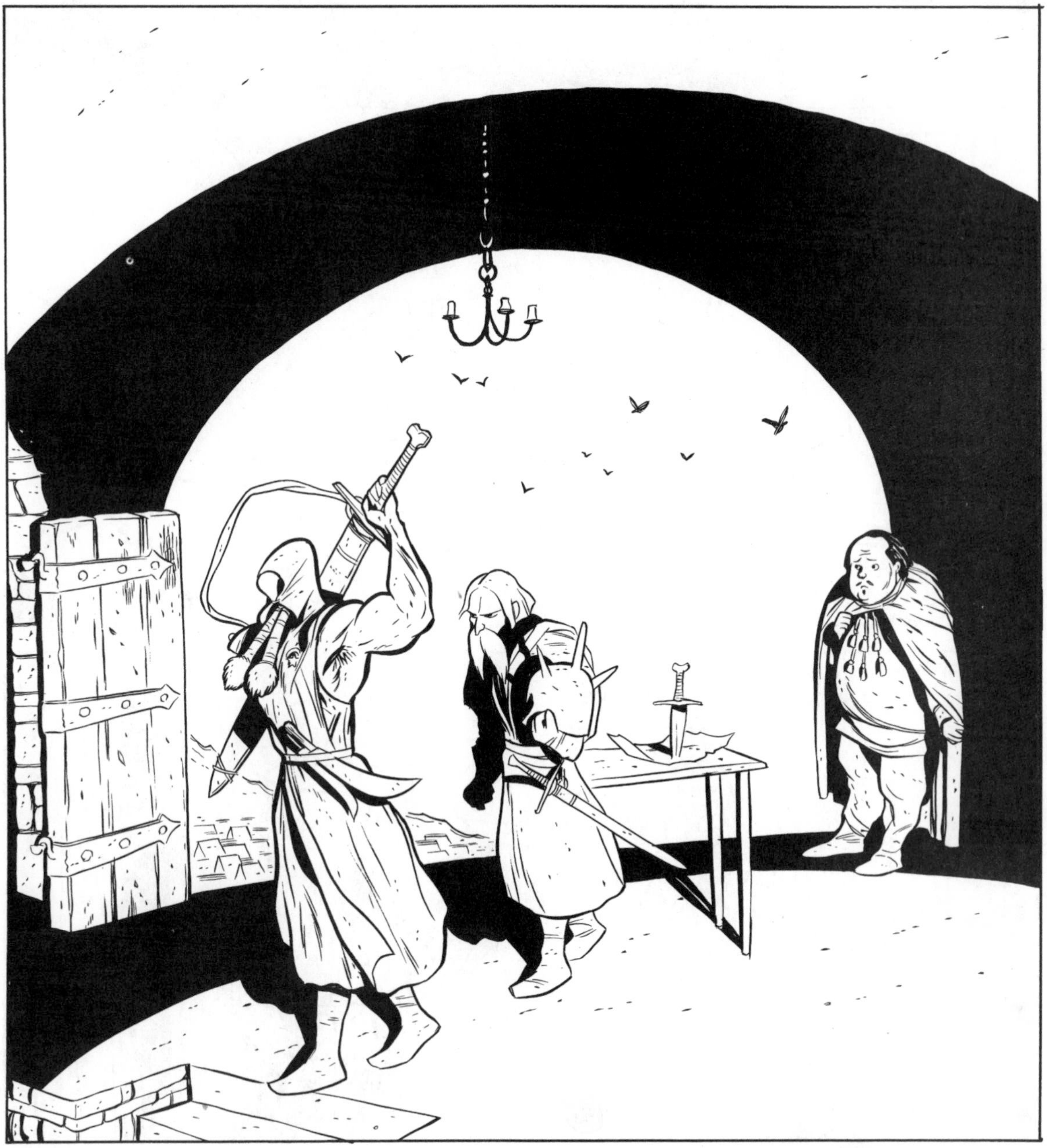

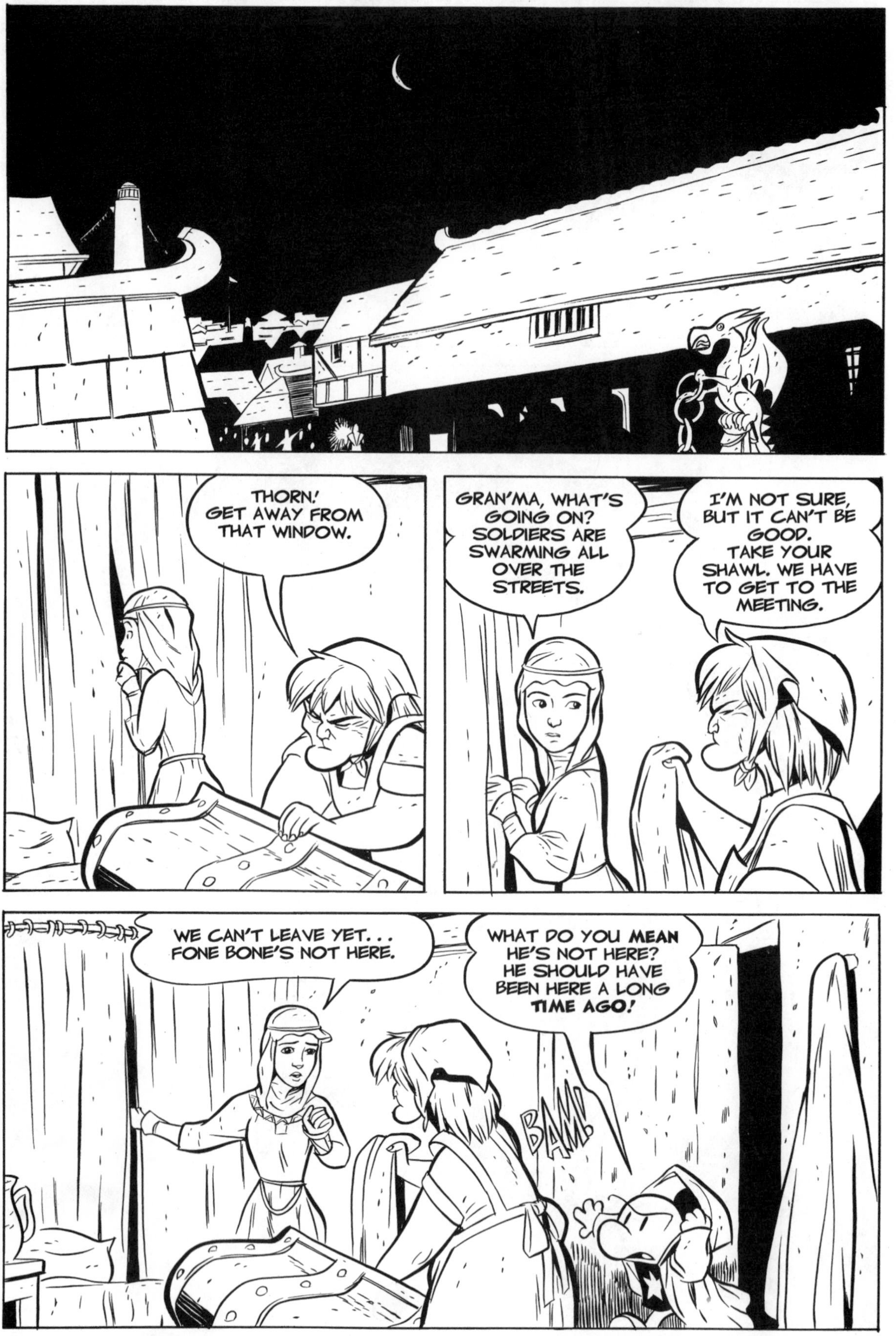
THORN! GET AWAY FROM THAT WINDOW.
GRAN'MA, WHAT'S GOING ON? SOLDIERS ARE SWARMING ALL OVER THE STREETS.
I'M NOT SURE, BUT IT CAN'T BE GOOD. TAKE YOUR SHAWL. WE HAVE TO GET TO THE MEETING.
WE CAN'T LEAVE YET... FONE BONE'S NOT HERE.
WHAT DO YOU **MEAN** HE'S NOT HERE? HE SHOULD HAVE BEEN HERE A LONG **TIME AGO!**
BAM!

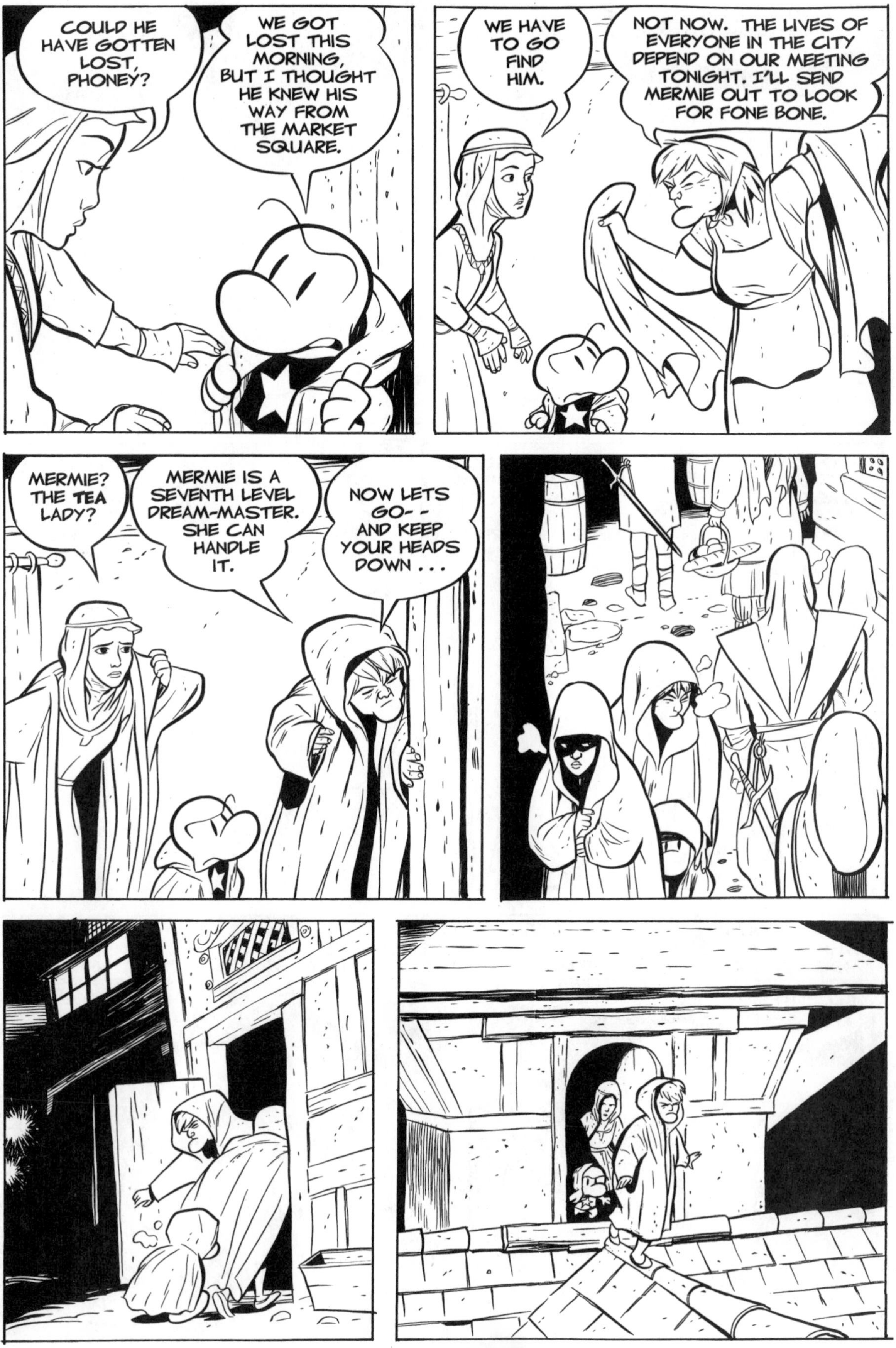
COULD HE HAVE GOTTEN LOST, PHONEY?
WE GOT LOST THIS MORNING, BUT I THOUGHT HE KNEW HIS WAY FROM THE MARKET SQUARE.
WE HAVE TO GO FIND HIM.
NOT NOW. THE LIVES OF EVERYONE IN THE CITY DEPEND ON OUR MEETING TONIGHT. I'LL SEND MERMIE OUT TO LOOK FOR FONE BONE.
MERMIE? THE TEA LADY?
MERMIE IS A SEVENTH LEVEL DREAM-MASTER. SHE CAN HANDLE IT.
NOW LETS GO- - AND KEEP YOUR HEADS DOWN . . .

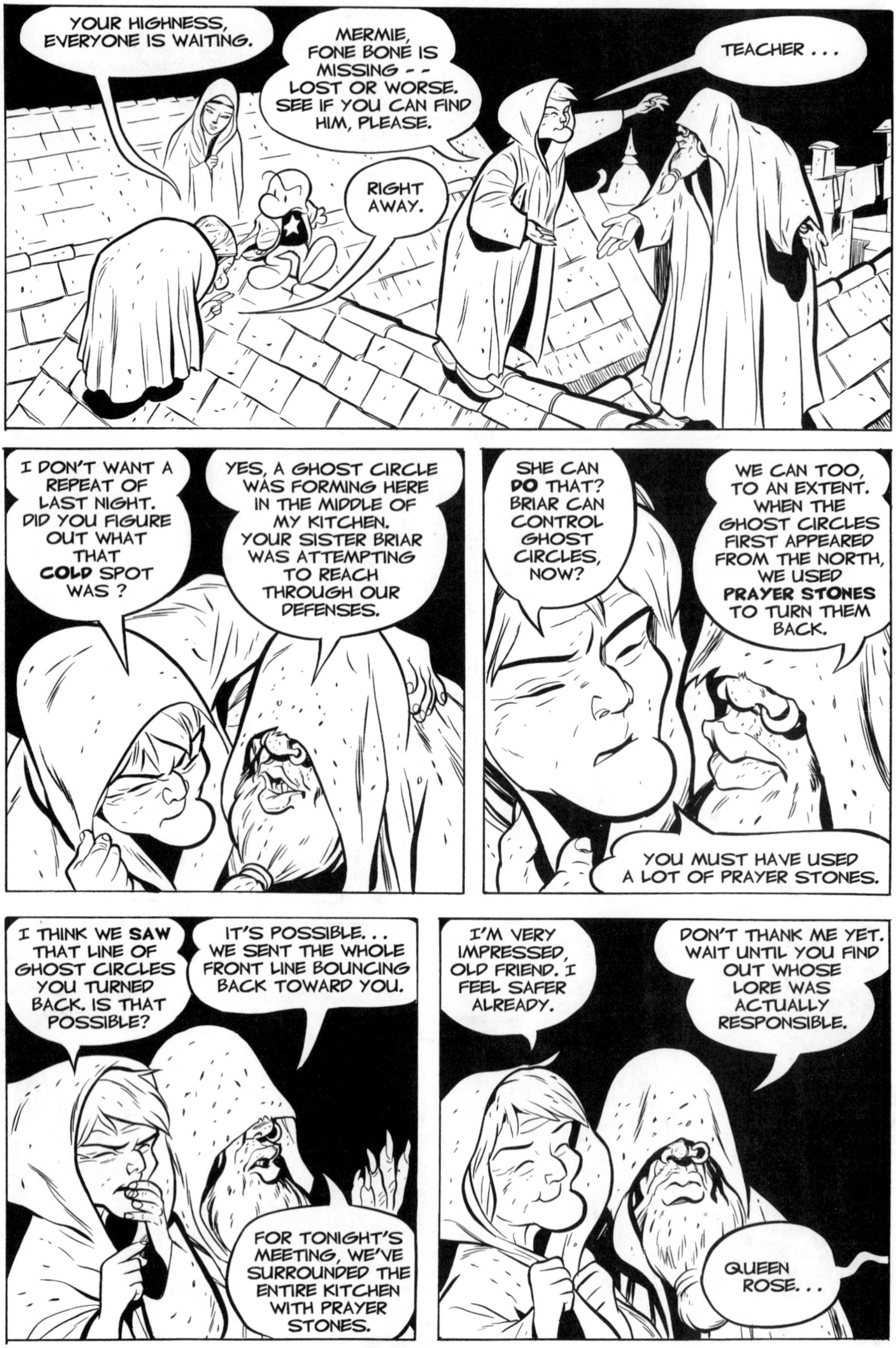
YOUR HIGHNESS, EVERYONE IS WAITING.
MERMIE, FONE BONE IS MISSING - - LOST OR WORSE. SEE IF YOU CAN FIND HIM, PLEASE.
RIGHT AWAY.
TEACHER . . .
I DON'T WANT A REPEAT OF LAST NIGHT. DID YOU FIGURE OUT WHAT THAT COLD SPOT WAS ?
YES, A GHOST CIRCLE WAS FORMING HERE IN THE MIDDLE OF MY KITCHEN. YOUR SISTER BRIAR WAS ATTEMPTING TO REACH THROUGH OUR DEFENSES.
SHE CAN DO THAT? BRIAR CAN CONTROL GHOST CIRCLES, NOW?
WE CAN TOO, TO AN EXTENT. WHEN THE GHOST CIRCLES FIRST APPEARED FROM THE NORTH, WE USED PRAYER STONES TO TURN THEM BACK.
YOU MUST HAVE USED A LOT OF PRAYER STONES.
I THINK WE SAW THAT LINE OF GHOST CIRCLES YOU TURNED BACK. IS THAT POSSIBLE?
IT'S POSSIBLE. . . WE SENT THE WHOLE FRONT LINE BOUNCING BACK TOWARD YOU.
FOR TONIGHT'S MEETING, WE'VE SURROUNDED THE ENTIRE KITCHEN WITH PRAYER STONES.
I'M VERY IMPRESSED, OLD FRIEND. I FEEL SAFER ALREADY.
DON'T THANK ME YET. WAIT UNTIL YOU FIND OUT WHOSE LORE WAS ACTUALLY RESPONSIBLE.
QUEEN ROSE. . .

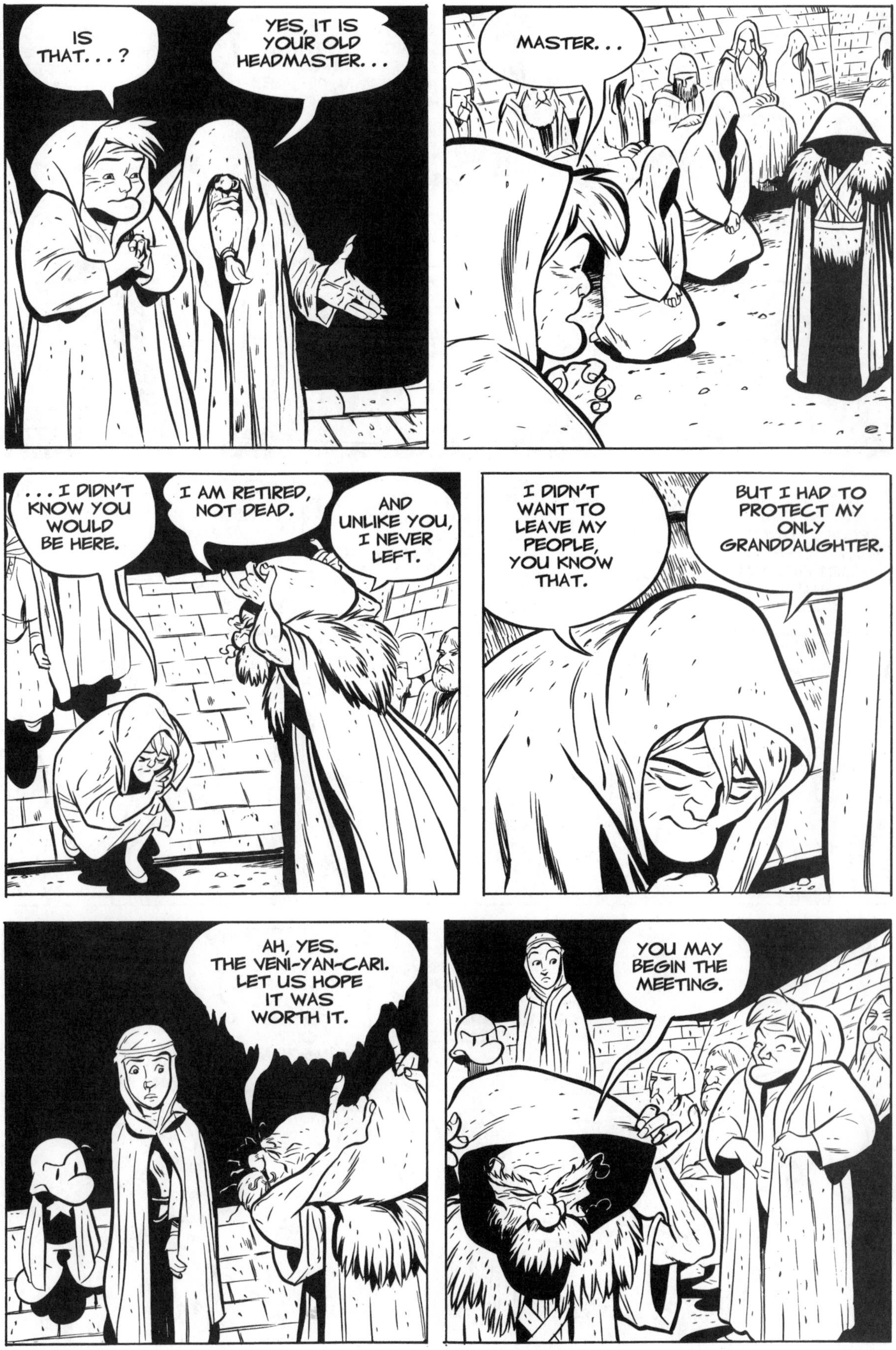
IS THAT...?
YES, IT IS YOUR OLD HEADMASTER...
MASTER...
...I DIDN'T KNOW YOU WOULD BE HERE.
I AM RETIRED, NOT DEAD.
AND UNLIKE YOU, I NEVER LEFT.
I DIDN'T WANT TO LEAVE MY PEOPLE, YOU KNOW THAT.
BUT I HAD TO PROTECT MY ONLY GRANDDAUGHTER.
AH, YES. THE VENI-YAN-CARI. LET US HOPE IT WAS WORTH IT.
YOU MAY BEGIN THE MEETING.

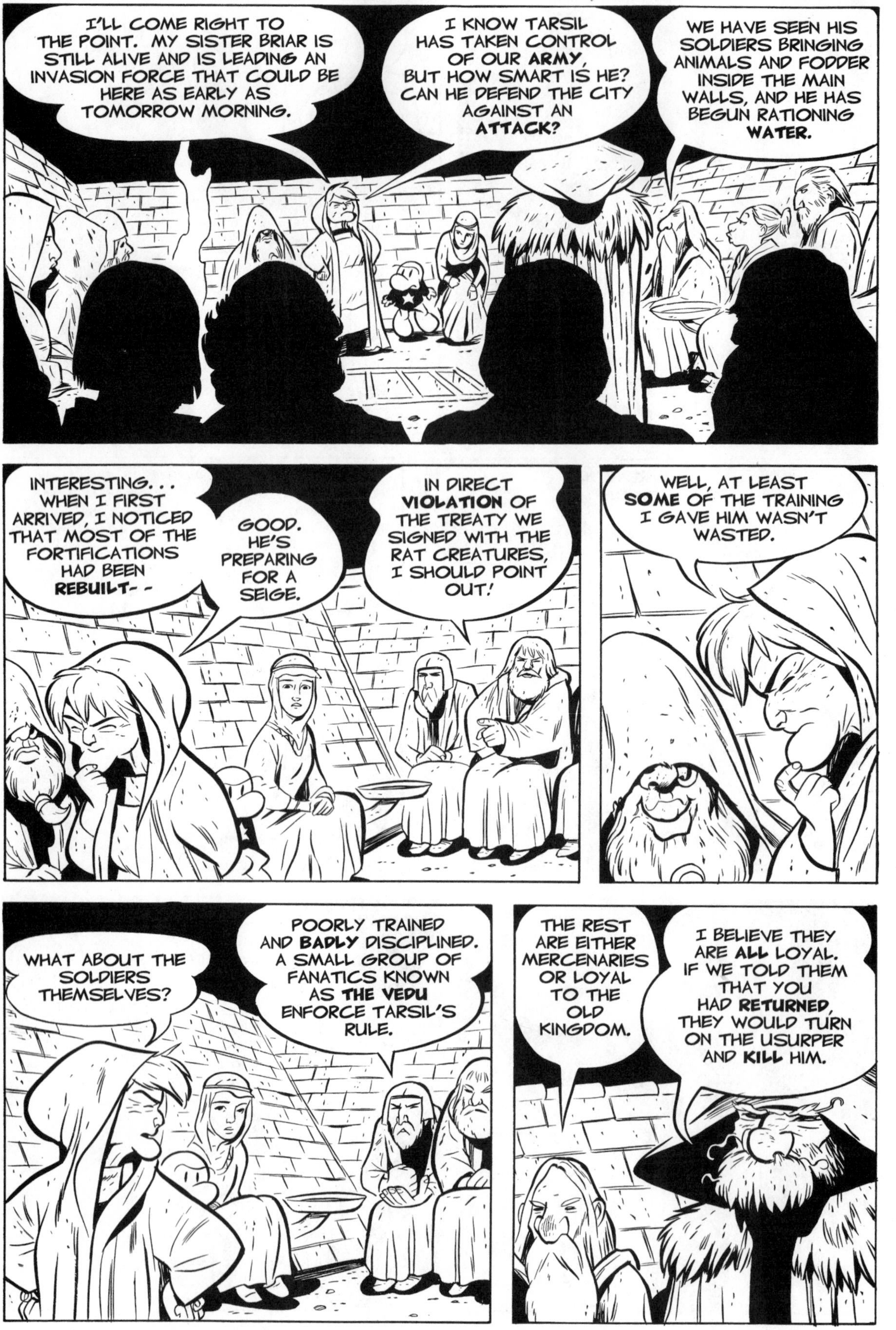
I'LL COME RIGHT TO THE POINT. MY SISTER BRIAR IS STILL ALIVE AND IS LEADING AN INVASION FORCE THAT COULD BE HERE AS EARLY AS TOMORROW MORNING.
I KNOW TARSIL HAS TAKEN CONTROL OF OUR **ARMY**, BUT HOW SMART IS HE? CAN HE DEFEND THE CITY AGAINST AN **ATTACK?**
WE HAVE SEEN HIS SOLDIERS BRINGING ANIMALS AND FODDER INSIDE THE MAIN WALLS, AND HE HAS BEGUN RATIONING **WATER.**
INTERESTING. . . WHEN I FIRST ARRIVED, I NOTICED THAT MOST OF THE FORTIFICATIONS HAD BEEN **REBUILT- -**
GOOD. HE'S PREPARING FOR A SEIGE.
IN DIRECT **VIOLATION** OF THE TREATY WE SIGNED WITH THE RAT CREATURES, I SHOULD POINT OUT!
WELL, AT LEAST **SOME** OF THE TRAINING I GAVE HIM WASN'T WASTED.
WHAT ABOUT THE SOLDIERS THEMSELVES?
POORLY TRAINED AND **BADLY** DISCIPLINED. A SMALL GROUP OF FANATICS KNOWN AS **THE VEDU** ENFORCE TARSIL'S RULE.
THE REST ARE EITHER MERCENARIES OR LOYAL TO THE OLD KINGDOM.
I BELIEVE THEY ARE **ALL** LOYAL. IF WE TOLD THEM THAT YOU HAD **RETURNED**, THEY WOULD TURN ON THE USURPER AND **KILL** HIM.

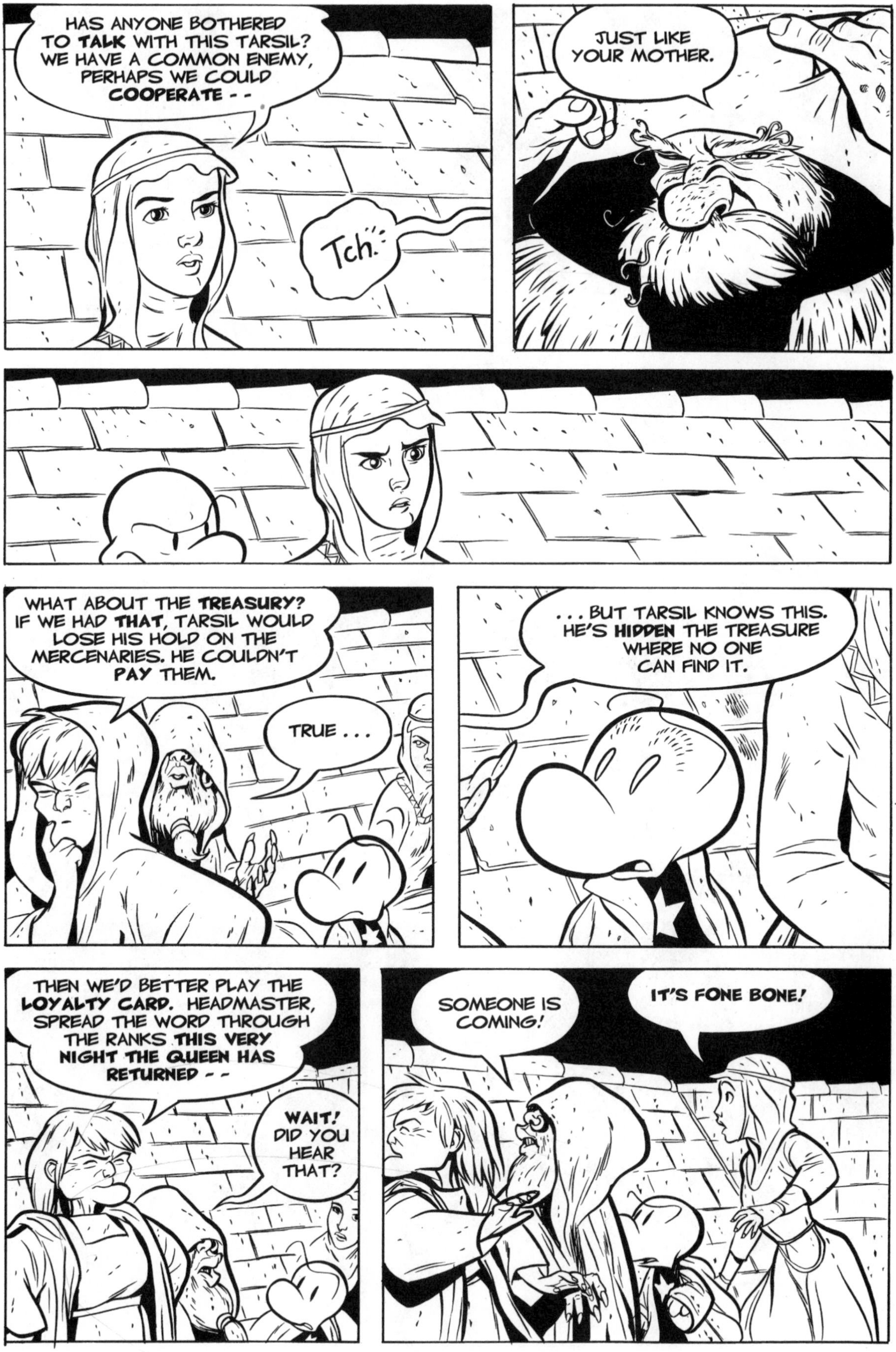
HAS ANYONE BOTHERED TO TALK WITH THIS TARSIL? WE HAVE A COMMON ENEMY, PERHAPS WE COULD COOPERATE - -
Tch.
JUST LIKE YOUR MOTHER.
WHAT ABOUT THE TREASURY? IF WE HAD THAT, TARSIL WOULD LOSE HIS HOLD ON THE MERCENARIES. HE COULDN'T PAY THEM.
TRUE . . .
. . . BUT TARSIL KNOWS THIS. HE'S HIDDEN THE TREASURE WHERE NO ONE CAN FIND IT.
THEN WE'D BETTER PLAY THE LOYALTY CARD. HEADMASTER, SPREAD THE WORD THROUGH THE RANKS THIS VERY NIGHT THE QUEEN HAS RETURNED - -
WAIT! DID YOU HEAR THAT?
SOMEONE IS COMING!
IT'S FONE BONE!

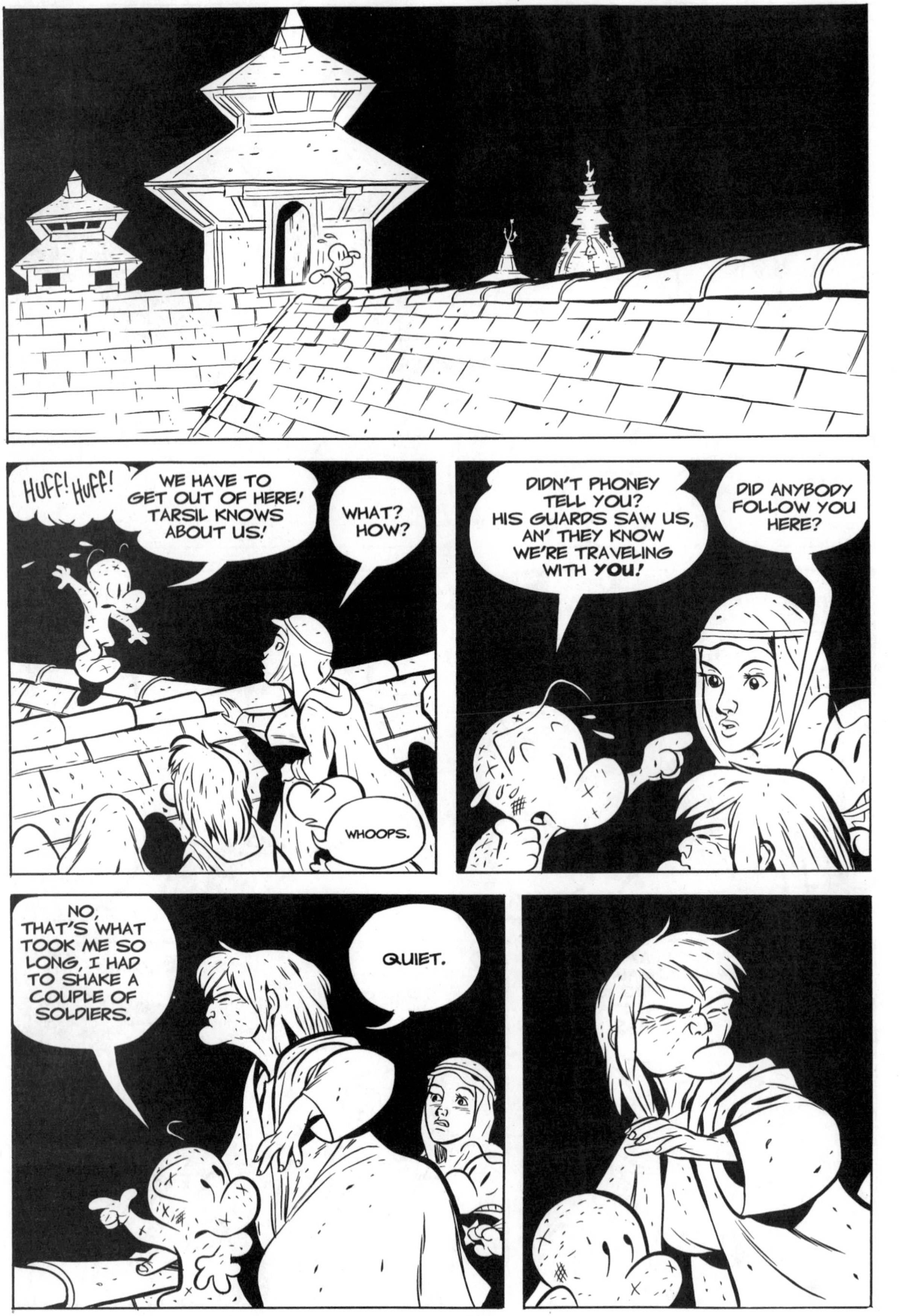
HUFF! HUFF!
WE HAVE TO GET OUT OF HERE! TARSIL KNOWS ABOUT US!
WHAT? HOW?
WHOOPS.
DIDN'T PHONEY TELL YOU? HIS GUARDS SAW US, AN' THEY KNOW WE'RE TRAVELING WITH **YOU!**
DID ANYBODY FOLLOW YOU HERE?
NO, THAT'S WHAT TOOK ME SO LONG, I HAD TO SHAKE A COUPLE OF SOLDIERS.
QUIET.

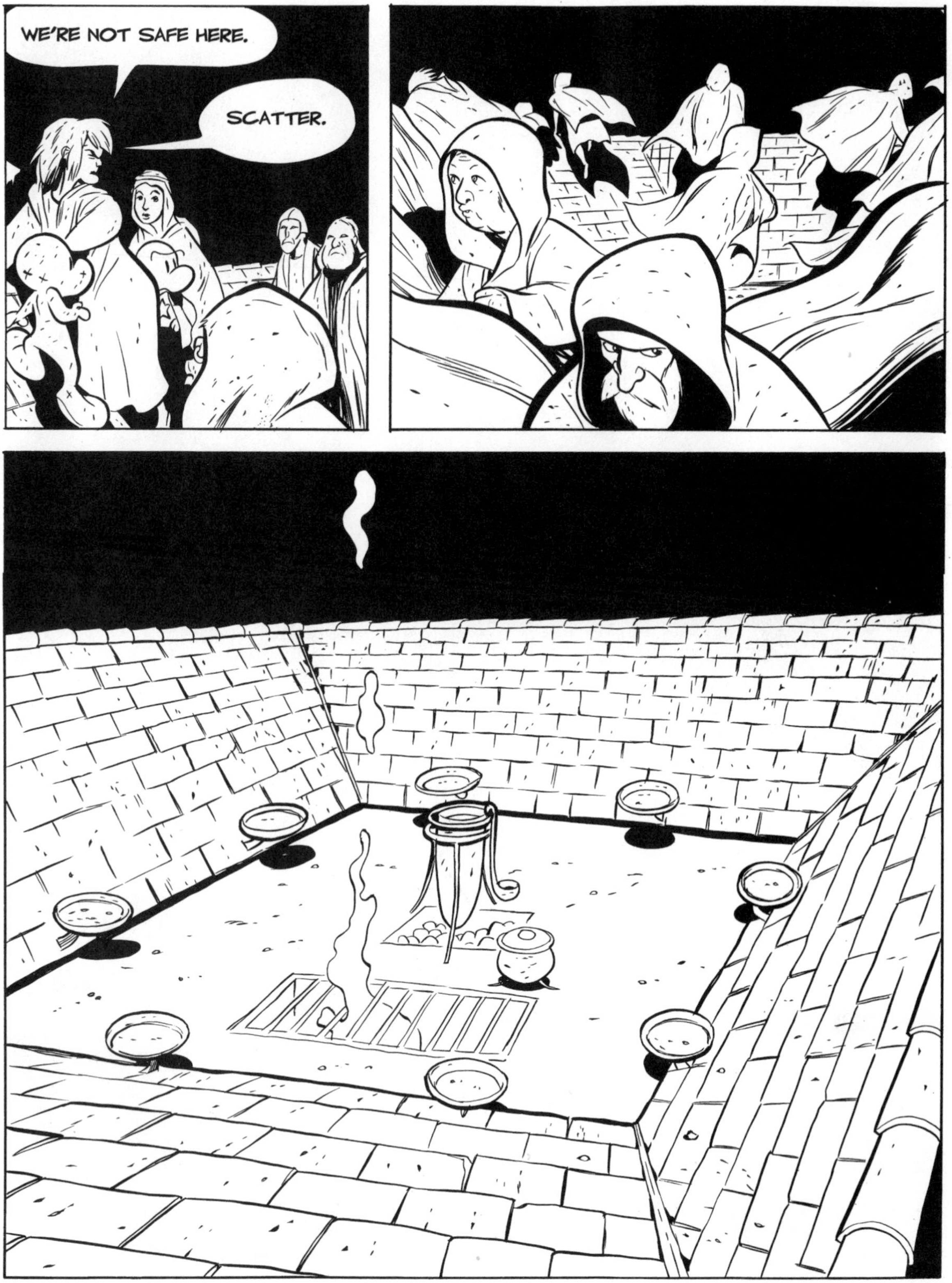
WE'RE NOT SAFE HERE.
SCATTER.

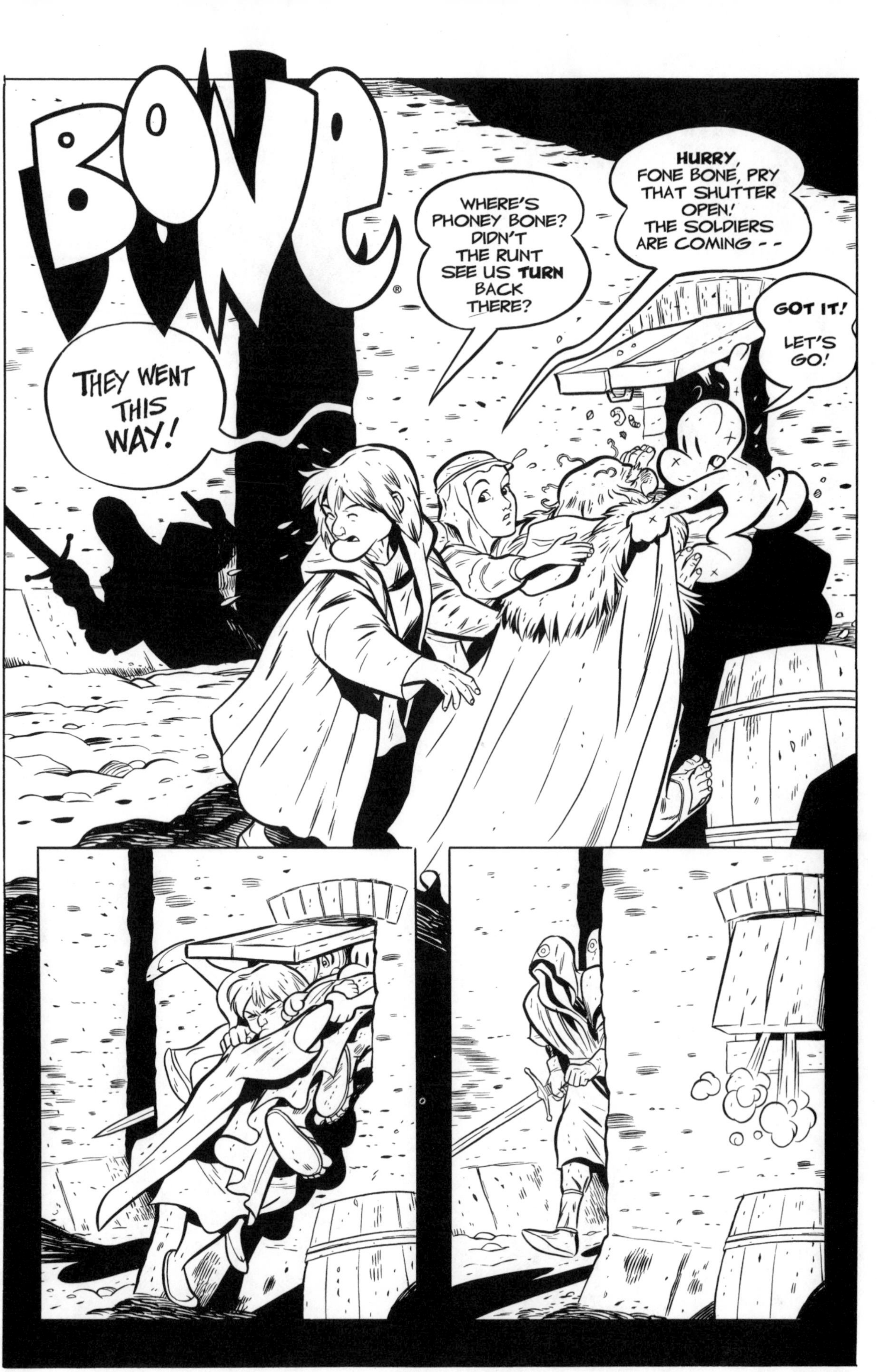
BONE®
WHERE'S PHONEY BONE? DIDN'T THE RUNT SEE US TURN BACK THERE?
HURRY, FONE BONE, PRY THAT SHUTTER OPEN! THE SOLDIERS ARE COMING - -
GOT IT! LET'S GO!
THEY WENT THIS WAY!

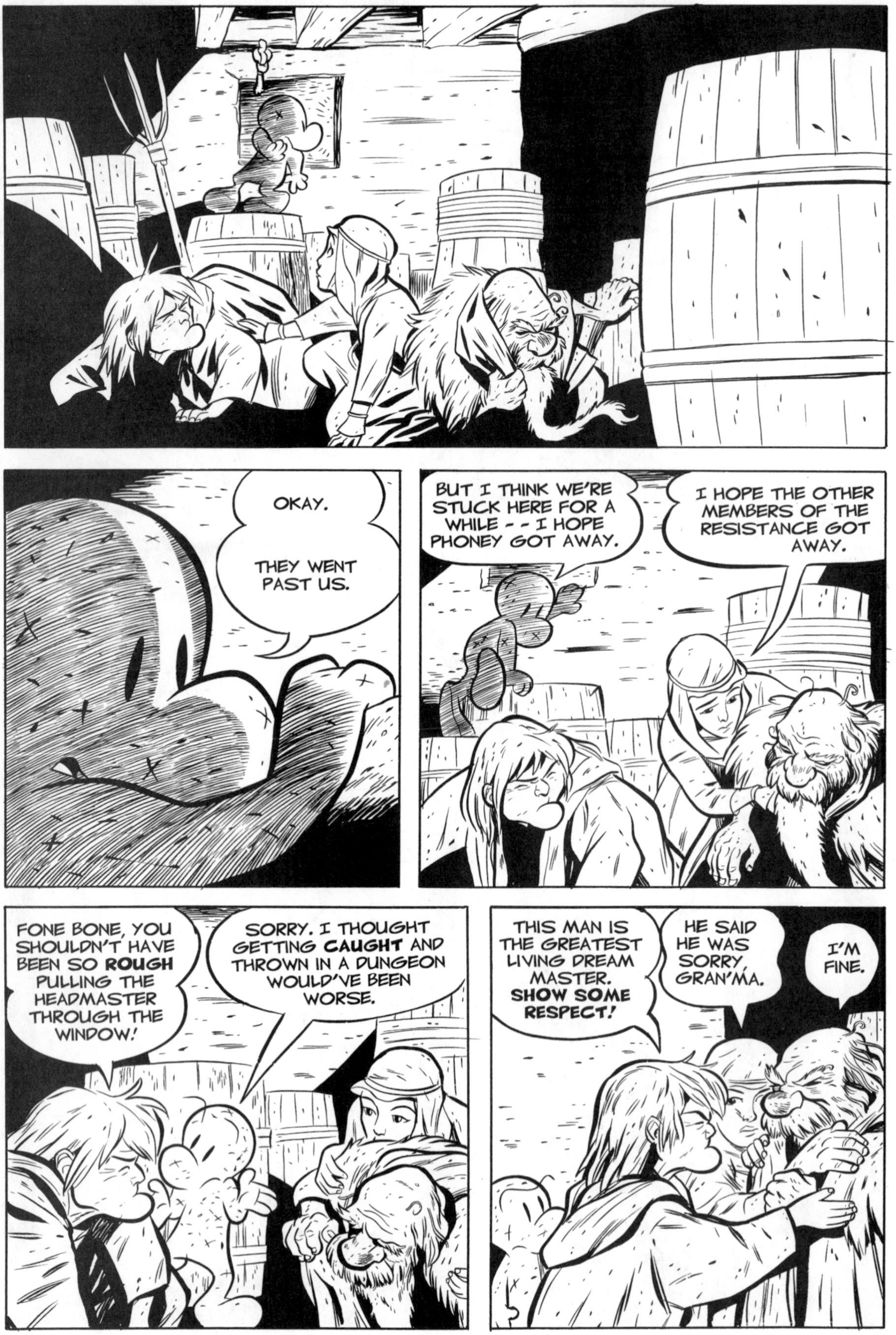
OKAY.
THEY WENT PAST US.
BUT I THINK WE'RE STUCK HERE FOR A WHILE - - I HOPE PHONEY GOT AWAY.
I HOPE THE OTHER MEMBERS OF THE RESISTANCE GOT AWAY.
FONE BONE, YOU SHOULDN'T HAVE BEEN SO **ROUGH** PULLING THE HEADMASTER THROUGH THE WINDOW!
SORRY. I THOUGHT GETTING **CAUGHT** AND THROWN IN A DUNGEON WOULD'VE BEEN WORSE.
THIS MAN IS THE GREATEST LIVING DREAM MASTER. **SHOW SOME RESPECT!**
HE SAID HE WAS SORRY, GRAN'MA.
I'M FINE.

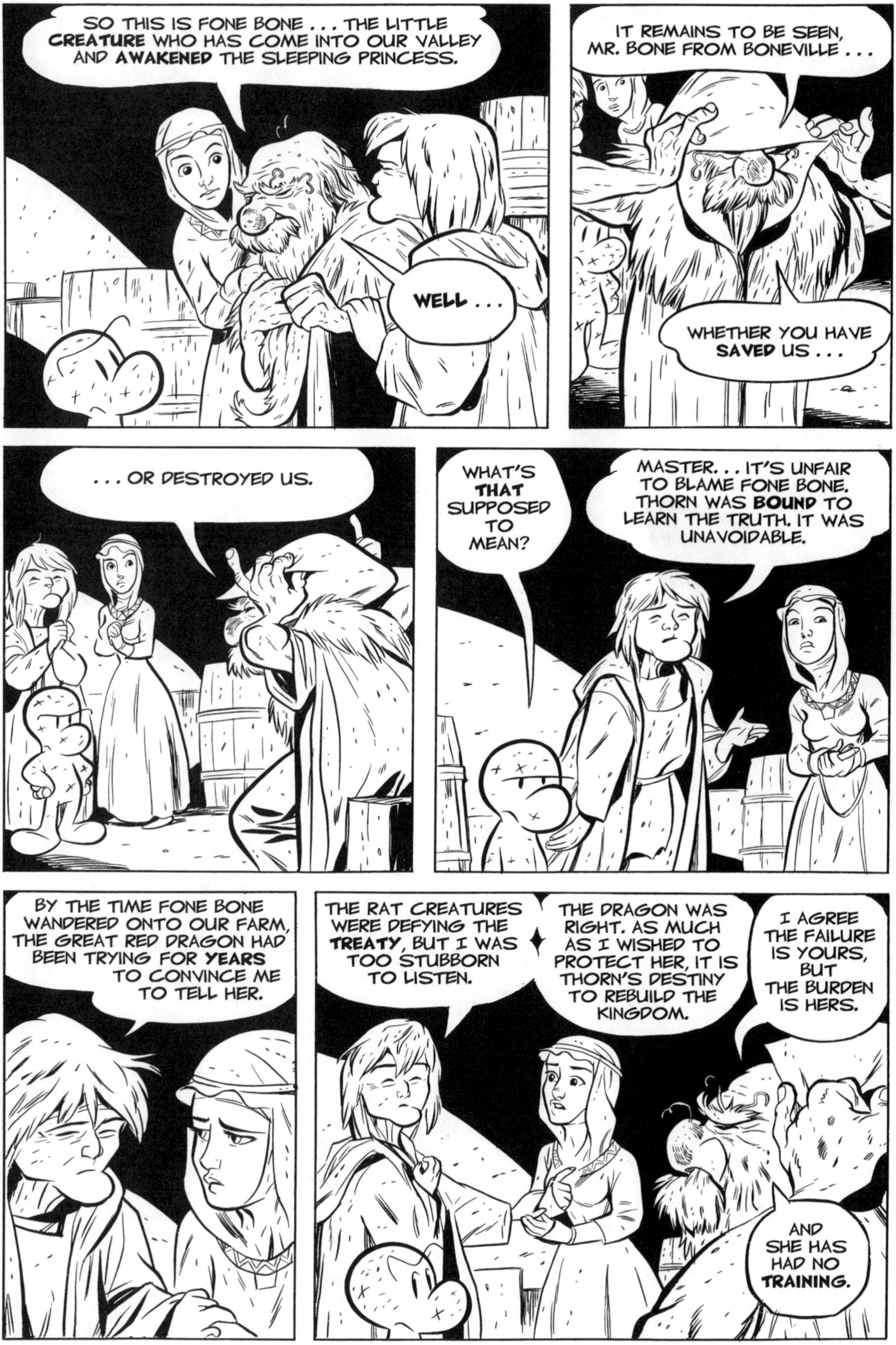

SO THIS IS FONE BONE . . . THE LITTLE CREATURE WHO HAS COME INTO OUR VALLEY AND AWAKENED THE SLEEPING PRINCESS.
WELL . . .
IT REMAINS TO BE SEEN, MR. BONE FROM BONEVILLE . . .
WHETHER YOU HAVE SAVED US . . .
. . . OR DESTROYED US.
WHAT'S THAT SUPPOSED TO MEAN?
MASTER. . . IT'S UNFAIR TO BLAME FONE BONE. THORN WAS BOUND TO LEARN THE TRUTH. IT WAS UNAVOIDABLE.
BY THE TIME FONE BONE WANDERED ONTO OUR FARM, THE GREAT RED DRAGON HAD BEEN TRYING FOR YEARS TO CONVINCE ME TO TELL HER.
THE RAT CREATURES WERE DEFYING THE TREATY, BUT I WAS TOO STUBBORN TO LISTEN.
THE DRAGON WAS RIGHT. AS MUCH AS I WISHED TO PROTECT HER, IT IS THORN'S DESTINY TO REBUILD THE KINGDOM.
I AGREE THE FAILURE IS YOURS, BUT THE BURDEN IS HERS.
AND SHE HAS HAD NO TRAINING.

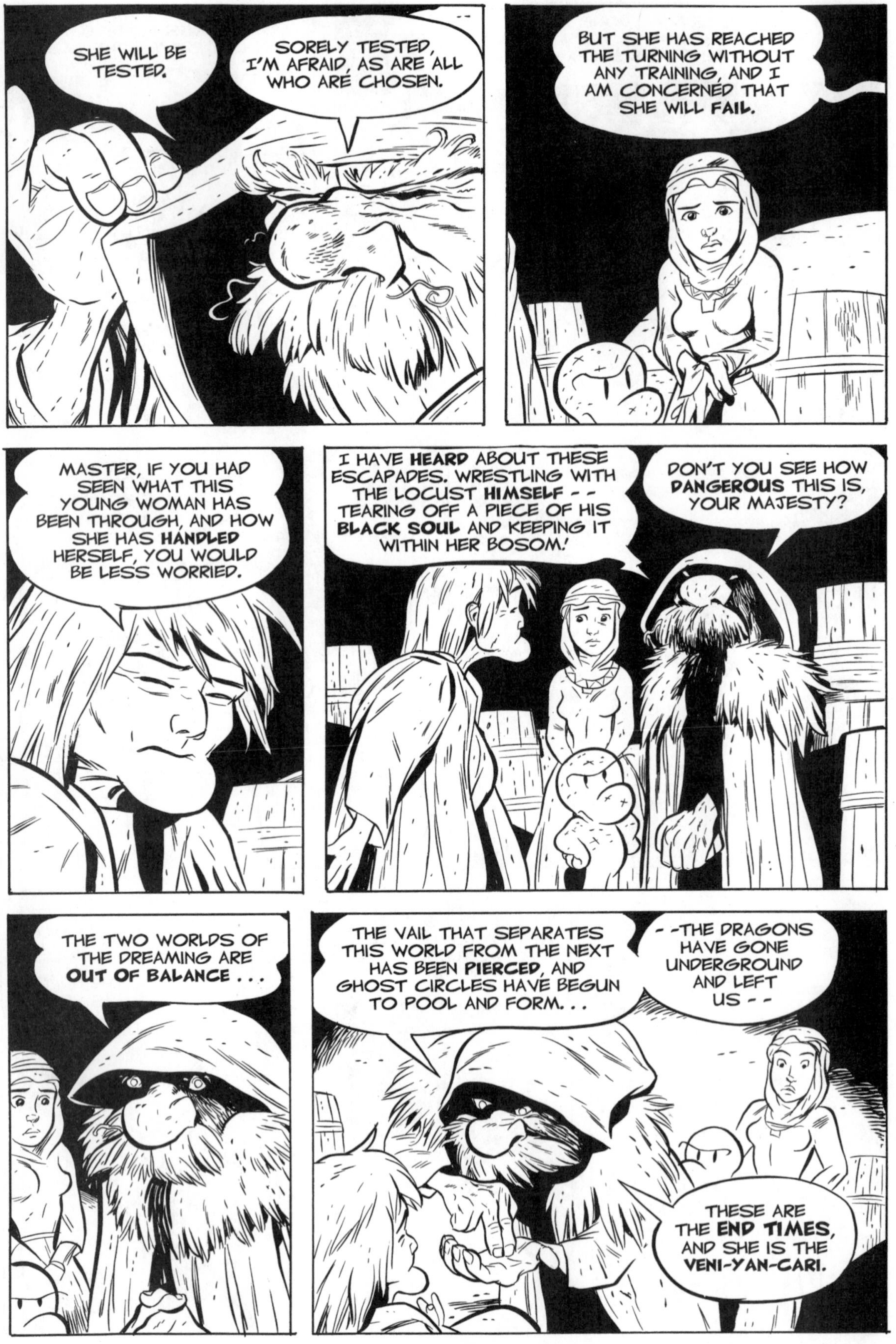
SHE WILL BE TESTED.
SORELY TESTED, I'M AFRAID, AS ARE ALL WHO ARE CHOSEN.
BUT SHE HAS REACHED THE TURNING WITHOUT ANY TRAINING, AND I AM CONCERNED THAT SHE WILL **FAIL.**
MASTER, IF YOU HAD SEEN WHAT THIS YOUNG WOMAN HAS BEEN THROUGH, AND HOW SHE HAS **HANDLED** HERSELF, YOU WOULD BE LESS WORRIED.
I HAVE **HEARD** ABOUT THESE ESCAPADES. WRESTLING WITH THE LOCUST **HIMSELF** -- TEARING OFF A PIECE OF HIS **BLACK SOUL** AND KEEPING IT WITHIN HER BOSOM!
DON'T YOU SEE HOW **DANGEROUS** THIS IS, YOUR MAJESTY?
THE TWO WORLDS OF THE DREAMING ARE **OUT OF BALANCE** . . .
THE VAIL THAT SEPARATES THIS WORLD FROM THE NEXT HAS BEEN **PIERCED**, AND GHOST CIRCLES HAVE BEGUN TO POOL AND FORM. . .
--THE DRAGONS HAVE GONE UNDERGROUND AND LEFT US --
THESE ARE THE **END TIMES**, AND SHE IS THE **VENI-YAN-CARI.**

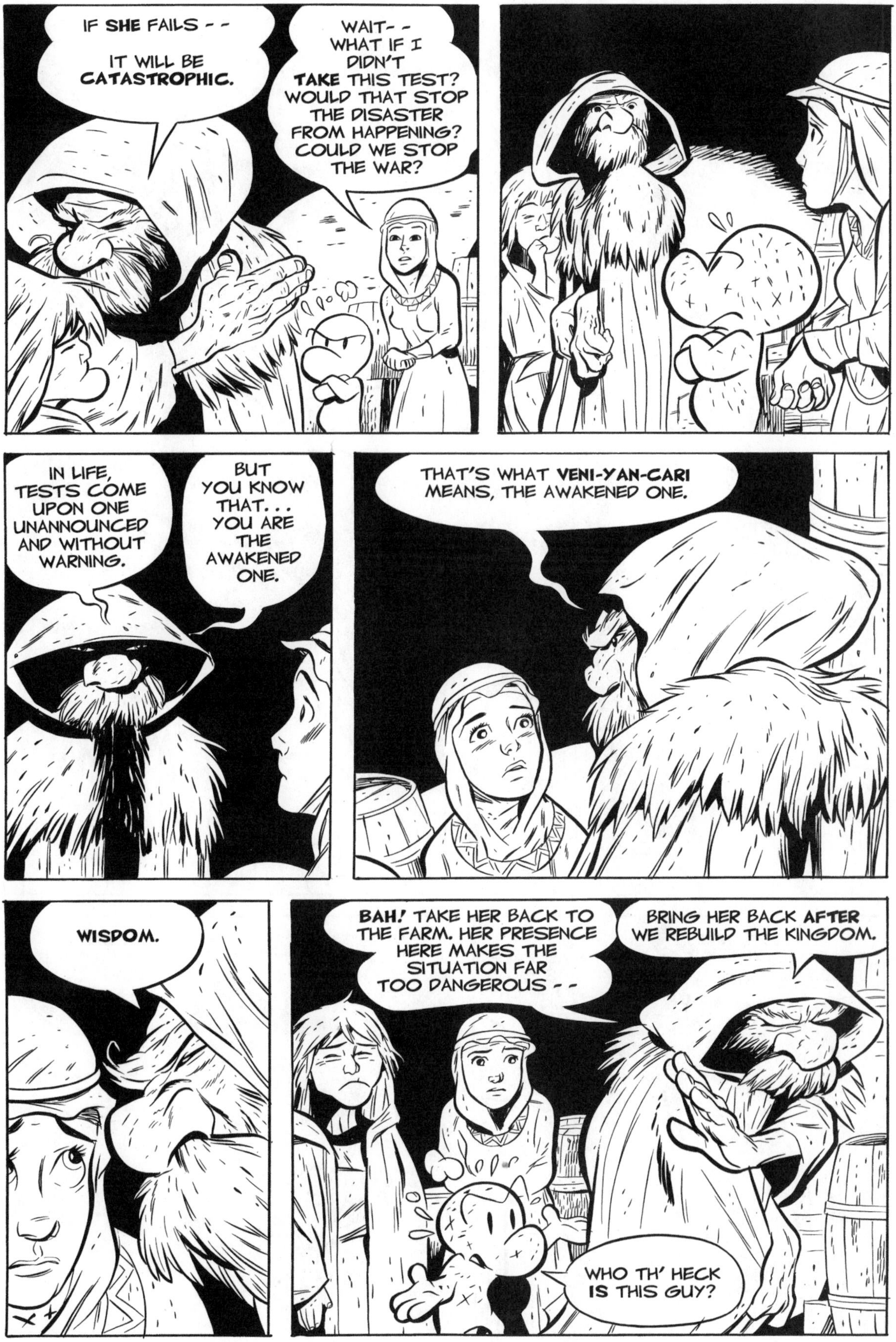
IF SHE FAILS - -
IT WILL BE CATASTROPHIC.
WAIT- - WHAT IF I DIDN'T TAKE THIS TEST? WOULD THAT STOP THE DISASTER FROM HAPPENING? COULD WE STOP THE WAR?
IN LIFE, TESTS COME UPON ONE UNANNOUNCED AND WITHOUT WARNING.
BUT YOU KNOW THAT. . . YOU ARE THE AWAKENED ONE.
THAT'S WHAT VENI-YAN-CARI MEANS, THE AWAKENED ONE.
WISDOM.
BAH! TAKE HER BACK TO THE FARM. HER PRESENCE HERE MAKES THE SITUATION FAR TOO DANGEROUS - -
BRING HER BACK AFTER WE REBUILD THE KINGDOM.
WHO TH' HECK IS THIS GUY?

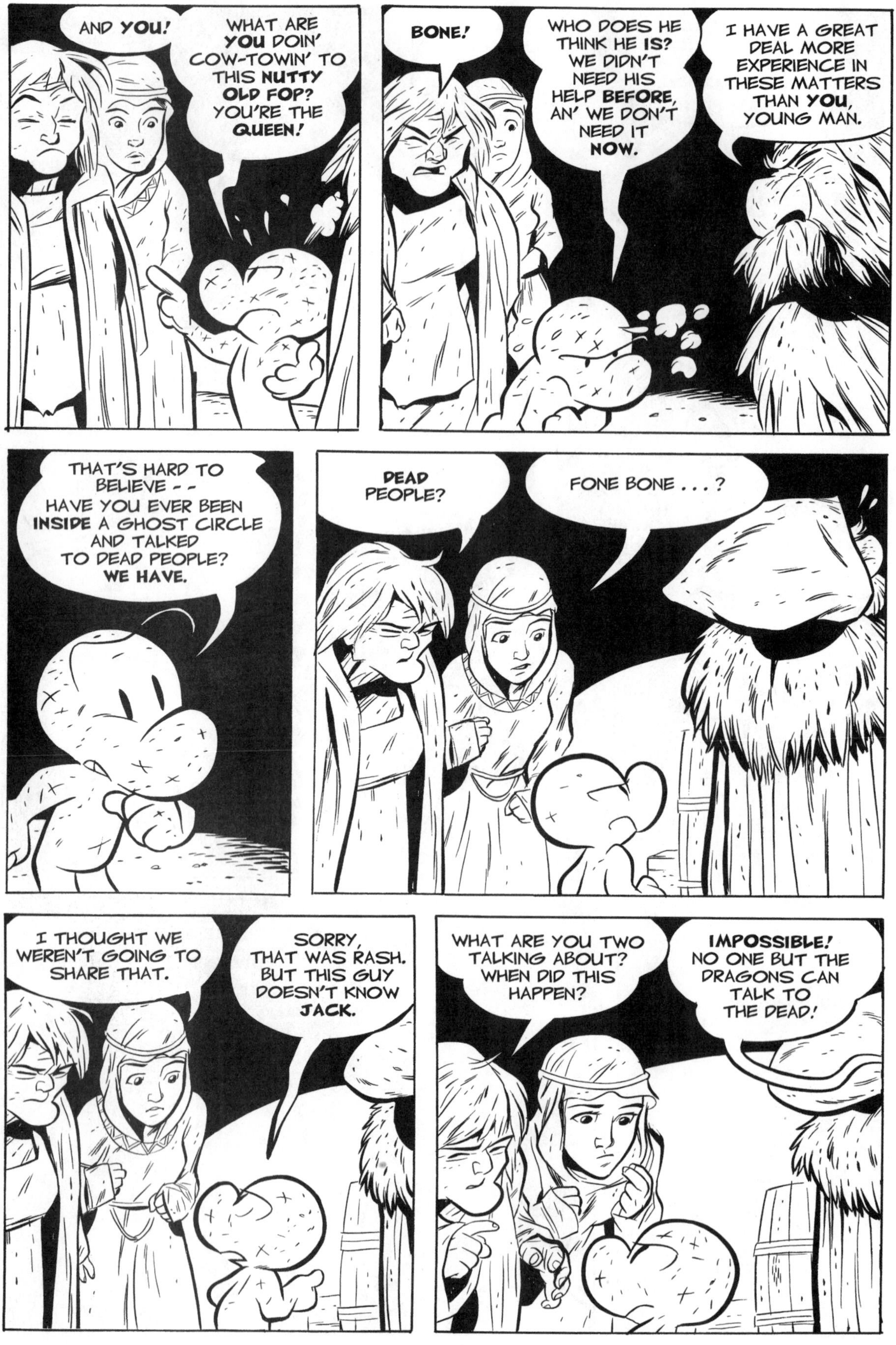
AND YOU!
WHAT ARE YOU DOIN' COW-TOWIN' TO THIS NUTTY OLD FOP? YOU'RE THE QUEEN!
BONE!
WHO DOES HE THINK HE IS? WE DIDN'T NEED HIS HELP BEFORE, AN' WE DON'T NEED IT NOW.
I HAVE A GREAT DEAL MORE EXPERIENCE IN THESE MATTERS THAN YOU, YOUNG MAN.
THAT'S HARD TO BELIEVE -- HAVE YOU EVER BEEN INSIDE A GHOST CIRCLE AND TALKED TO DEAD PEOPLE? WE HAVE.
DEAD PEOPLE?
FONE BONE . . . ?
I THOUGHT WE WEREN'T GOING TO SHARE THAT.
SORRY, THAT WAS RASH. BUT THIS GUY DOESN'T KNOW JACK.
WHAT ARE YOU TWO TALKING ABOUT? WHEN DID THIS HAPPEN?
IMPOSSIBLE! NO ONE BUT THE DRAGONS CAN TALK TO THE DEAD!

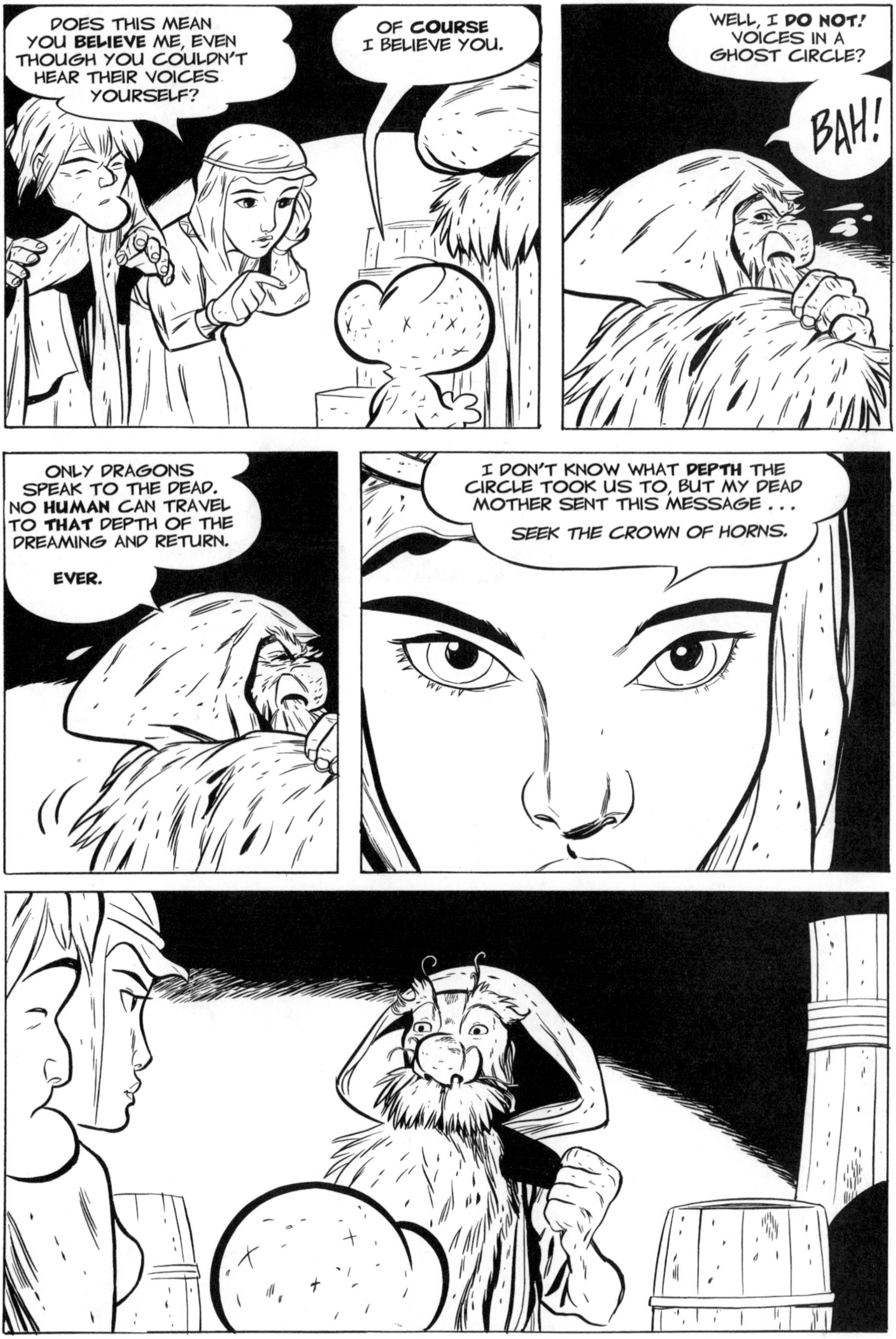
DOES THIS MEAN YOU BELIEVE ME, EVEN THOUGH YOU COULDN'T HEAR THEIR VOICES YOURSELF?
OF COURSE I BELIEVE YOU.
WELL, I DO NOT! VOICES IN A GHOST CIRCLE?
BAH!
ONLY DRAGONS SPEAK TO THE DEAD. NO HUMAN CAN TRAVEL TO THAT DEPTH OF THE DREAMING AND RETURN.
EVER.
I DON'T KNOW WHAT DEPTH THE CIRCLE TOOK US TO, BUT MY DEAD MOTHER SENT THIS MESSAGE . . .
SEEK THE CROWN OF HORNS.

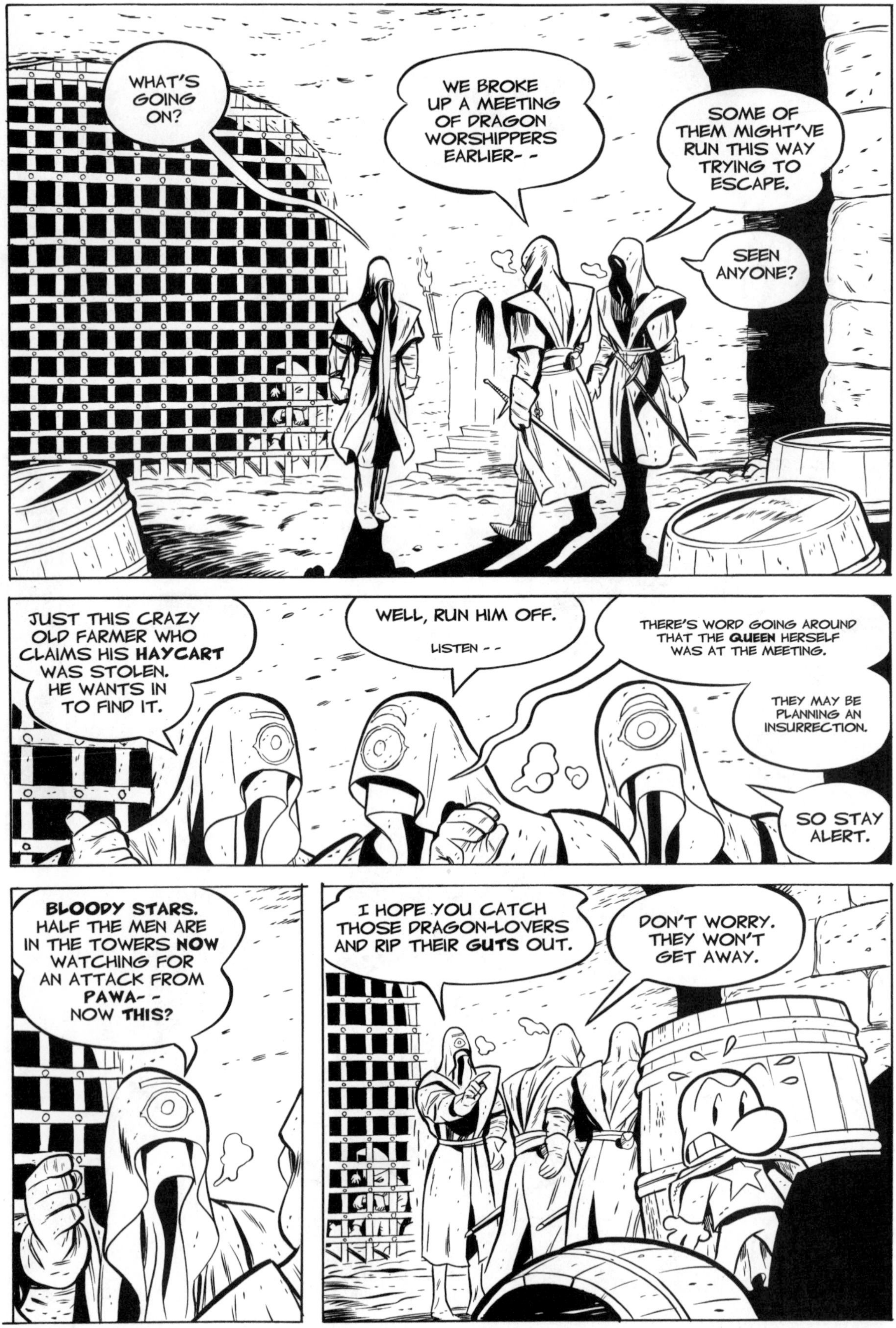
WHAT'S GOING ON?
WE BROKE UP A MEETING OF DRAGON WORSHIPPERS EARLIER- -
SOME OF THEM MIGHT'VE RUN THIS WAY TRYING TO ESCAPE.
SEEN ANYONE?
JUST THIS CRAZY OLD FARMER WHO CLAIMS HIS HAYCART WAS STOLEN. HE WANTS IN TO FIND IT.
WELL, RUN HIM OFF.
LISTEN - -
THERE'S WORD GOING AROUND THAT THE QUEEN HERSELF WAS AT THE MEETING.
THEY MAY BE PLANNING AN INSURRECTION.
SO STAY ALERT.
BLOODY STARS. HALF THE MEN ARE IN THE TOWERS NOW WATCHING FOR AN ATTACK FROM PAWA- - NOW THIS?
I HOPE YOU CATCH THOSE DRAGON-LOVERS AND RIP THEIR GUTS OUT.
DON'T WORRY. THEY WON'T GET AWAY.

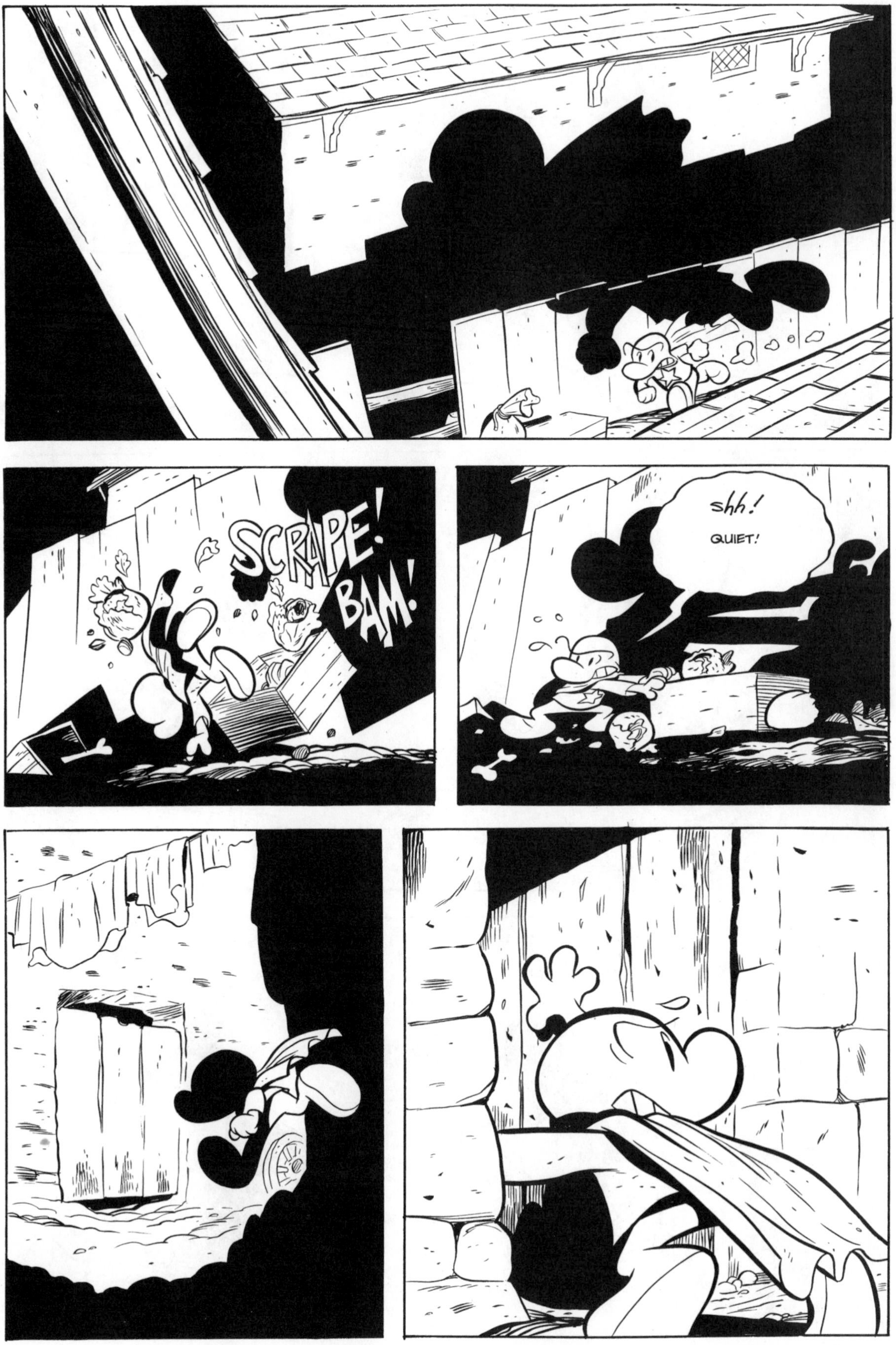
SCRAPE!
BAM!
shh!
QUIET!

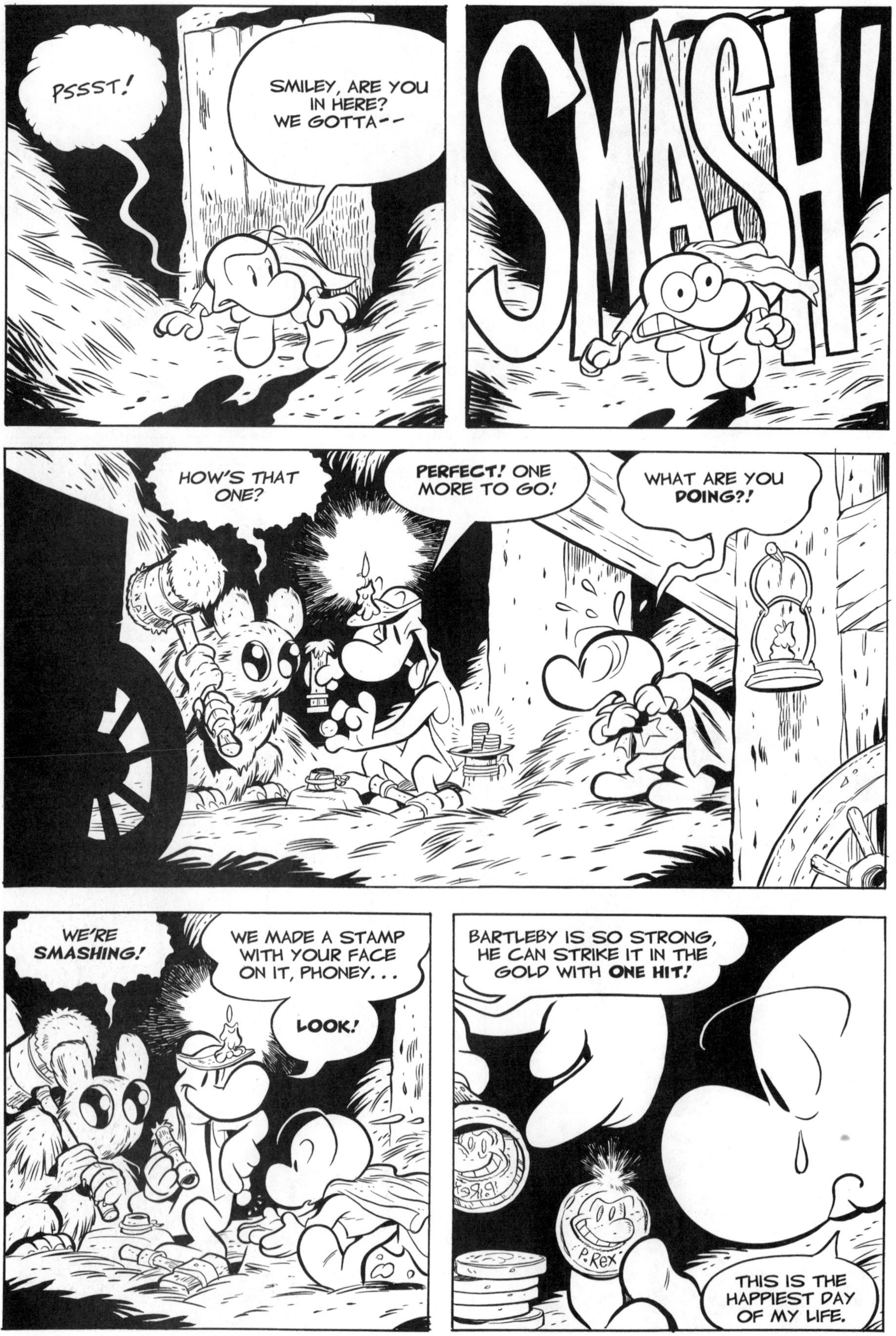
PSSST!
SMILEY, ARE YOU IN HERE? WE GOTTA--
SMASH!
HOW'S THAT ONE?
PERFECT! ONE MORE TO GO!
WHAT ARE YOU **DOING?!**
WE'RE **SMASHING!**
WE MADE A STAMP WITH YOUR FACE ON IT, PHONEY...
LOOK!
BARTLEBY IS SO STRONG, HE CAN STRIKE IT IN THE GOLD WITH **ONE HIT!**
P. Rex
THIS IS THE HAPPIEST DAY OF MY LIFE.

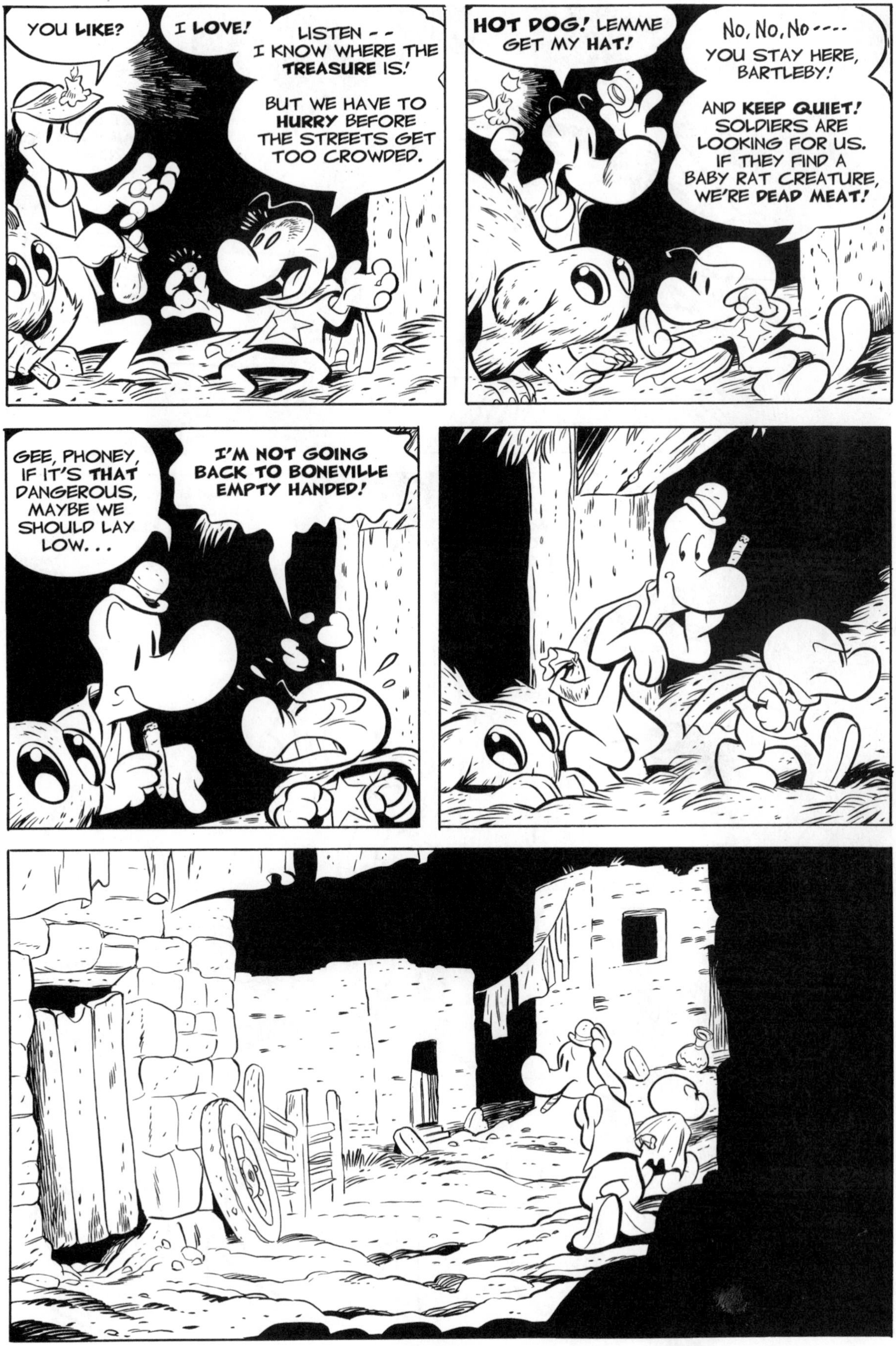
YOU LIKE?
I LOVE!
LISTEN - - I KNOW WHERE THE TREASURE IS!
BUT WE HAVE TO HURRY BEFORE THE STREETS GET TOO CROWDED.
HOT DOG! LEMME GET MY HAT!
No, No, No ----
YOU STAY HERE, BARTLEBY!
AND KEEP QUIET! SOLDIERS ARE LOOKING FOR US. IF THEY FIND A BABY RAT CREATURE, WE'RE DEAD MEAT!
GEE, PHONEY, IF IT'S THAT DANGEROUS, MAYBE WE SHOULD LAY LOW...
I'M NOT GOING BACK TO BONEVILLE EMPTY HANDED!

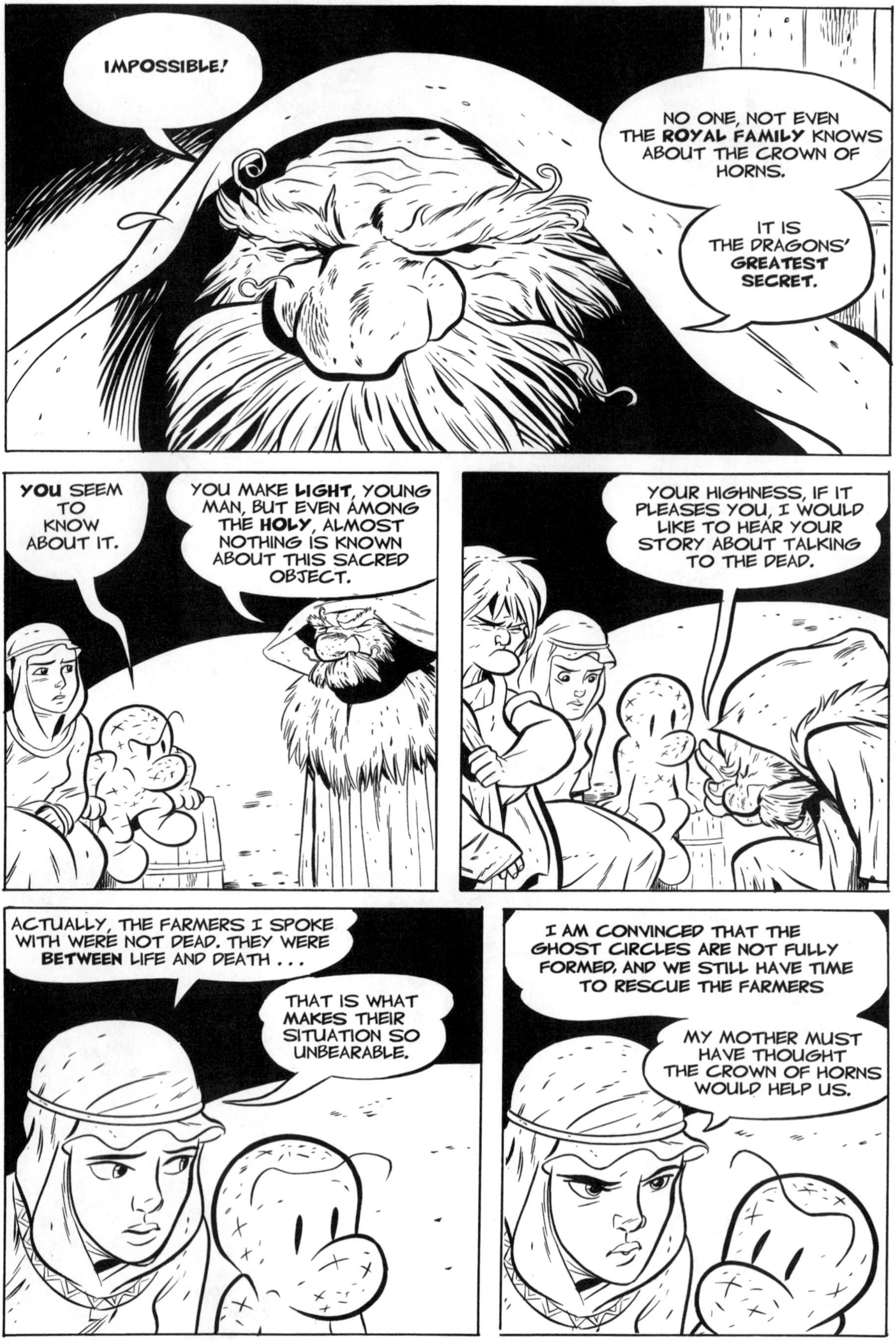
IMPOSSIBLE!
NO ONE, NOT EVEN THE ROYAL FAMILY KNOWS ABOUT THE CROWN OF HORNS.
IT IS THE DRAGONS' GREATEST SECRET.
YOU SEEM TO KNOW ABOUT IT.
YOU MAKE LIGHT, YOUNG MAN, BUT EVEN AMONG THE HOLY, ALMOST NOTHING IS KNOWN ABOUT THIS SACRED OBJECT.
YOUR HIGHNESS, IF IT PLEASES YOU, I WOULD LIKE TO HEAR YOUR STORY ABOUT TALKING TO THE DEAD.
ACTUALLY, THE FARMERS I SPOKE WITH WERE NOT DEAD. THEY WERE BETWEEN LIFE AND DEATH . . .
THAT IS WHAT MAKES THEIR SITUATION SO UNBEARABLE.
I AM CONVINCED THAT THE GHOST CIRCLES ARE NOT FULLY FORMED, AND WE STILL HAVE TIME TO RESCUE THE FARMERS
MY MOTHER MUST HAVE THOUGHT THE CROWN OF HORNS WOULD HELP US.

MY GOODNESS. I'M NOT CERTAIN I CAN HELP **YOU**, PRINCESS. ALMOST NOTHING IS KNOWN ABOUT IT...

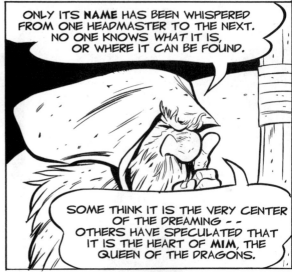

ONLY ITS **NAME** HAS BEEN WHISPERED FROM ONE HEADMASTER TO THE NEXT. NO ONE KNOWS WHAT IT IS, OR WHERE IT CAN BE FOUND.

SOME THINK IT IS THE VERY CENTER OF THE DREAMING -- OTHERS HAVE SPECULATED THAT IT IS THE HEART OF **MIM**, THE QUEEN OF THE DRAGONS.

THERE IS ONE LINE OF THINKING WHICH SUGGESTS THAT AS THE CENTER OF THE DREAMING --

THE CROWN OF HORNS WOULD BE THE **ANTITHESIS** OF THE LOCUST.

HMM. IF WE COULD RESTORE **BALANCE** TO THE DREAMING, THE GHOST CIRCLES MIGHT VANISH.

YEAH, BUT **HOW**?

WELL, SINCE BRIAR USED THE LOCUST TO PUSH THINGS OUT OF BALANCE, I SUPPOSE WE SHOULD **START** BY FINDING THE CROWN OF HORNS.

WISDOM.

NO, NO, NO, **NO**. DON'T YOU SEE?

THIS IS EXACTLY THE LACK OF TRAINING I WAS **TALKING** ABOUT! DO YOU KNOW WHAT HAPPENS WHEN YOU BRING **OPPOSITES** TOGETHER?

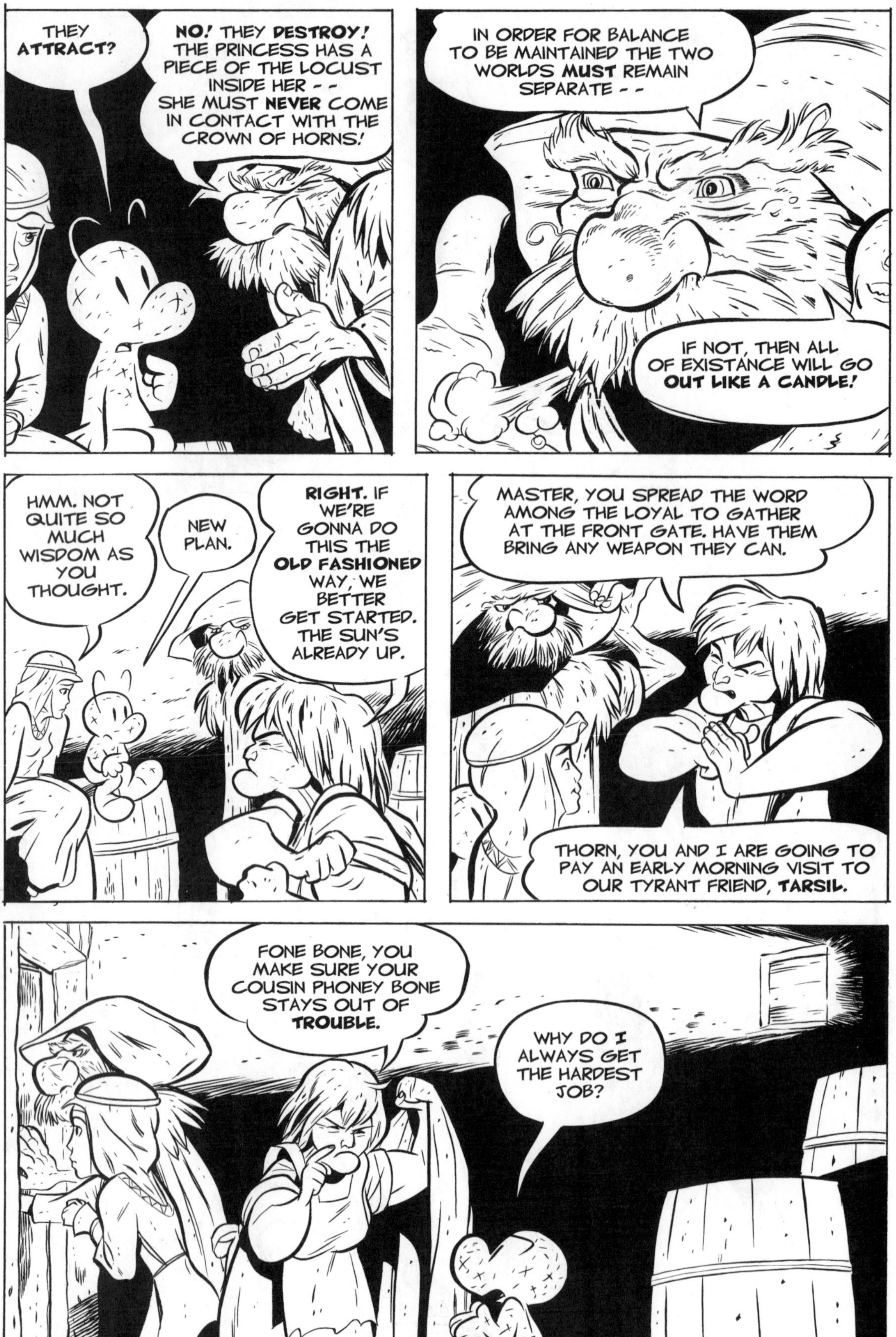
THEY ATTRACT?
NO! THEY DESTROY! THE PRINCESS HAS A PIECE OF THE LOCUST INSIDE HER - - SHE MUST NEVER COME IN CONTACT WITH THE CROWN OF HORNS!
IN ORDER FOR BALANCE TO BE MAINTAINED THE TWO WORLDS MUST REMAIN SEPARATE - -
IF NOT, THEN ALL OF EXISTANCE WILL GO OUT LIKE A CANDLE!
HMM. NOT QUITE SO MUCH WISDOM AS YOU THOUGHT.
NEW PLAN.
RIGHT. IF WE'RE GONNA DO THIS THE OLD FASHIONED WAY, WE BETTER GET STARTED. THE SUN'S ALREADY UP.
MASTER, YOU SPREAD THE WORD AMONG THE LOYAL TO GATHER AT THE FRONT GATE. HAVE THEM BRING ANY WEAPON THEY CAN.
THORN, YOU AND I ARE GOING TO PAY AN EARLY MORNING VISIT TO OUR TYRANT FRIEND, TARSIL.
FONE BONE, YOU MAKE SURE YOUR COUSIN PHONEY BONE STAYS OUT OF TROUBLE.
WHY DO I ALWAYS GET THE HARDEST JOB?

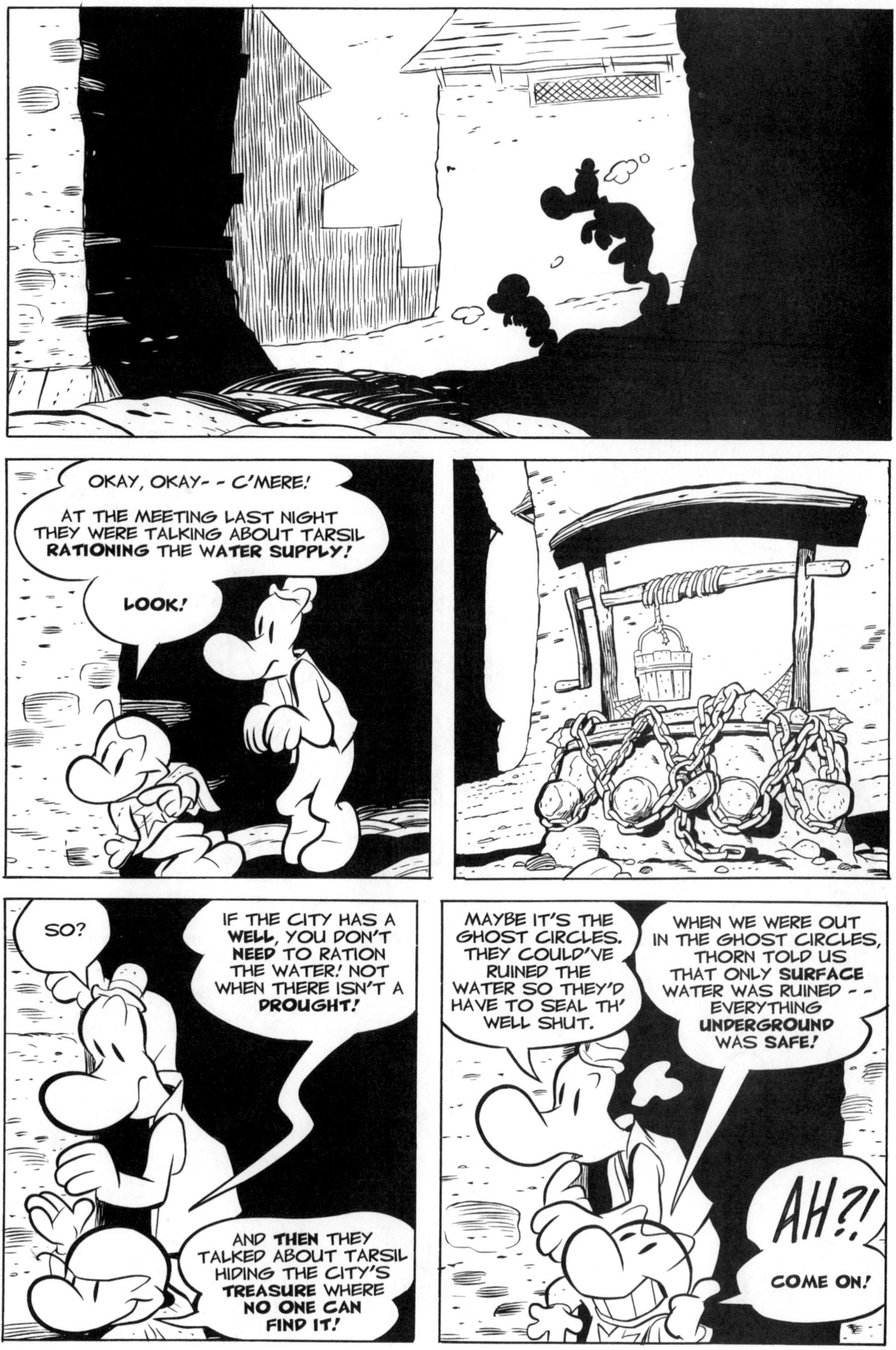

OKAY, OKAY- - C'MERE!
AT THE MEETING LAST NIGHT THEY WERE TALKING ABOUT TARSIL RATIONING THE WATER SUPPLY!
LOOK!
SO?
IF THE CITY HAS A WELL, YOU DON'T NEED TO RATION THE WATER! NOT WHEN THERE ISN'T A DROUGHT!
AND THEN THEY TALKED ABOUT TARSIL HIDING THE CITY'S TREASURE WHERE NO ONE CAN FIND IT!
MAYBE IT'S THE GHOST CIRCLES. THEY COULD'VE RUINED THE WATER SO THEY'D HAVE TO SEAL TH' WELL SHUT.
WHEN WE WERE OUT IN THE GHOST CIRCLES, THORN TOLD US THAT ONLY SURFACE WATER WAS RUINED - - EVERYTHING UNDERGROUND WAS SAFE!
AH?!
COME ON!

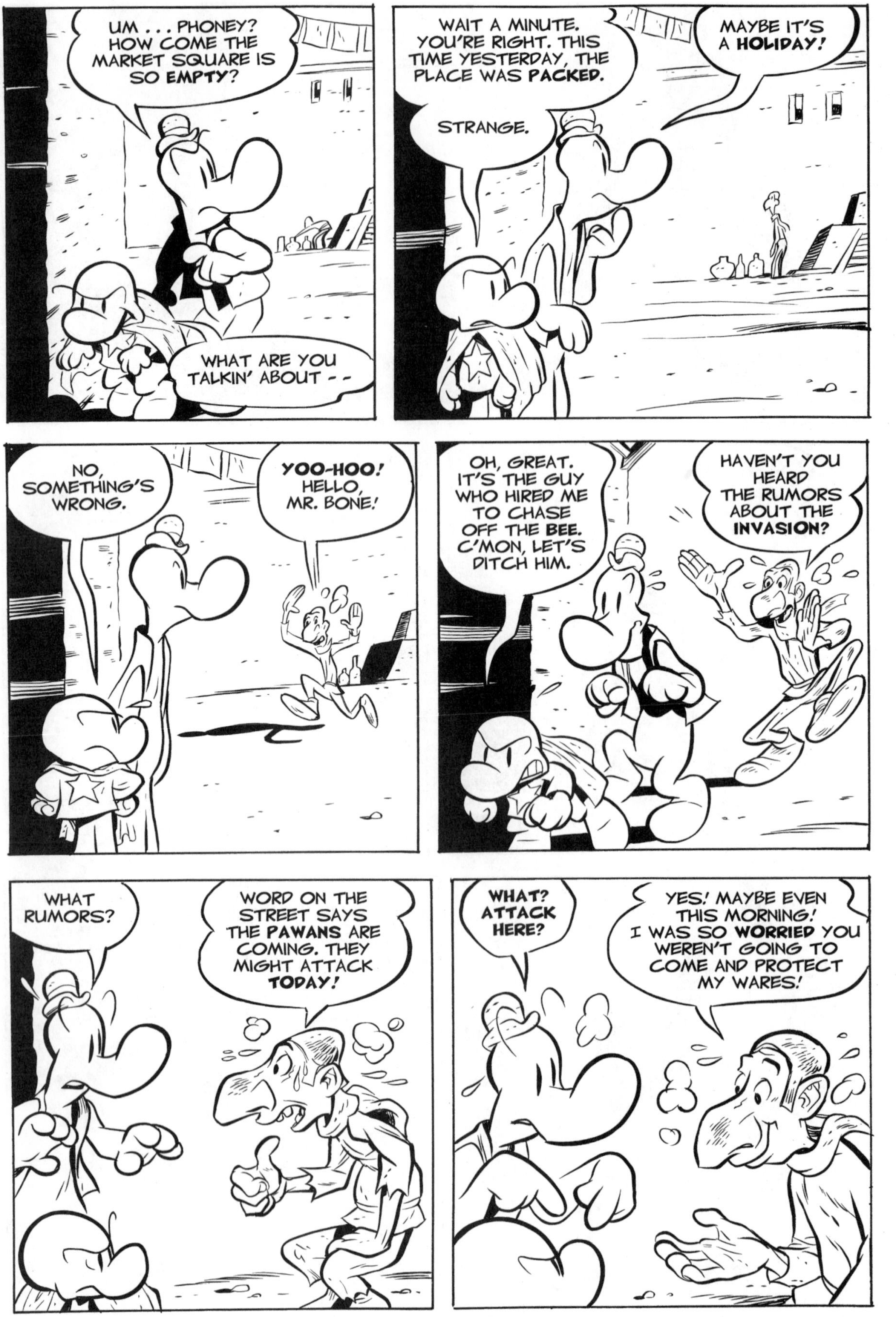
UM . . . PHONEY? HOW COME THE MARKET SQUARE IS SO **EMPTY**?
WHAT ARE YOU TALKIN' ABOUT - -
WAIT A MINUTE. YOU'RE RIGHT. THIS TIME YESTERDAY, THE PLACE WAS **PACKED**.
STRANGE.
MAYBE IT'S A **HOLIDAY!**
NO, SOMETHING'S WRONG.
YOO-HOO! HELLO, MR. BONE!
OH, GREAT. IT'S THE GUY WHO HIRED ME TO CHASE OFF THE **BEE**. C'MON, LET'S DITCH HIM.
HAVEN'T YOU HEARD THE RUMORS ABOUT THE **INVASION?**
WHAT RUMORS?
WORD ON THE STREET SAYS THE **PAWANS** ARE COMING. THEY MIGHT ATTACK **TODAY!**
WHAT? ATTACK HERE?
YES! MAYBE EVEN THIS MORNING! I WAS SO **WORRIED** YOU WEREN'T GOING TO COME AND PROTECT MY WARES!

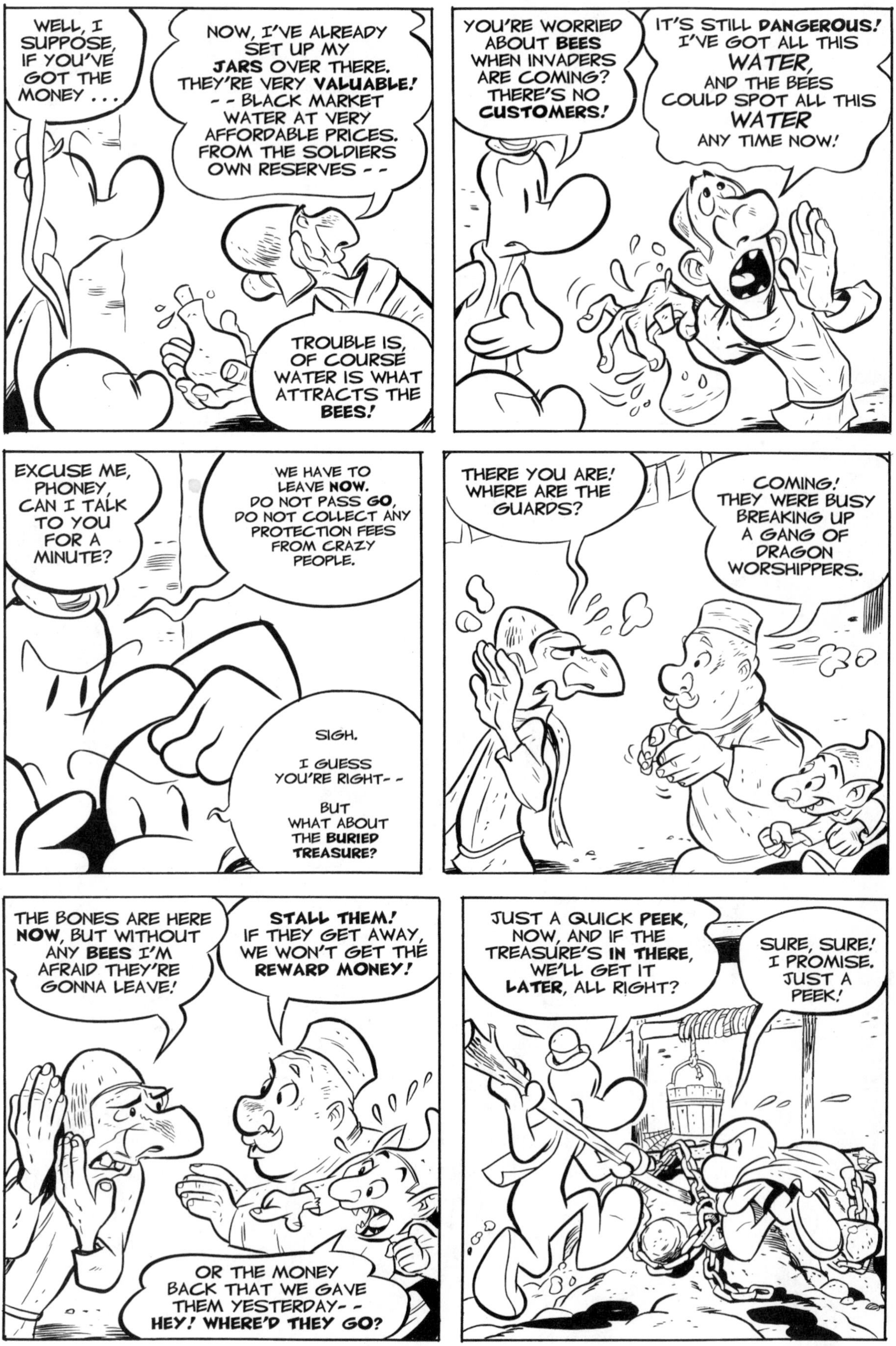
WELL, I SUPPOSE, IF YOU'VE GOT THE MONEY . . .
NOW, I'VE ALREADY SET UP MY JARS OVER THERE. THEY'RE VERY VALUABLE! - - BLACK MARKET WATER AT VERY AFFORDABLE PRICES. FROM THE SOLDIERS OWN RESERVES - -
TROUBLE IS, OF COURSE WATER IS WHAT ATTRACTS THE BEES!
YOU'RE WORRIED ABOUT BEES WHEN INVADERS ARE COMING? THERE'S NO CUSTOMERS!
IT'S STILL DANGEROUS! I'VE GOT ALL THIS WATER, AND THE BEES COULD SPOT ALL THIS WATER ANY TIME NOW!
EXCUSE ME, PHONEY, CAN I TALK TO YOU FOR A MINUTE?
WE HAVE TO LEAVE NOW. DO NOT PASS GO, DO NOT COLLECT ANY PROTECTION FEES FROM CRAZY PEOPLE.
SIGH.
I GUESS YOU'RE RIGHT- -
BUT WHAT ABOUT THE BURIED TREASURE?
THERE YOU ARE! WHERE ARE THE GUARDS?
COMING! THEY WERE BUSY BREAKING UP A GANG OF DRAGON WORSHIPPERS.
THE BONES ARE HERE NOW, BUT WITHOUT ANY BEES I'M AFRAID THEY'RE GONNA LEAVE!
STALL THEM! IF THEY GET AWAY, WE WON'T GET THE REWARD MONEY!
OR THE MONEY BACK THAT WE GAVE THEM YESTERDAY- - HEY! WHERE'D THEY GO?
JUST A QUICK PEEK, NOW, AND IF THE TREASURE'S IN THERE, WE'LL GET IT LATER, ALL RIGHT?
SURE, SURE! I PROMISE. JUST A PEEK!

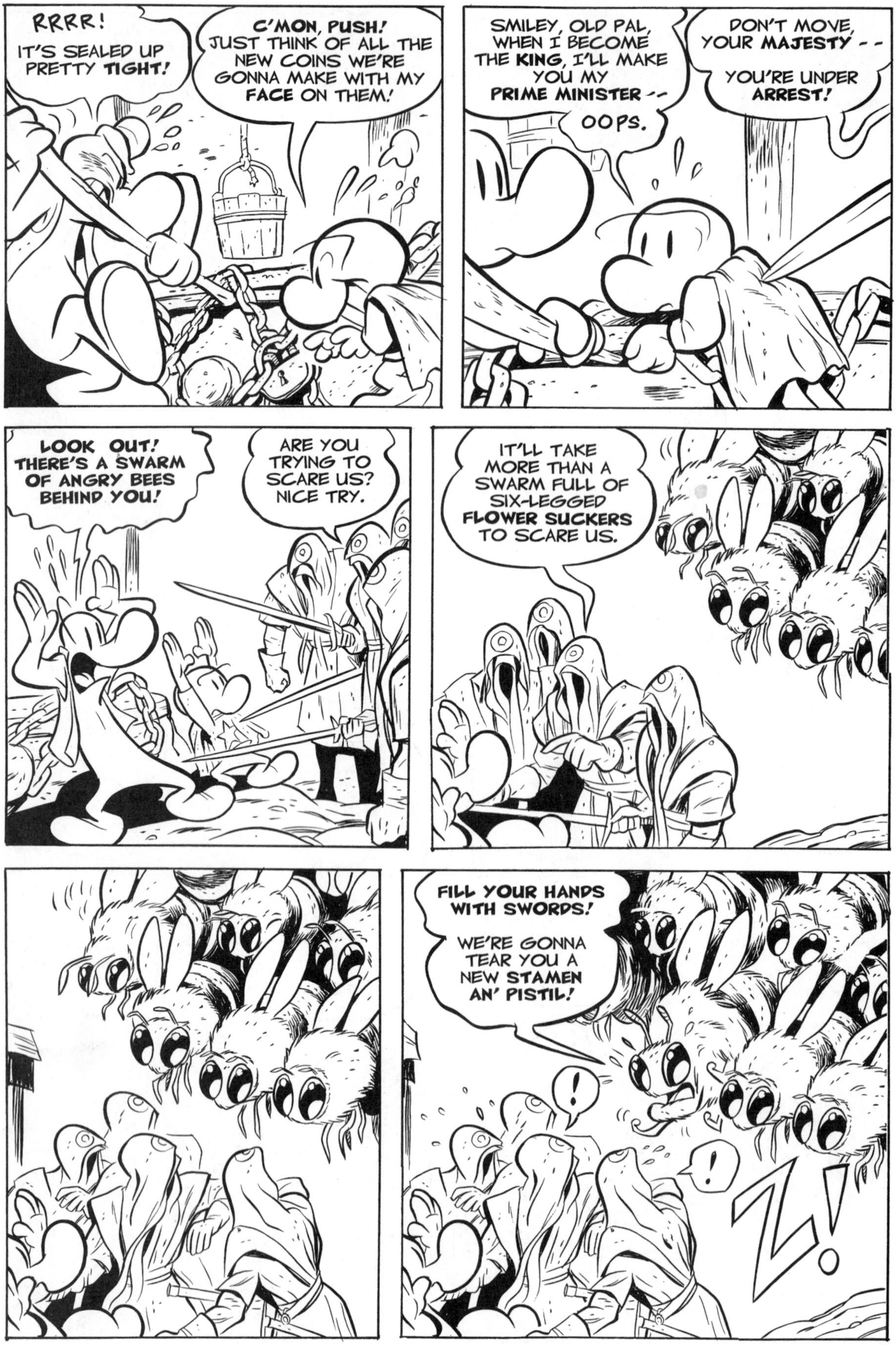
RRRR!
IT'S SEALED UP PRETTY TIGHT!
C'MON, PUSH! JUST THINK OF ALL THE NEW COINS WE'RE GONNA MAKE WITH MY FACE ON THEM!
SMILEY, OLD PAL, WHEN I BECOME THE KING, I'LL MAKE YOU MY PRIME MINISTER --
OOPS.
DON'T MOVE, YOUR MAJESTY --
YOU'RE UNDER ARREST!
LOOK OUT! THERE'S A SWARM OF ANGRY BEES BEHIND YOU!
ARE YOU TRYING TO SCARE US? NICE TRY.
IT'LL TAKE MORE THAN A SWARM FULL OF SIX-LEGGED FLOWER SUCKERS TO SCARE US.
FILL YOUR HANDS WITH SWORDS!
WE'RE GONNA TEAR YOU A NEW STAMEN AN' PISTIL!
!
!
Z!

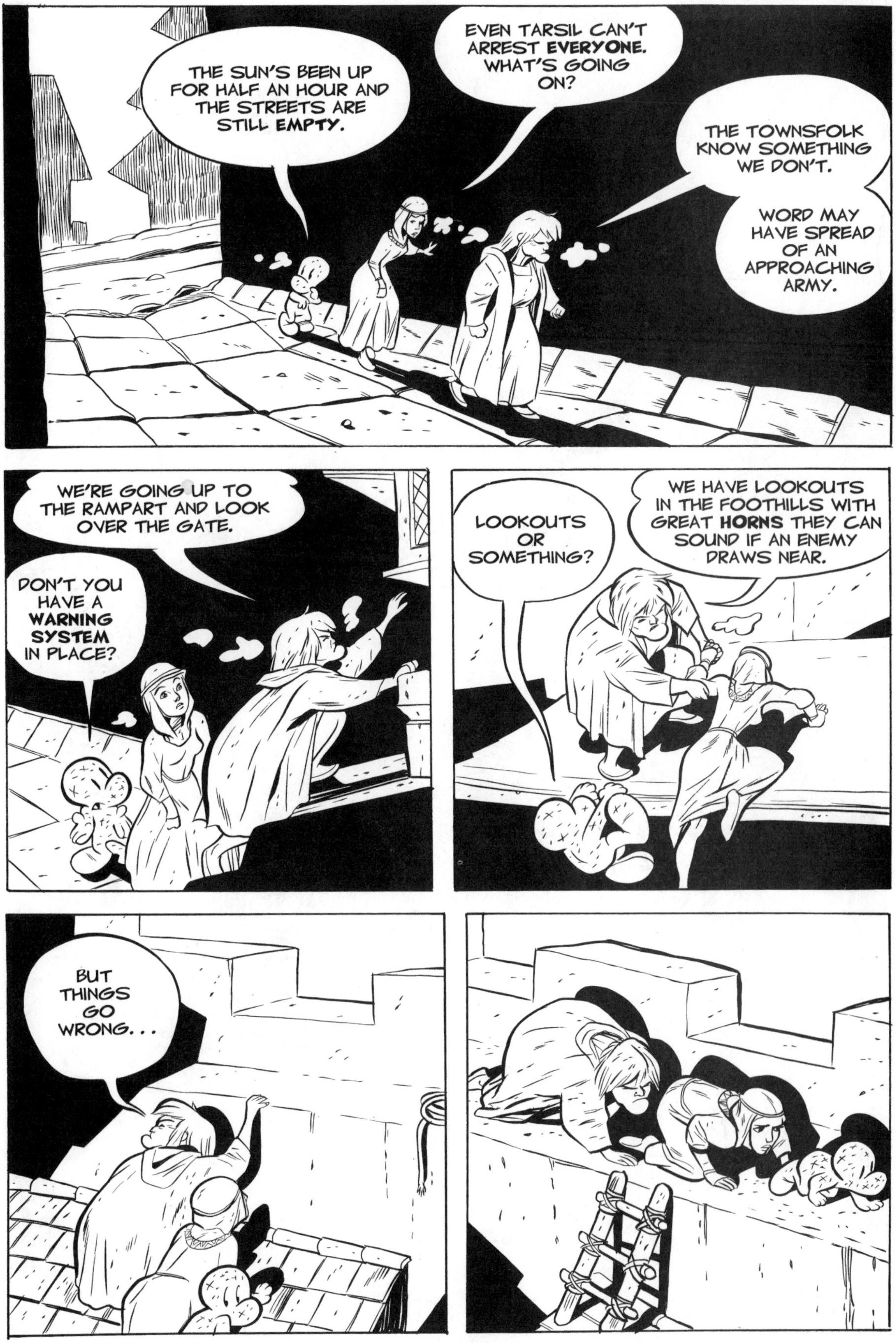
THE SUN'S BEEN UP FOR HALF AN HOUR AND THE STREETS ARE STILL EMPTY.
EVEN TARSIL CAN'T ARREST EVERYONE. WHAT'S GOING ON?
THE TOWNSFOLK KNOW SOMETHING WE DON'T.
WORD MAY HAVE SPREAD OF AN APPROACHING ARMY.
WE'RE GOING UP TO THE RAMPART AND LOOK OVER THE GATE.
DON'T YOU HAVE A WARNING SYSTEM IN PLACE?
LOOKOUTS OR SOMETHING?
WE HAVE LOOKOUTS IN THE FOOTHILLS WITH GREAT HORNS THEY CAN SOUND IF AN ENEMY DRAWS NEAR.
BUT THINGS GO WRONG...

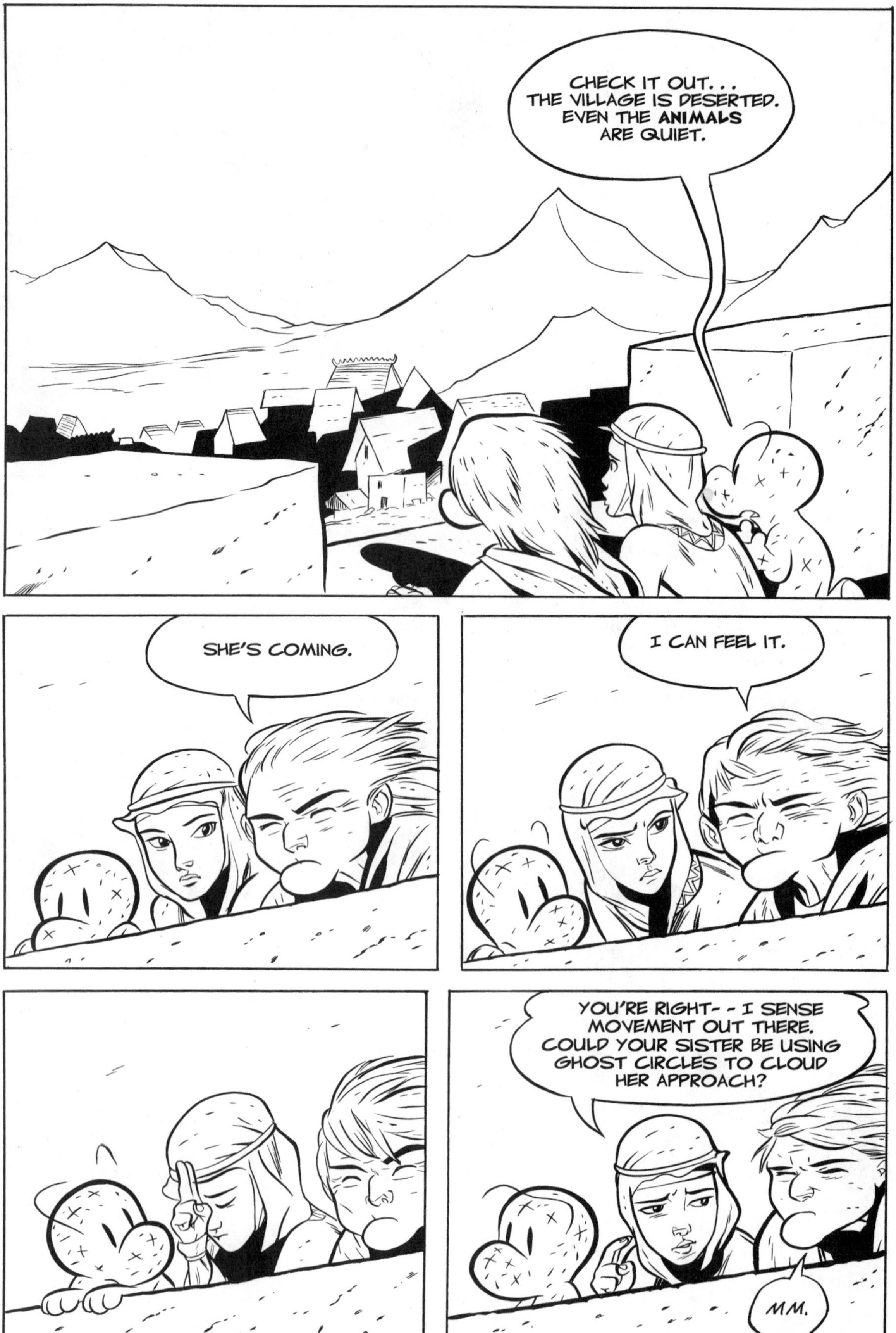
CHECK IT OUT. . .
THE VILLAGE IS DESERTED.
EVEN THE **ANIMALS**
ARE QUIET.
SHE'S COMING.
I CAN FEEL IT.
YOU'RE RIGHT- - I SENSE MOVEMENT OUT THERE. COULD YOUR SISTER BE USING GHOST CIRCLES TO CLOUD HER APPROACH?
MM.

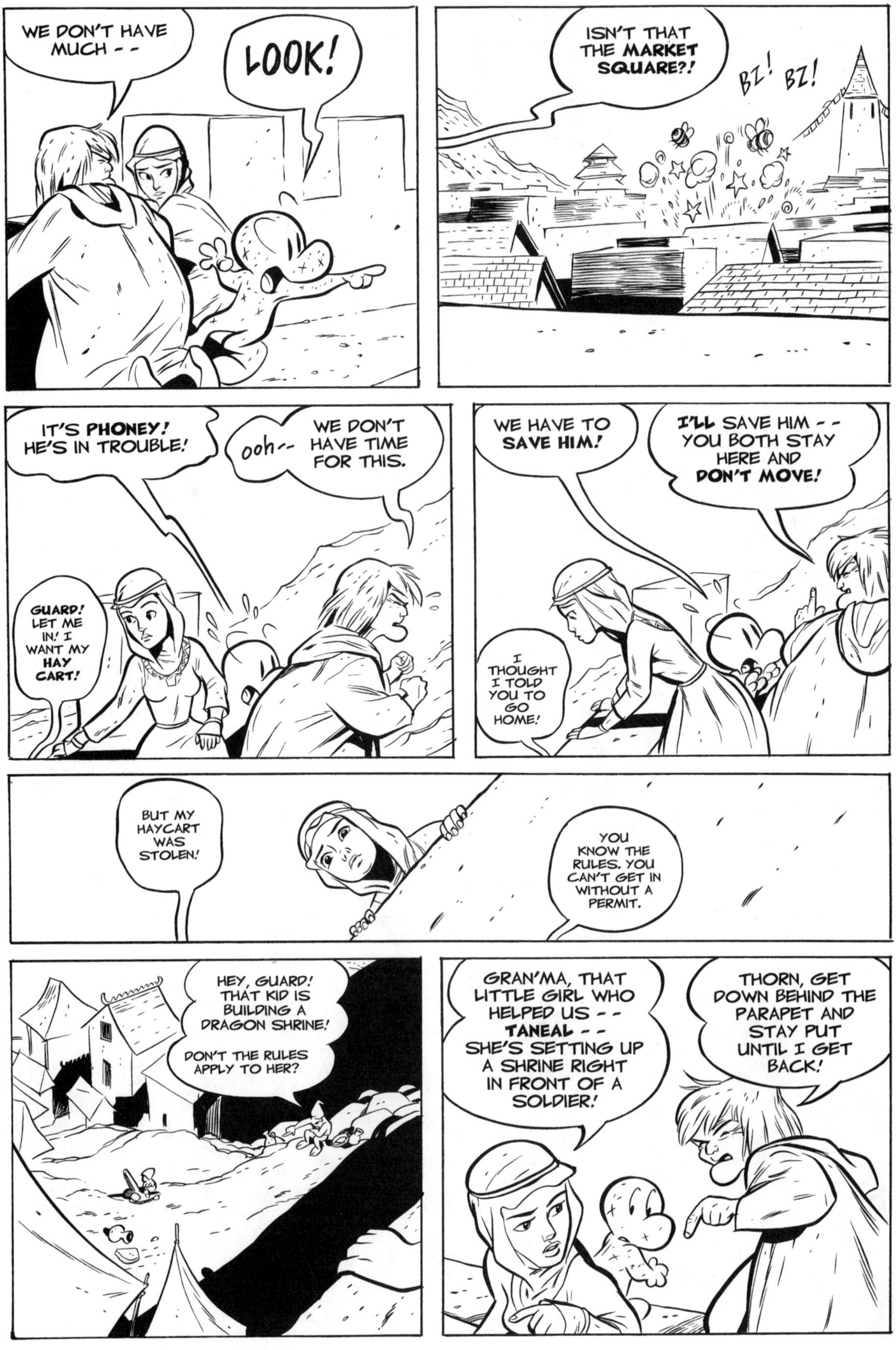

WE DON'T HAVE MUCH - -
LOOK!
ISN'T THAT THE MARKET SQUARE?!
BZ! BZ!
IT'S PHONEY! HE'S IN TROUBLE!
ooh- -
WE DON'T HAVE TIME FOR THIS.
GUARD! LET ME IN! I WANT MY HAY CART!
WE HAVE TO SAVE HIM!
I'LL SAVE HIM - - YOU BOTH STAY HERE AND DON'T MOVE!
I THOUGHT I TOLD YOU TO GO HOME!
BUT MY HAYCART WAS STOLEN!
YOU KNOW THE RULES. YOU CAN'T GET IN WITHOUT A PERMIT.
HEY, GUARD! THAT KID IS BUILDING A DRAGON SHRINE!
DON'T THE RULES APPLY TO HER?
GRAN'MA, THAT LITTLE GIRL WHO HELPED US - - TANEAL - - SHE'S SETTING UP A SHRINE RIGHT IN FRONT OF A SOLDIER!
THORN, GET DOWN BEHIND THE PARAPET AND STAY PUT UNTIL I GET BACK!

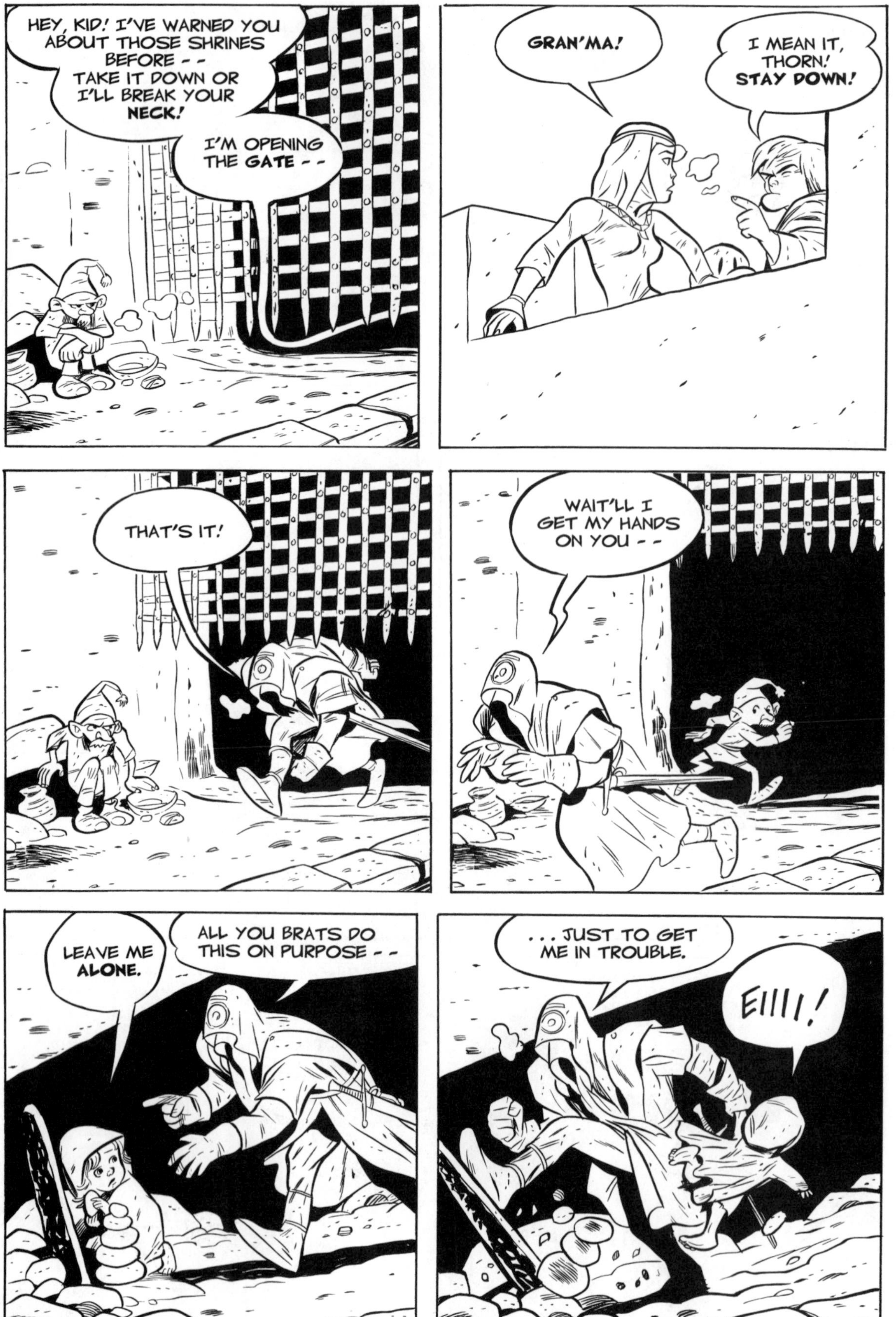
HEY, KID! I'VE WARNED YOU ABOUT THOSE SHRINES BEFORE -- TAKE IT DOWN OR I'LL BREAK YOUR **NECK**!
I'M OPENING THE **GATE** --
GRAN'MA!
I MEAN IT, THORN! **STAY DOWN!**
THAT'S IT!
WAIT'LL I GET MY HANDS ON YOU --
LEAVE ME **ALONE.**
ALL YOU BRATS DO THIS ON PURPOSE --
... JUST TO GET ME IN TROUBLE.
EIIII!

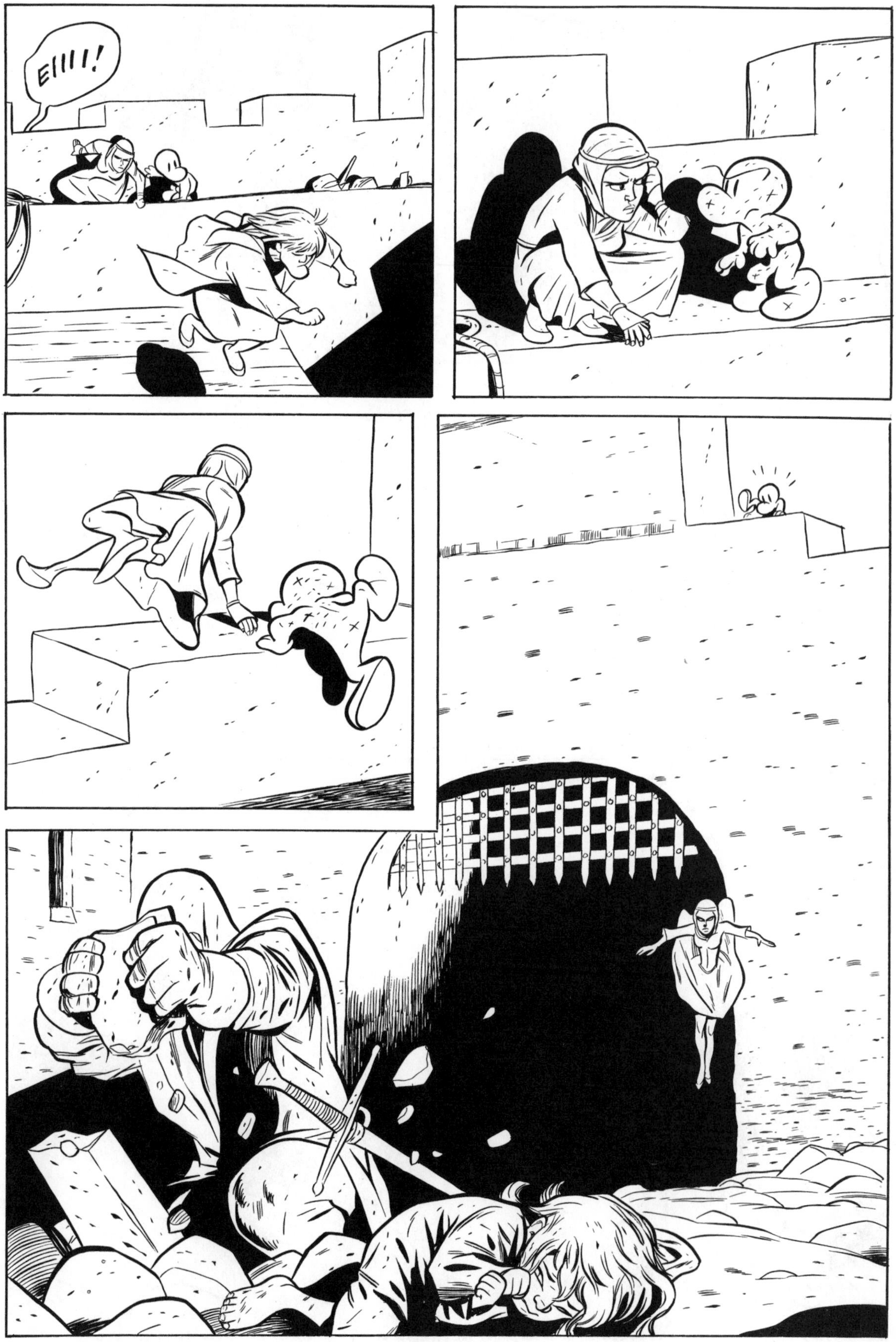
EIIII!

GET AWAY, RAT!

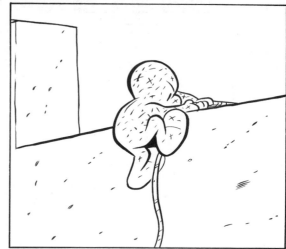

I WARNED YOU---

HEY!

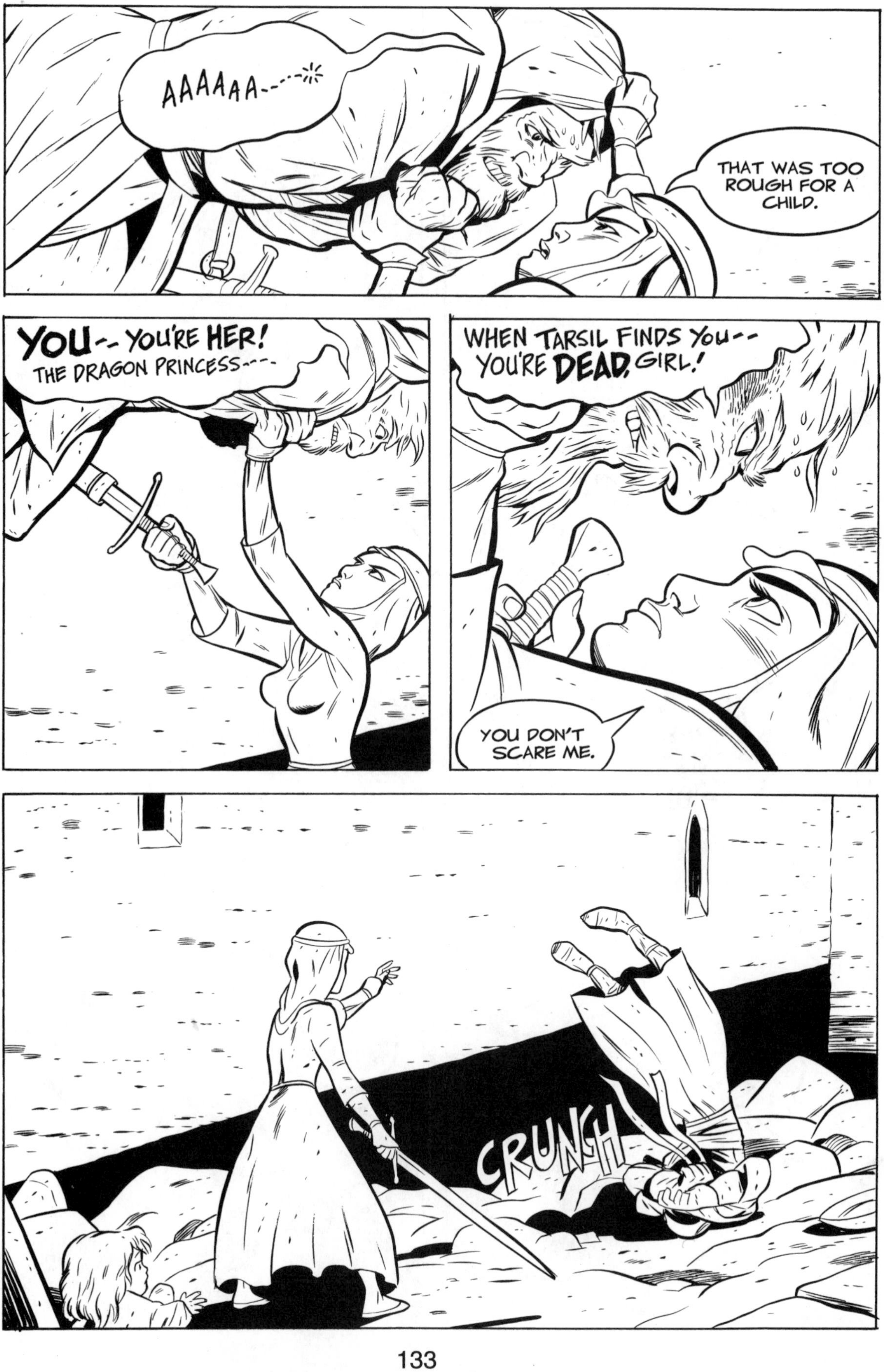
AAAAAA---
THAT WAS TOO ROUGH FOR A CHILD.
YOU-- YOU'RE HER! THE DRAGON PRINCESS---
WHEN TARSIL FINDS YOU-- YOU'RE DEAD, GIRL!
YOU DON'T SCARE ME.
CRUNCH

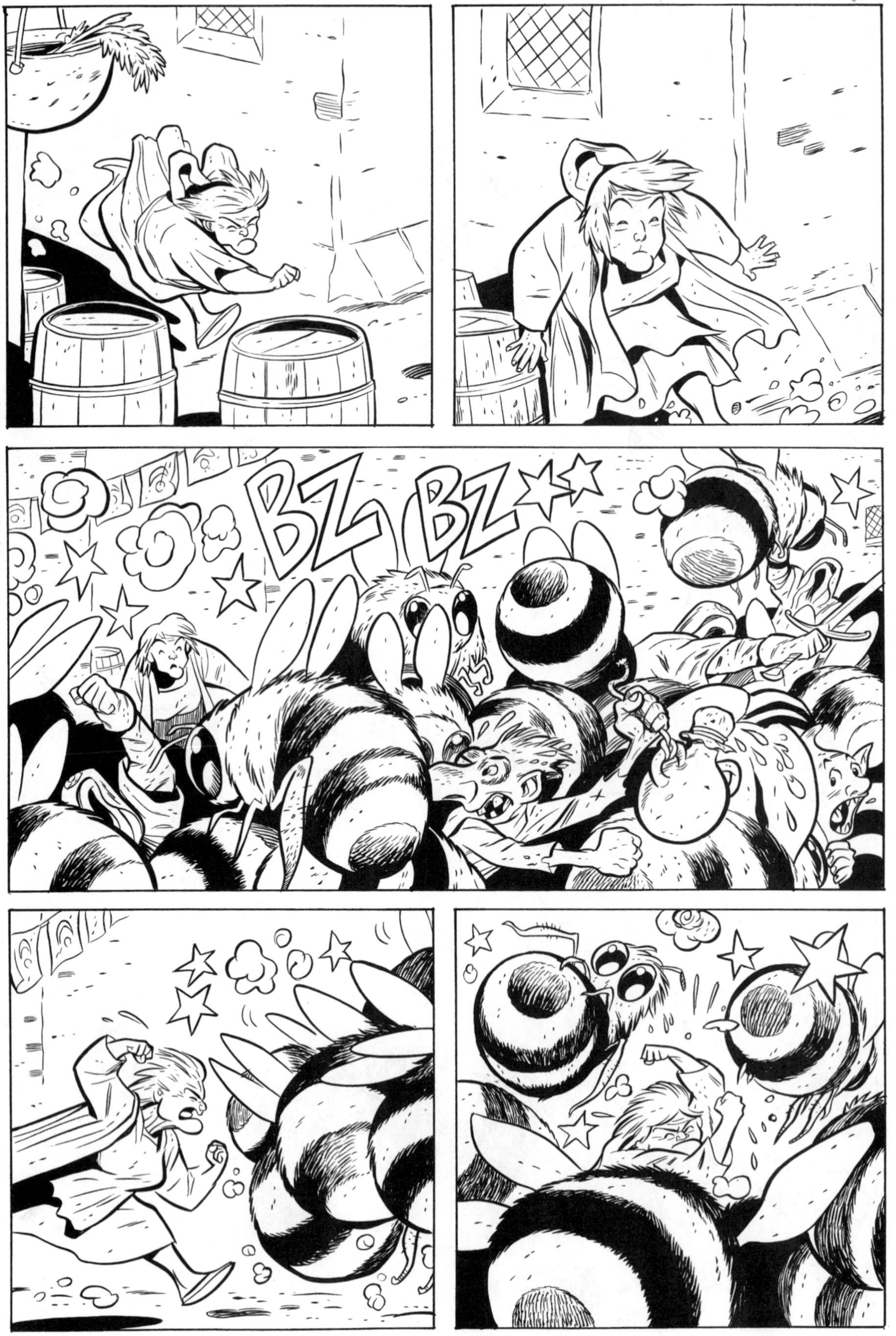
BZ BZ

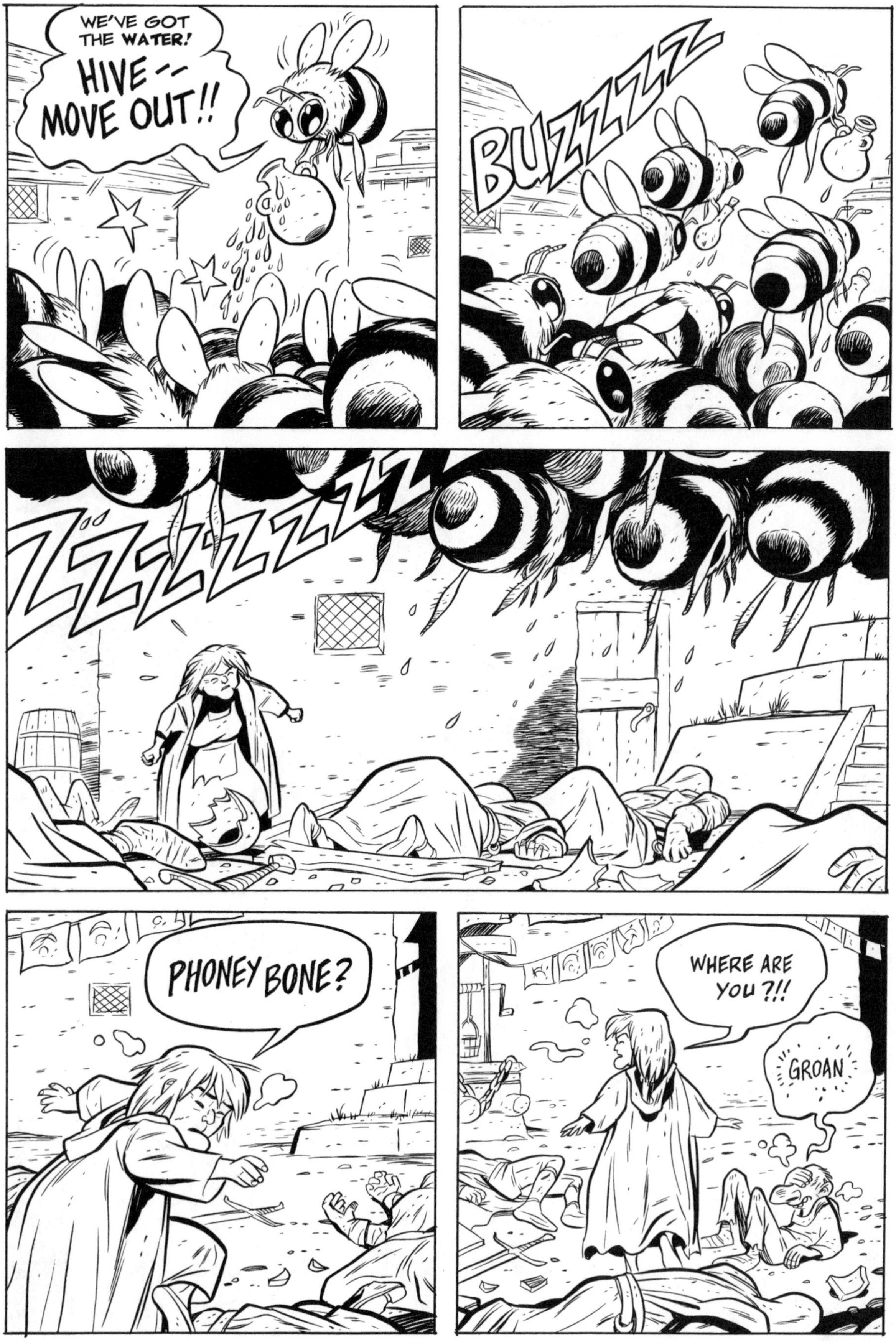
WE'VE GOT THE WATER!
HIVE -- MOVE OUT!!
BUZZZZZ
ZZZZZZZZZ
PHONEY BONE?
WHERE ARE YOU ?!!
GROAN

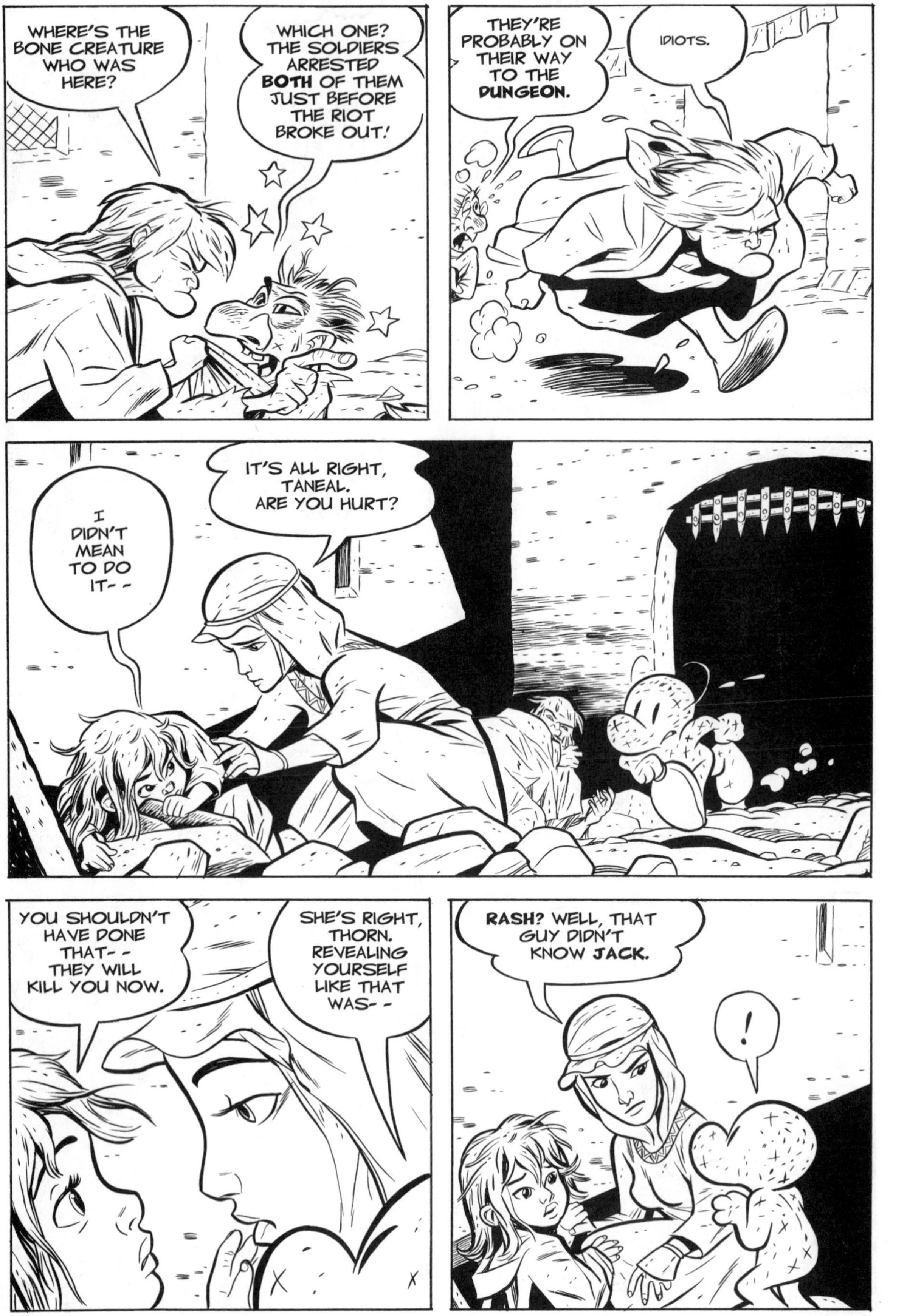

WHERE'S THE BONE CREATURE WHO WAS HERE?
WHICH ONE? THE SOLDIERS ARRESTED **BOTH** OF THEM JUST BEFORE THE RIOT BROKE OUT!
THEY'RE PROBABLY ON THEIR WAY TO THE **DUNGEON.**
IDIOTS.
IT'S ALL RIGHT, TANEAL. ARE YOU HURT?
I DIDN'T MEAN TO DO IT- -
YOU SHOULDN'T HAVE DONE THAT- - THEY WILL KILL YOU NOW.
SHE'S RIGHT, THORN. REVEALING YOURSELF LIKE THAT WAS- -
RASH? WELL, THAT GUY DIDN'T KNOW **JACK.**
!

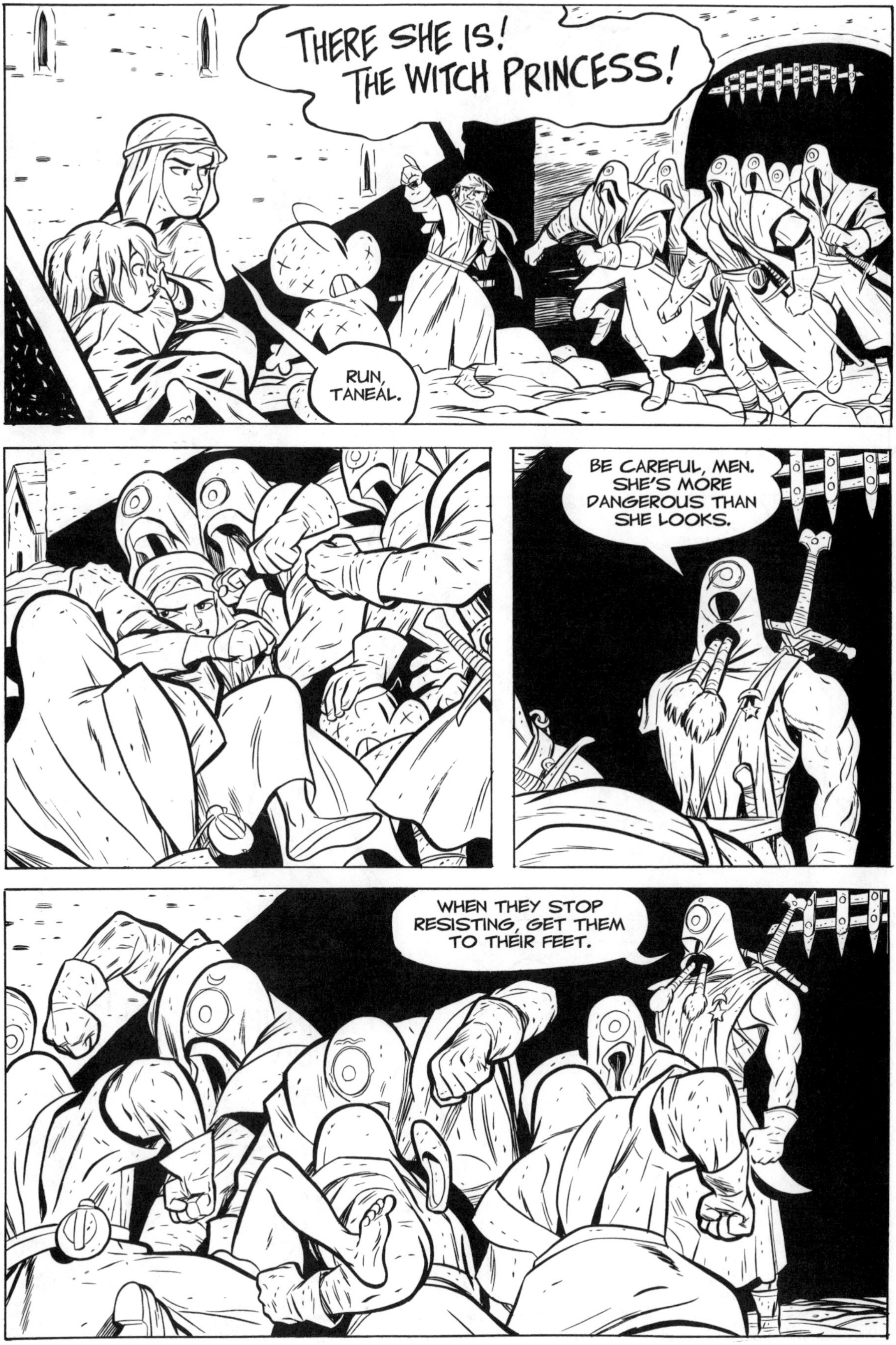
THERE SHE IS! THE WITCH PRINCESS!
RUN, TANEÁL.
BE CAREFUL, MEN. SHE'S MORE DANGEROUS THAN SHE LOOKS.
WHEN THEY STOP RESISTING, GET THEM TO THEIR FEET.

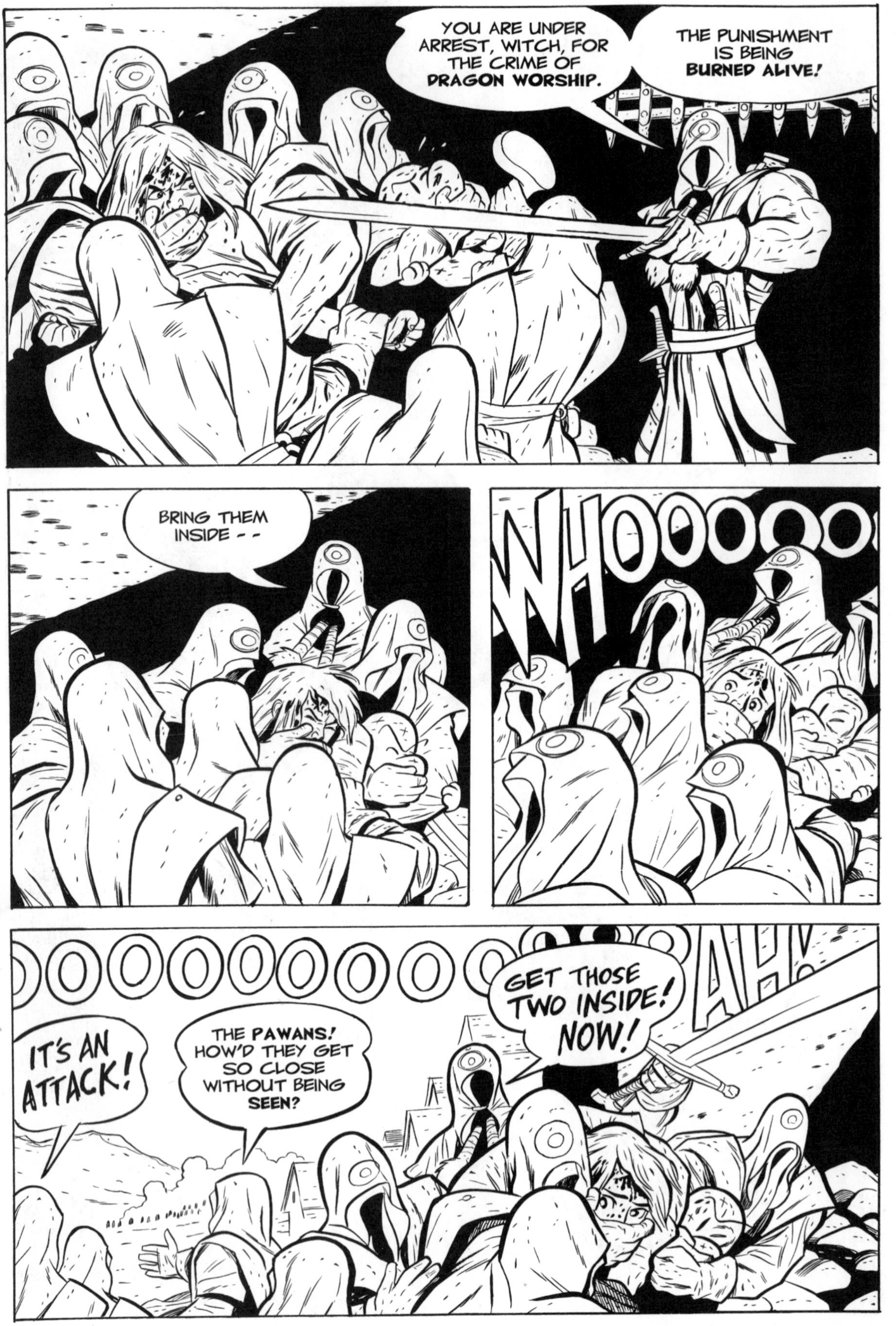
YOU ARE UNDER ARREST, WITCH, FOR THE CRIME OF DRAGON WORSHIP.
THE PUNISHMENT IS BEING BURNED ALIVE!
BRING THEM INSIDE - -
WHOOOOO
OOOOOOOOOOOOOOOOAH!
GET THOSE TWO INSIDE! NOW!
IT'S AN ATTACK!
THE PAWANS! HOW'D THEY GET SO CLOSE WITHOUT BEING SEEN?

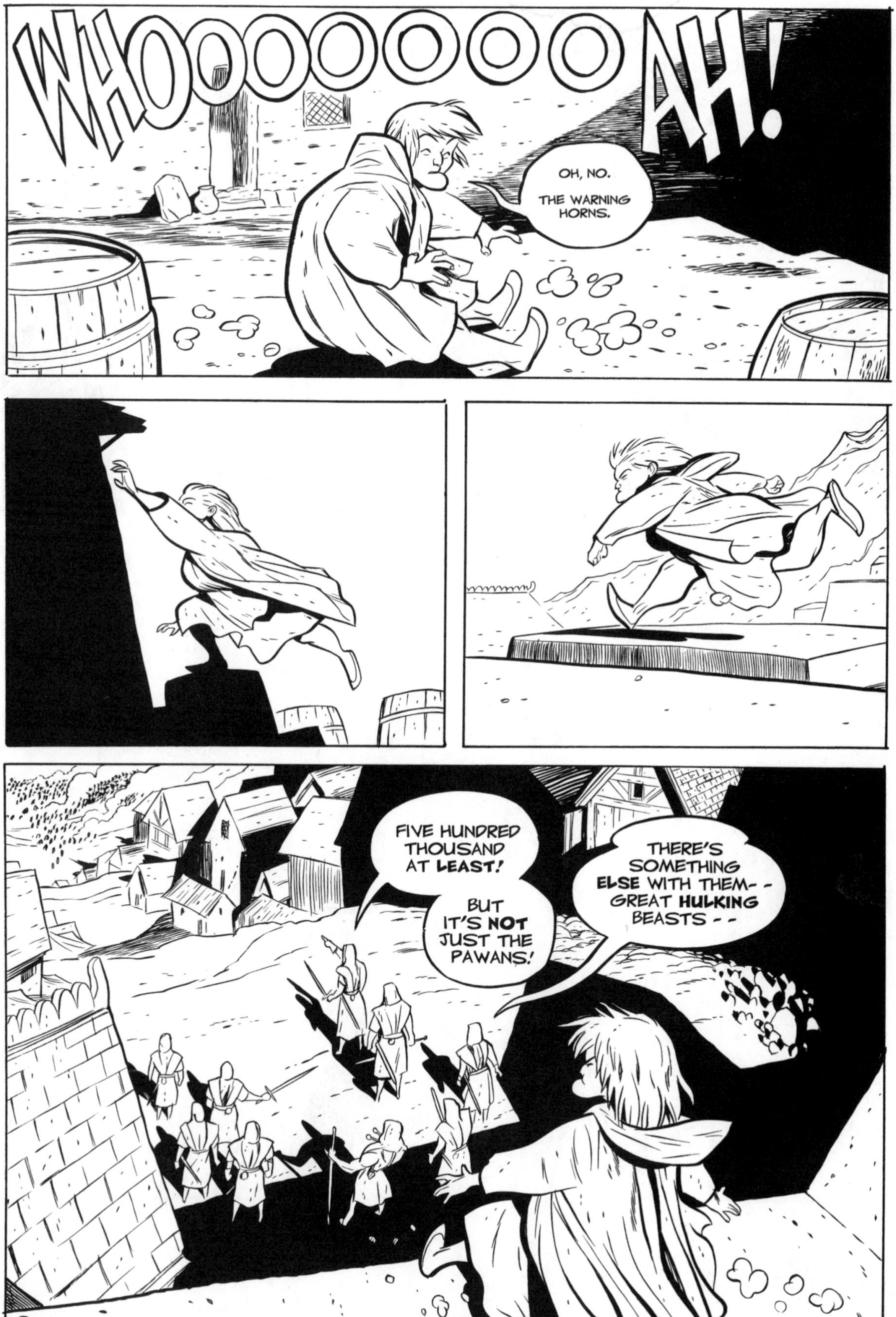
WHOOOOOOOAH!
OH, NO.
THE WARNING HORNS.
FIVE HUNDRED THOUSAND AT LEAST!
BUT IT'S NOT JUST THE PAWANS!
THERE'S SOMETHING ELSE WITH THEM- - GREAT HULKING BEASTS - -

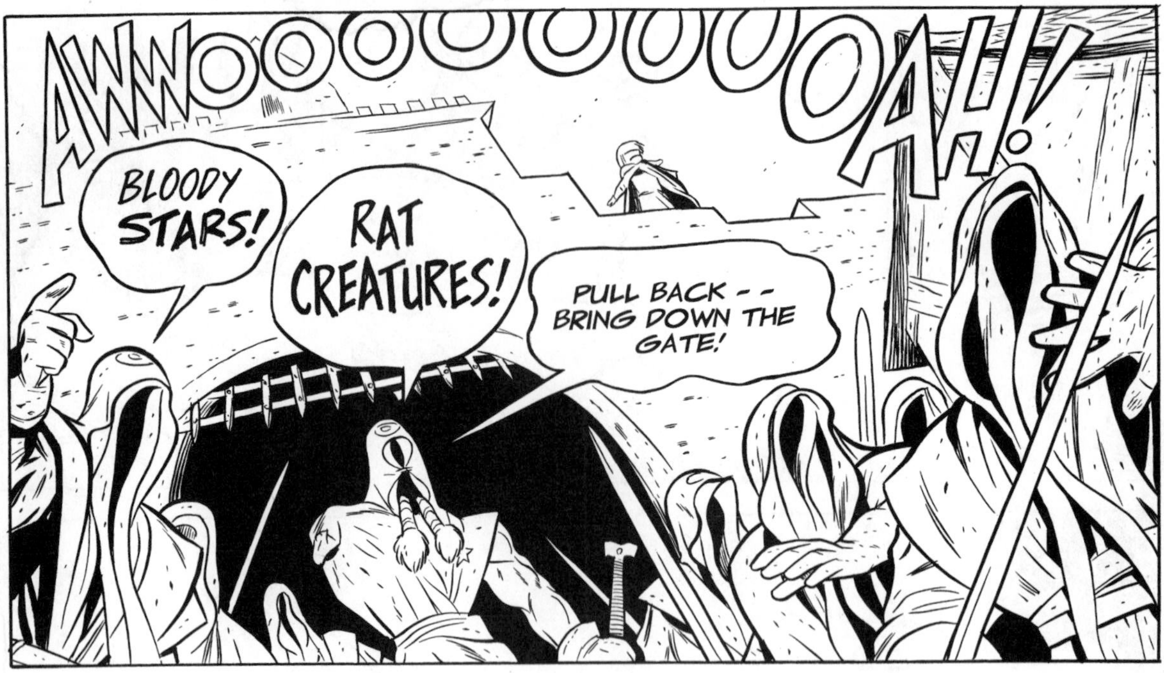
AWWOOOOOOOOOAH!
BLOODY STARS!
RAT CREATURES!
PULL BACK -- BRING DOWN THE GATE!

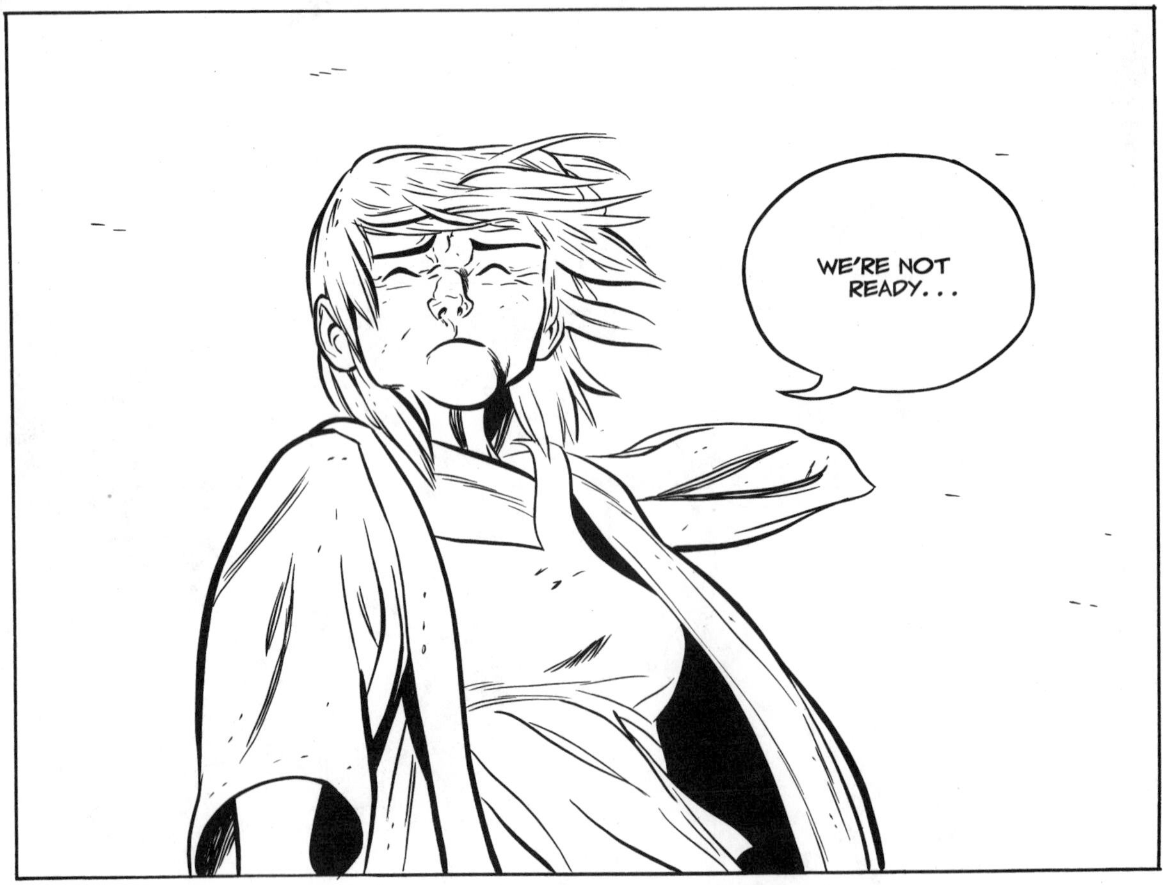
WE'RE NOT READY...

Artist and writer Jeff Smith has spent much of the last ten years working on his epic adventure novel about three modern Bone cousins who spend a year lost in a pre-technological kingdom. The BONE series is currently printed in fifteen languages around the world and has earned its author numerous awards, including Eisner Awards for best story and Best Writer/Artist, Harvey Awards for Best Humor publication and Best Cartoonist, as well as many international awards in Germany, France, Spain, Finland, Norway, and Italy. BONE is a 2002 YALSA/American Library Association Book Choice.

Most recently, Smith completed scripts and layouts for the graphic novel ROSE with fantasy artist Charles Vess, and is currently at work on the final BONE novel, CROWN OF HORNS, in Columbus, Ohio where he and his wife Vijaya live with their Great Dane, Euclid.

OTHER BOOKS BY JEFF SMITH

THE FIRST TRILOGY

BONE VOLUME ONE: OUT FROM BONEVILLE

BONE VOLUME TWO: THE GREAT COW RACE

BONE VOLUME THREE: EYES OF THE STORM

THE SECOND TRILOGY

BONE VOLUME FOUR: THE DRAGONSLAYER

BONE VOLUME FIVE: ROCKJAW, MASTER OF THE EASTERN BORDER

BONE VOLUME SIX: OLD MAN'S CAVE

THE THIRD TRILOGY

BONE VOLUME SEVEN: GHOST CIRCLES

BONE VOLUME EIGHT: TREASURE HUNTERS

PREQUELS

STUPID, STUPID RAT TAILS: THE ADVENTURES OF BIG JOHNSON BONE, FRONTIER HERO
(WRITTEN BY TOM SNIEGOSKI, DRAWN BY JEFF SMITH)

ROSE
(WRITTEN BY JEFF SMITH, PAINTED BY CHARLES VESS)

the dragon's
stair

Dorengard

great
falls

old forest

B...

hot

old

Athei...